A
Sea Vagabond's
World

Also by Bernard Moitessier

Sailing to the Reefs
Cape Horn: The Logical Route
The Long Way
Tamata and the Alliance

A Sea Vagabond's World

boats and sails
distant shores
islands and lagoons

BERNARD MOITESSIER

Translated by William Rodarmor

S
sheridan house

First published 1998 by
Sheridan House, Inc.
145 Palisade Street
Dobbs Ferry, NY 10522

First published in France under the title
Voile, Mers Lointaines, Iles et Lagons
by Editions Arthaud

Library of Congress Cataloging-in-Publication Data

Moitessier, Bernard.
[Voile, mers lointaines, iles et lagons. English]
A sea vagabond's world: boats and sails, distant
shores, islands and lagoons /
Bernard Moitessier: translated by William Rodarmor.
p. cm.
Includes bibliographical references and index.
ISBN 1-57409-021-6 (alk. paper)
1. Moitessier, Bernard. 2. Sailing. 3. Sailboats.
4. Adventure and adventurers—France—Biography.
I. Title.
G530.M715M65313 1998
910.4'5—dc21 98-12995
CIP

Editor: Janine Simon

Printed in the United States of America

ISBN 1-57409-021-6

This translation is dedicated to the memory of my friend Bernard Moitessier. In helping me become both a French translator and a solo sailor, he changed my life.

William Rodarmor

I want to thank the people who helped Bernard with this book, and especially Patrick Pont and Emlie Ifrah; as well as all those who gave me advice, criticism, or moral support since his death in giving the work its present shape. I am particularly thinking of Antoine, Louis Batier, Céline Casalis, Bernard Champon, Odile Chevalier, Iléana Draghici, Daniel Drion, Anne Falconer, Gérard Janichon, Daniel and Joëlle Gazanion, Goudis, Michka, Nicole Van De Kerchove, Hugo Verlomme, Eric Vibart, and finally Frédérique Potier, Christine de Colombel, and Pascal Tournaire.

Véronique Lerebours Pigeonnière

"The act of dreaming is important in itself.
I wish you an endless flood of dreams
and the intense desire to make some of them come true.
I wish you love for what should be loved
and forgetting for what should be forgotten.
I wish you passions.
I wish you silences.
I wish you bird song on awakening
and the laughter of children.
I wish you resistance to being swallowed up,
to indifference,
to the negative virtues of our age.
Above all, I wish you to be yourself."

Jacques Brel

I am a citizen of the most beautiful nation on earth. A nation whose laws are harsh yet simple, a nation that never cheats, which is immense and without borders, where life is lived in the present. In this limitless nation, this nation of wind, light, and peace, there is no other ruler besides the sea.

Contents

Foreword

"Now I would like to write a technical book about the sea and boats and life on a desert island, but in three dimensions," Bernard Moitessier said in August 1993 in Polynesia, on the island of Tahaa in the Iles Sous-le-Vent. He had just finished *Tamata and the Alliance*, a book that had taken him eight and a half years of almost daily work, and which stands as the fabulous legacy of a humanist who was by turns sailor, writer, and gardener.

"Man is a fallen god who remembers the heavens," he also told me. "I'm absolutely sure that people are going to get fed up with sailing technology, and will want to return to the basics."

Bernard was always something of a pioneer and a visionary, so where simplicity was concerned, I took his word for it. "Simplicity is hard to attain and learn," wrote Luc Sola, after meeting Bernard in Tahiti, "but it is especially hard to understand." For Bernard however, simplicity was his entire being, everything he had, and the thing he wanted to share one last time.

This book project wasn't actually a new one. Bernard had been talking about it for years. He carried a little notebook in which he carefully wrote down tips, maneuvers, and advice from sailing pals on solving particular problems, as well as his own experiences, which he shared along the way in his books' technical appendices and in the articles he wrote for sailing magazines. He hoped to collect all those scattered elements in a single volume and offer them to the future "birds of the open seas," to help them through the various stages from the dream of sailing away to discovering some desert island, without forgetting what is essential.

In June 1994, fifteen days before he died, Bernard proposed the project to his publisher, Charles-Henri Flammarion. He didn't have the time to bring it about, but I knew the framework and the message, and I had his material.

Our paths first crossed in August 1985, when I came aboard TAMATA in Moorea. I was an honored and intimate witness to Bernard's last sailing voyages, and had the pleasure of being introduced to beachcomber life on Suvorov and Caroline atolls. I had learned to sail at Les Glénans school, then started cruising and racing in the English Channel and the Atlantic. But with Bernard, I discovered a new way to sail, in which everything became very simple and basic.

So I decided to pick up the torch and gather his material. In a way, this book synthesizes Bernard Moitessier's sailing knowledge, and, above all, illustrates his "barehanded" approach to the sea. It is pragmatic. Based on writings spread over three decades, the book doesn't pretend to offer technical solutions for the ages. To the contrary, it's intended to show that regardless of the headlong evolution of sailing technology, the sea remains the sea, and a sailor's basic instincts never change.

Bernard was part fish, but he was also part monkey, which is very useful at sea, and his methods reflect his physical capabilities. Above all, he had reached a state of perfect partnership with his boat. He lived in symbiosis with the universe he had chosen as his life's framework, and which was limited only by the horizon, "which retreats as you sail toward it." That partnership was marked by modesty and respect for the rules of the game imposed by the sea. Bernard didn't brave the elements; he merged with them.

I also thought it would be useful to recall Bernard's great sailing voyages and the evolution of his boats, from youthful mistakes to his conceiving of JOSHUA, not as a reference, but so the reader can understand why the author made the choices he did. In the way sailors gather below decks to swap stories and learn from each other's experiences, I have occasionally quoted excerpts from his writings in order to clarify some procedure or other.

In closing, I'll let Bernard have the last word: "Make use of the experience of others, but without ever imitating them. You won't become accomplished that way. And even if you could succeed by using someone else's style, it wouldn't be any good. It wouldn't be you."

Véronique Lerebours Pigeonnière
April 25, 1995

The call of the open sea

My teachers and the gods

This book is the natural result of a life spent at sea and at anchor with other sailboats, mainly in the tropics.

I first set out solo many years ago, on a fine northeast monsoon morning, with MARIE-THÉRÈSE's bow pointed toward the wide horizon. I was leaving my native Vietnam forever, brushing its dust from my bare feet. As a sailor, I already had a lot going for me. My first teachers, the fishermen of my village on the Gulf of Siam, had given everything you can give to someone you cherish who is drawn to the sea as if by a magnet. All I lacked was a little theory—and maybe some maturity. But in my very depths my soul was strong and I was beloved by the gods, and therefore ready to take on the Dragons of the Sky and Sea bare-handed.

The gods . . . They started to watch over me very early on. I can still see myself as a boy of eight or nine halfway up a coconut tree that rose to the heavens. Far below, the boy's two brothers were playing at shooting at sand crabs with his magic slingshot. The boy was furious; he was the only one allowed to touch, or even come near the slingshot, which the gods had blessed.

The boy continued to climb. His fatigue was immense. Having reached the top, he chose a coconut and pulled—and pulled and pulled. The tough stem creaked, but the nut clung tight to its cluster. Climbing a coconut tree requires a physical effort that few people can imagine. Doing it twice leads to total exhaustion.

Very far below, Assam, the boy's Chinese *amah*, shouted for him to come down right away. His mother,

her eyes wide with terror, watched this child she loved more than her own life, who was about to kill himself.

For the third time, the boy's slim hand reached for the nut, which had become sacred, and he tried with all his might to pull it loose. Just then, the gods passing by in the Asian sky loved the child, came close, and blew away his fatigue with the warmth of their friendship. And on the third try, the woody stem snapped and the beautiful green coconut bounced all the way down to the sea beside the village of his childhood, the village of his roots, where you could see, far, far away, blue-rimmed islands resting on the horizon like seabirds with fantastic wings.

Created by a colossal effort, the Alliance had just been born, the undissolvable union—which is essential to any real creation—of thought, sweat, and faith.

I have met other teachers along the way, the sea has continued to shape me and my attraction for the sea has never faltered. The gods who came to watch over me have kept me company to the end of the road. If I have sometimes drawn their anger, it was out of carelessness, pride, or stupidity—which caused my first two shipwrecks, and also the last one.

When I left Vietnam, I had only read Alain Gerbault, Eric de Bisschop, and Henri de Monfried. A short list, but sufficient, since each of them had sailed on very different kinds of boats: Western-style sailboats, Chinese junks, catamarans, Arab dhows. For me, Slocum, Voss, and Pidgeon came later; at the time, I didn't even know those great masters' names.

Where theory was concerned—celestial navigation in particular—it was no picnic. Little by little, helped by friends I made along the way, I first learned to master the sextant by bringing the sun down to brush the roof of a building in Singapore, then the nasty navigation tables a few years later on Mauritius and Saint Helena.

The sea and encounters taught me. In the course of my nomadic existence the determination ripened within me, like a sprouting seed, to transmit my knowledge to my fellow sailors through writing, to which I devoted time, patience, and a great deal of seriousness. In the course of my encounters and meetings, I filled notebooks in which I stored up tips, shortcuts, solutions to problems I had worked out, or which trustworthy friends told me about. Those notes fleshed out the technical appendices of my four books and various magazine articles I wrote (such as those written between 1959 and 1965 for my friend Pierre Lavat at *Bateaux* magazine).

The book you are holding is the one I would have liked to have had when I first set out on SNARK, and later on MARIE-THÉRÈSE: a book full of experiences that would have helped solve my problems as I undertook my great adventure. This book describes the stages, initial learning, mistakes (which teach you more than successes), things I tried, friends' ideas, anecdotes of life events that illustrate points that strike me as useful . . . in short, everything that can help you along.

The sea will always be the sea, full of enigmas and new lessons.*

But let's be clear about one thing: I am not giving advice. I am only saying how I look at the sea, how it manifests itself to my eyes, why I do this or that, and how I manage to tack between the Dragons that guard the Treasure of the Enchanted Island protected by the great salt water.

*All quotations, unless otherwise identified, are by Bernard Moitessier, excerpted from his earlier books—*Tamata and the Alliance, The Long Way, Cape Horn: The Logical Route,* and *Sailing to the Reefs*—or from interviews and private correspondence.

Salut et fraternité
Bernard Moitessier

boats and sails...

Preparing for the great adventure

A few words of advice, just the same

Because of my various books, I've received many letters from people—not all of them young—who felt the call of the open sea. They asked more or less directly, depending on their temperaments, for my advice on getting ready for the great departure.

If you can, stay. Leave, if you must.

There is one fundamental question you have to ask yourself at the outset: "Do I really want to live and travel on a sailboat?" Once you've answered that question, without hiding your head in the sand, things will become clear, because you won't be kidding yourself.

I tell everyone pretty much the same thing. Don't needlessly complicate your life. Give top priority to the essentials. Firmly put aside anything superfluous. Given a choice between something simple and something complicated, choose what is simple without hesitation; sooner or later, what is complicated will almost always lead to problems—needless expense, loss of time, and waste of energy.

There are different philosophies of sailing. Mine is to do everything as simply as possible, so you can set out to sea in the quickest time and for the least expense.

This philosophy of simplicity has guided me like a guardian angel ever since I first set sail. Make do with what you have, and don't have eyes bigger than your stomach.

Theory

Unless you are solidly grounded in sailing theory and practice, I think it wise to start very modestly at

What really helped me was the training I got in Asia, where people sail with practically nothing, bare-handed, meaning without any equipment and always improvising; so everything is simple, and you learn how to make do, as simply as possible.

the beginning. Others have shared their experiences in books. I think the book published by the Glénans sailing school, *The Glénans Manual of Sailing,* covers the basics very well. I also very much like Antoine's book, *Mettre les Voiles.* Those two books will help clear the way for you. I also know of an excellent American book, written by Larry and Lin Pardey, *The Self-Sufficient Sailor.*

First practical steps

Together with what you learn in books, don't hesitate to get your feet wet by sailing a small dinghy such as an Optimist. You'll learn a tremendous amount. You may think, "Me, in an Optimist? That's a kid's boat! People will make fun of me!" To that I would say, "Beware of pride!"

A few years ago in Tahiti, my friends René and Jocelyne had acquired a 27-foot sloop. He was 33 and a real athlete; he did martial arts, parachute-jumping, body surfing, and some diving, among other things. At 25, Jocelyne wasn't the least bit interested in sports, but she had good common sense. Neither had ever done any sailing—except for a trip to Moorea with a bunch of friends aboard a 60-foot ketch—and they asked me to show them the ropes. The Arue yacht club agreed to lend us a Caravelle, a big, dry-sailing centerboard boat that at first glance seemed ideal. But when we got to the yacht club, we were greeted by a swarm of 10- to 12-year-old children who were about to go out on Optimists. We watched as they cleared the harbor area. One of the kids, though obviously at a loss, managed to get out into the channel despite the crowding and jeers of his friends. An hour later, the children returned like a swarm of bees. And we saw something eye-opening: the hapless kid of an hour before had been transformed. He was doing just as well as the others, yelling "starboard" at any challengers, deftly handling the crosswinds in the narrow channel before raising his centerboard and sailing up to the ramp.

The main thing is to know how to handle a boat; later on, you go sailing.

We helped him stow his gear and asked, "How long have you been sailing an Optimist?" Answer: "This is my first time." In a blinding flash, we were struck by the obvious. So René, Jocelyne, and I immediately set sail, each aboard one of those marvelous dinghies. Close reach, reach, beam reach, coming about, jibing, backing with reverse rudder. We checked to see how well the boats hove to with the sail sheeted in and the tiller down at 45 degrees. The wind rose and we watched for gusts, learning to anticipate shifts as a force 4 wind raised little whitecaps on the lagoon. René and Jocelyne were beginning to take charge of their boats. Just for the heck of it, we started racing. It was terrific fun; we were in seventh heaven!

When we headed back a couple of hours later, nobody could have said which of us had sailed the most miles in his life. It was extraordinary: in a single outing, René and Jocelyne had grasped the essentials, because each was responsible for everything, from beginning to end. When you're sailing alone, you pay for the slightest mistake or lapse of attention. But an Optimist is a forgiving boat, and it gives you fair warning; you really have to work to turn one over. A 14-foot 420, on the other hand, is a temperamental racing dinghy that I feel is much too fast and unpredictable for a beginner. If nothing else is available, sailing a 420 is obviously a lot better than sitting on the yacht club terrace. But as soon as the wind rises a notch, a 420 will dump you without giving you the time to understand why or how. So I don't think it's the best way to quickly learn to sail well.

As for learning in a group aboard a Caravelle, a number of things can make this inconvenient and a waste of time. You have a skipper at the helm—who may or not be a good teacher—and a crew, the people who do the work. The two most eager students usually grab the jib sheets and the others become "moveable ballast": they aren't very motivated, and their attention wanders as soon as they start getting bored or cold. Meanwhile, the two people at the sheets start thinking it's high time they took a turn at the tiller. But you don't get the tiller just like that; you have to earn it, you have to deserve it. "Trim your jib a little better," says the skipper. "No, not like that! Are you asleep, or what? How did I ever get such a crew? And you want to take the helm, too?"

All right, I'm exaggerating a little. But still, that's

the heart of the problem. In an Optimist, you get to take the tiller right away and you catch on very fast. I know of no better basic training. I consider this modest cockleshell the royal road to blue-water cruising. Aboard an Optimist, your senses sharpen naturally. The only voices you hear are whispered by the hull, sail, wind, and rocks. Through those instantly understandable messages, an Optimist will teach you the fundamental reflexes that will be needed aboard any other craft, large or small. Whether you're on the poop deck of a 2,000-ton three-master, in the cockpit of a 30-foot cutter, or on a 420 or a Caravelle, the basics are absolutely the same, the only difference being a matter of extrapolation depending on tonnage. And a beginner will learn the basics much better and faster aboard a dinghy.

Of course, I've met excellent sailors who had never set foot in a sailing dinghy or even tried their hand at crewing on a day sail before setting off for the great adventure aboard 25- to 45-foot boats. They learned as they went along, and I salute them. But how many others have given up because they tried to rush things? The sea and the gods don't like excessive haste, lack of preparation, or a casual or careless attitude—especially concerning the really important things.

A few final words on this subject. During her three cruising-school seasons in the Sixties, some 350 people crewed aboard JOSHUA. About 30 percent of these were complete novices. The other 70 percent had some experience: they had taken sailing-school classes at Les Glénans, or they owned cruising boats. And I noticed a distinct difference between the two categories of non-beginners. The ones who had gone through the Glénans school—even if they had only sailed on a 16-foot Vaurien—very quickly got the hang of handling 15-ton JOSHUA. Whereas if they hadn't sailed dinghies, the cruising-boat owners were almost always overwhelmed by events—to the point where I often wondered whether they ever used the sails on their boats, or relied mainly on their motors. And I hope that despite the passage of time and the rush of technology, Les Glénans still maintains its grand 1960s tradition, when sailing was the rule.

Choosing a type of boat, and further practice

This is the second stage in preparing for the great departure. Choosing a boat is a delicate problem, and I don't think that the ideal boat really exists. Our own experience is what actually shapes the outline of our next boat, which will be a bit closer to that ideal, though without, I think, ever attaining it.

A boat is freedom, not just a way to reach a goal.

Be careful, though; take it easy. Here too, I think it's prudent not to rush ahead if you have any alternatives. Beware of falling in love; it blinds you at first, only to leave you unhappy and at a loss aboard a boat that may not match your real hopes. Before deciding on this or that kind of boat, it's best to have a general notion of what might best suit you. The smart thing is to do some sailing on several types of boats. Hang around marinas during your vacations and weekends armed only with a small sea-bag, a good dose of nerve, and enormous determination. The gods love this sort of thing.

The more you sail on different kinds of boats, cruisers and racers, in summer and in winter, the clearer your thinking will become. It may take several seasons, but the effort won't be wasted. You will be reaching three goals at the same time: you'll get to know different kinds of boats; learn all sorts of things about sailing (reefing, sail-trimming tips, tidal currents, marine charts, buoyage systems, *Sailing Directions,* charts, etc.); and clear up many mysteries at little cost.

It may seem hard to get that first "Yes" from an owner that will allow you—with no other references than your smiling face—to crew on a boat that is preparing to weigh anchor. But, as my old friend René Tournoüer used to say: "You already have the 'No'. So there's really no risk in insisting, to get yourself a 'Yes'."

Abadie gave me* TITETTE*'s tiller. This was my first great outing at sea. Abadie was resting below; he trusted me. Sailing by night in that apparent darkness, while knowing where the island was . . . it was a magic that renewed within me my alliance with the universe. The stars were speaking, as were the sea, the wind, and the island cloaked by night.

Choosing the boat's material

If you want to go far and keep your boat for a long time, I don't think anything beats metal construction.

I am convinced that a solid boat, even a very small one, the size of a 19-foot Corsaire d'Herbulot, could be sailed solo from Tahiti to the Falklands by way of Cape Horn without risk to life or limb, if it were built of metal. If you drop a well-plugged bottle in the middle of a hurricane, it will float just fine. The same is basically true of a boat. If it is built of metal, well designed and watertight, it could be knocked over by breaking waves ten times in a row without sinking. The rest is merely details and adjusting to circumstances.

To show how strong metal construction can be, here is what happened when JOSHUA was driven aground in Cabo San Lucas, in December 1982.

During the night of the hurricane, 26 boats, almost all of them production fiberglass models, wound up on shore. At dawn, the beach looked like a huge garbage dump: half-boats, quarter-boats, big sheets of fiberglass, debris everywhere—a total disaster. During that night, JOSHUA went aground at low tide and a 50-foot fiberglass ketch was driven on top of her. This big boat was destroyed in a couple of hours, whereas mine came through with some serious bumps but not a single crack. Two other boats, beached at high tide, survived the disaster. One was a 40-foot ultralight racer made of molded plywood; her keel was knocked askew, but could be repaired. The other was a sturdy 30-foot cutter of traditional plank construction on laminated ribs; she took some bad knocks, but no fatal ones. If they had gone aground at low- or mid-tide, the waves would have destroyed them like the others. Several fiberglass boats that went on the beach at high tide stayed there, beyond repair.

For me, a boat comes down to three main elements: a watertight hull and deck, masts that stand upright, and a solidly hung rudder.

STEEL

Amateur construction is possible

I know of six or seven steel boats that were very well built by competent amateurs whose main tools were a torch and welding gear. This type of construction is especially fast compared to wood or fiberglass.

Other advantages: it is rigid and watertight

Ah, steel . . . watertight bulkheads, tanks welded right to the hull, incomparable rigidity, welded chainplates, and an absolutely watertight boat that you clean with a broom and dustpan instead of a bilge pump.

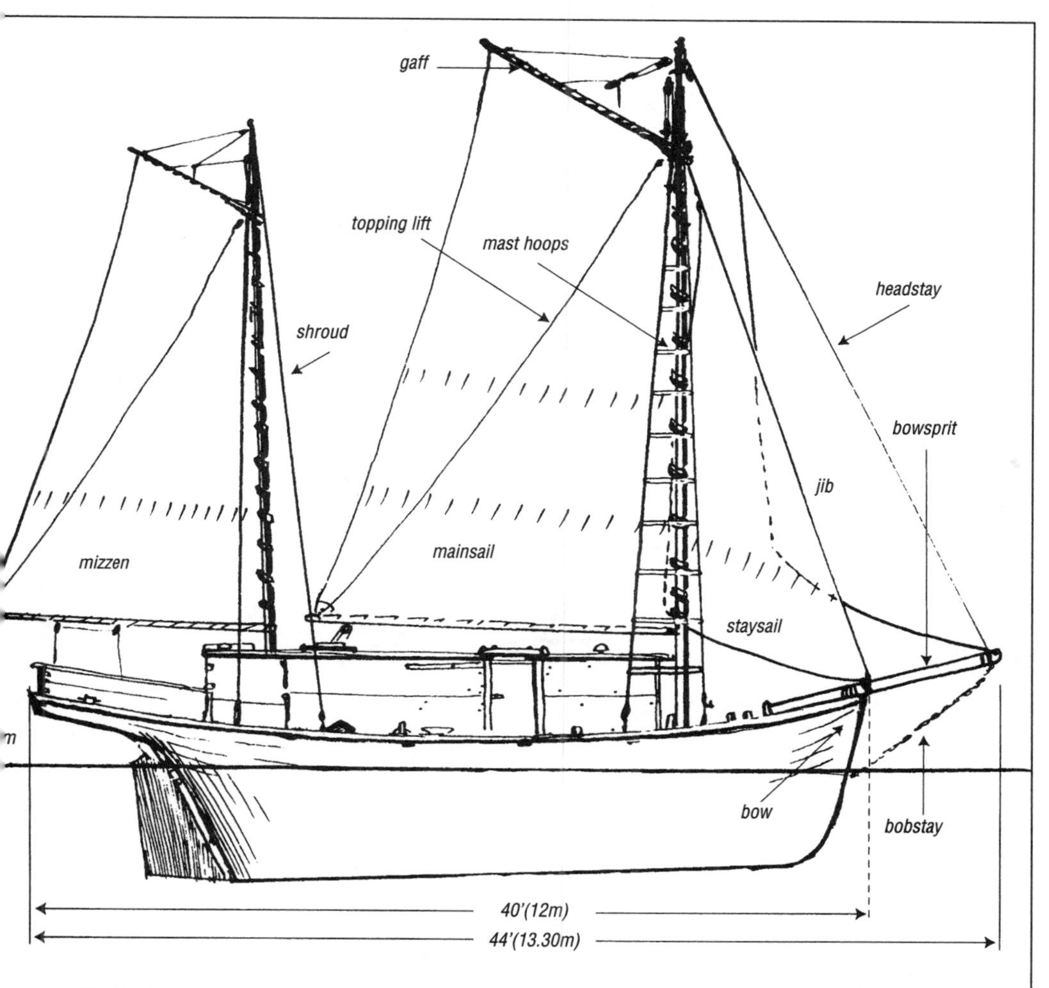

1950 Snark

Wooden gaff-rigged ketch. A Malaysian boat, known as a *proa*—which is very different from a junk—built in Borneo for fishing. She had a bowsprit and not much freeboard. Length 40'; beam 14'; draft 6'.

SNARK was making 25 gallons of water a day by the time we reached Singapore . . . Without quite sinking, we managed to bring her back to Saigon, which we had left six months before. All that remained was to sell poor SNARK. She was rotten from the tops of her masts to the bottom of her keel, by way of her hull and ribs! Devoured by shipworms, too, the poor old thing!

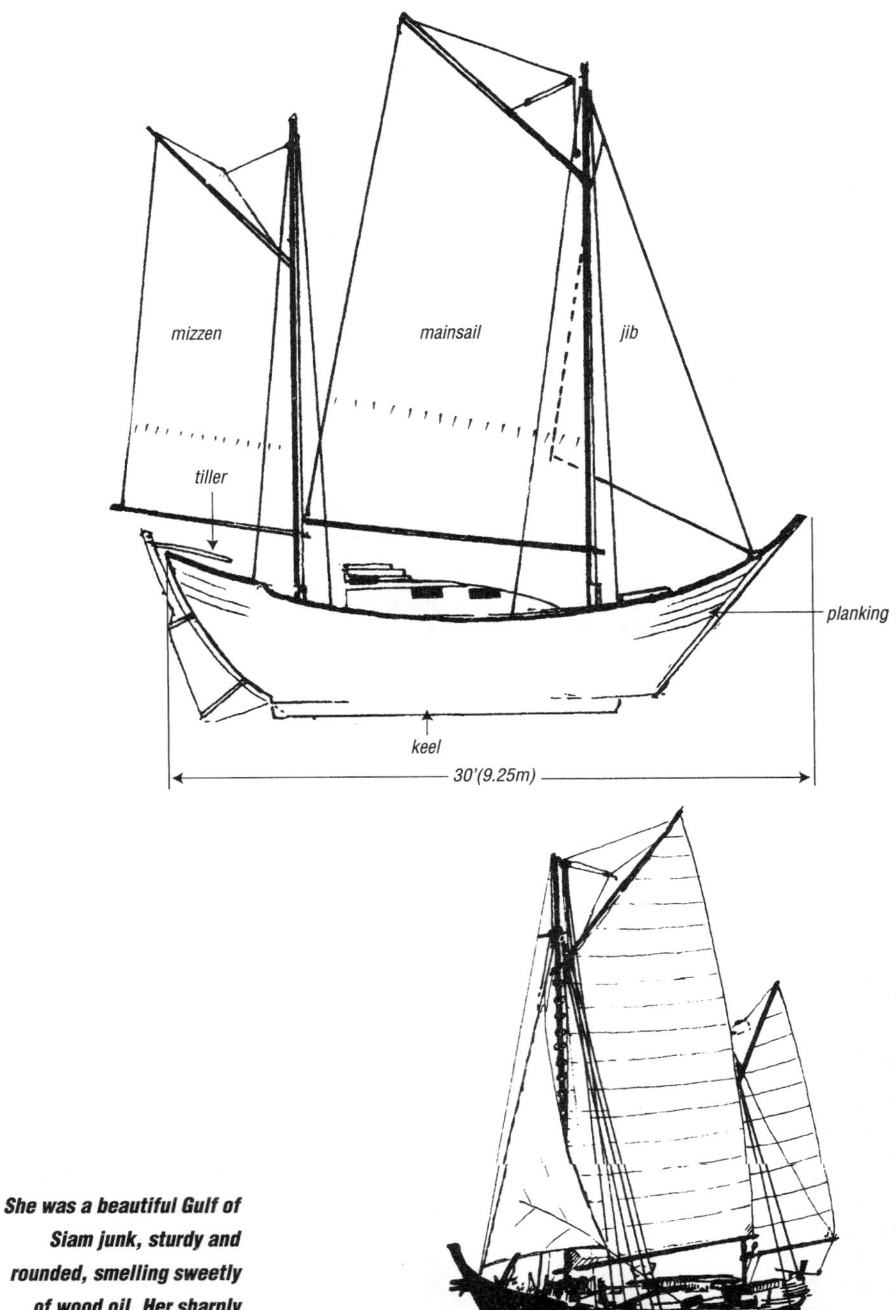

She was a beautiful Gulf of Siam junk, sturdy and rounded, smelling sweetly of wood oil. Her sharply angled bow gracefully extended her strong sheer forward, pointing to the sky, the horizon . . . and the lands beyond that horizon.

1952
Marie-Thérèse

A traditional wooden junk, gaff-rigged, with a very tall, slender bow and internal ballast. Length 30'; beam 10'.

1955
Marie-Thérèse II

Of Asian inspiration and built by eye, without any plans, she had rounded lines. *Marie-Thérèse II* was a ketch, initially gaff-rigged, then Marconi. Handsome mahogany keel, bow, and stem pieces; jackfruit and guava wood ribs; laminated deck beams. She had 880 pounds (400 kg) of exterior ballast; the rest was interior and fixed. Length 27'; width 10'; draft 5'.

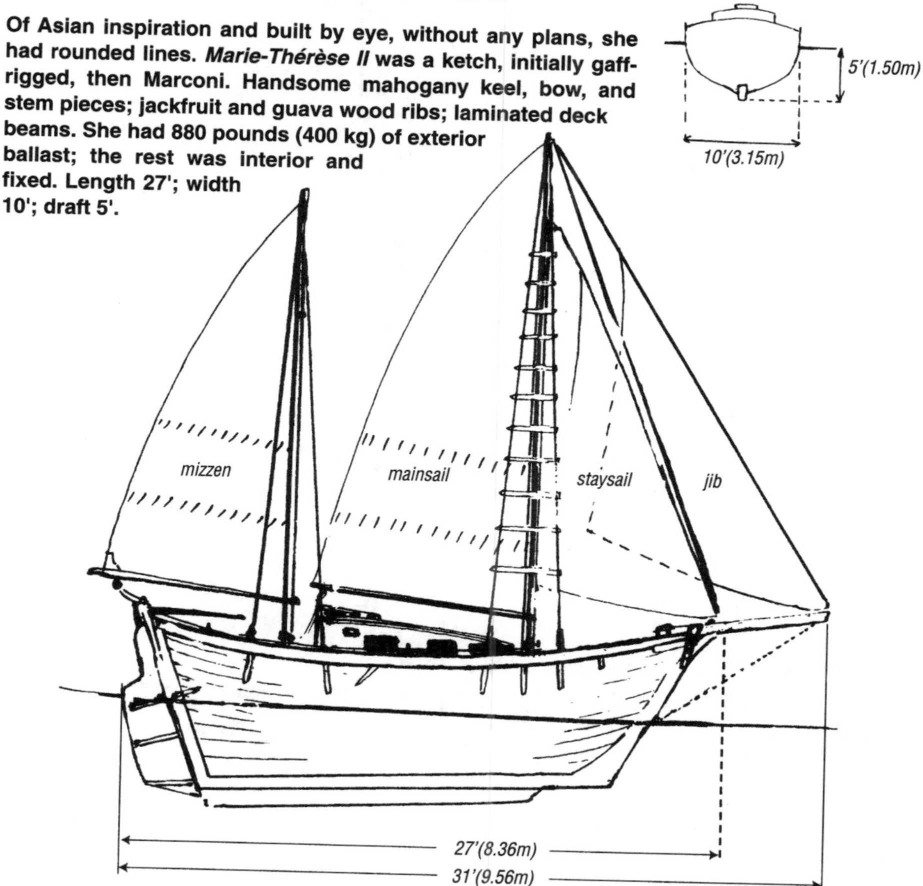

Maintaining my wooden boats presented some tricky problems that required solid credentials: you had to be a "doctor of rot," "doctor of shipworms," and "doctor of leaks" . . . Despite my instinctive distrust, I was forced to compare wood and steel. Working on a freighter taking me back from the Caribbean to France in 1958, those three doctorates were replaced by a scraper, a can of paint, and a big brush, with no further qualifications required beyond a little good will . . . I learned that a steel boat's topsides don't rust when they are maintained in the time-honored merchant marine way: painting, painting, and more painting, using quick-drying paint, since you're always in a hurry to get underway.

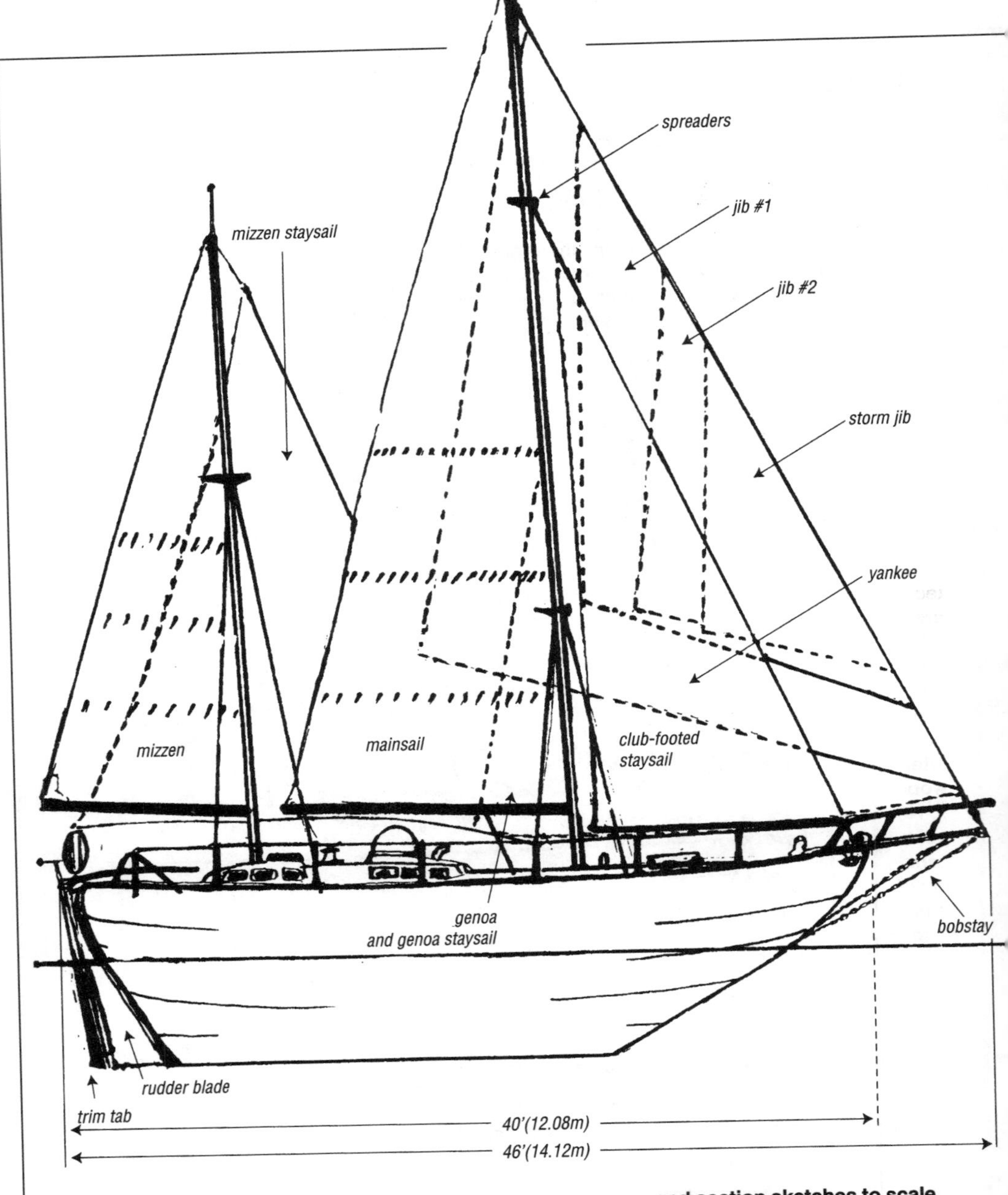

1961 Joshua

Joshua **is a 40-foot steel ketch designed by Jean Knocker and built for me by Jean Fricaud in his yard at Chauffailles. Steel had turned out to be the best answer to my concerns about maintenance and strength. From our very first meeting, Knocker put me at ease. I made plan and section sketches to scale. He then drew the waterlines, corrected my mistakes to conform to the requirements of naval architecture, and produced a real architect's plan that suited my wishes. This work together stretched over fourteen months, until the plans were done to his and my satisfaction.**

Needless to say, Knocker put in a great deal of work, given the number of requirements I had for the boat:

1. Good upwind performance. From the point of view of sailing close-hauled, my previous boats weren't much good. And when the seas were stronger than the wind, performance became pitiful, especially with a bit of contrary current. That state of affairs can lead to catastrophe, because it is very tiring to tack day and night. Fatigue leads to exhaustion, and that can put a boat on the rocks.

2. Shallow draft (things are getting complicated already). This is an element of both safety and pleasure in coral seas, where a boat drawing only 4'6" can get much closer to shore and enter little protected coves whose passes are too shallow for a boat with 6-foot draft. Knocker suggested a very elegant solution involving a centerboard, but I wouldn't hear of a centerboard well, since at the time I intended to use cold-molded wood construction.

3. Norwegian stern. I prefer a pointed Norwegian stern because it can very effectively divide, direct, and ease a breaking sea's violent push when running.

4. Very comfortable interior, but divided between two totally independent cabins (another difficulty, since the Norwegian stern makes the aft cabin less roomy).

5. Marconi ketch rig (this is awkward for the aft cabin, because of the mizzen mast).

6. Stern-hung rudder, which lets you directly connect a self-steering device.

As you see, the architect found himself confronted with an imbroglio of demands, which made his task very difficult. Good windward performance requires a fairly deep draft. Also, the least possible windage, whereas I wanted to be able to stand up anywhere in the main cabin, and in part of the aft cabin. But Knocker was able to overcome these serious difficulties.

Joshua: Length 40' plus a 6-foot bowsprit; length at the waterline 36'; beam 12'; draft 5'. Steel used: frames: 2" x 3/16" flat iron. Keel: 9/32" plate for the sides, 13/16" for the bottom. Stem and sternpost: 3" x 13/16" flat iron. Strakes: 3/16". Garboard: 7/32". Deck frames: 2" x 3/16" flat iron, on edge.

1982

If JOSHUA were 32 feet long and well laid out, she would be plenty of boat for two people, plenty to set out to sea on, and would require less time and money to maintain and outfit . . .

1983
Tamata

Tamata is a 32-foot hard-chine steel cutter with a transom and bowsprit. I once thought a transom dangerous when running in high seas, but hundreds of sailboats have proven that it is as good as a Norwegian stern in the high latitudes. And of course a transom means more room on deck and inside. I had wanted a boat that would be 30 feet long, maximum. John and Ned Hutton, the builders, only had plans for a 46- to 50-foot boat on hand, and the choice had to be made quickly. By extrapolating, they were able to bring the size down, but not under 32 feet. In her behavior under sail, *Tamata* isn't the ideal boat, but she is better than no boat at all. The cutter rig allows a divided headsail, so you can handle heavy weather, maneuver under mainsail alone in port, sail close-hauled under staysail alone—in a word, simplicity. But I loyally chose a bowsprit, which greatly increases the sail area for light winds.

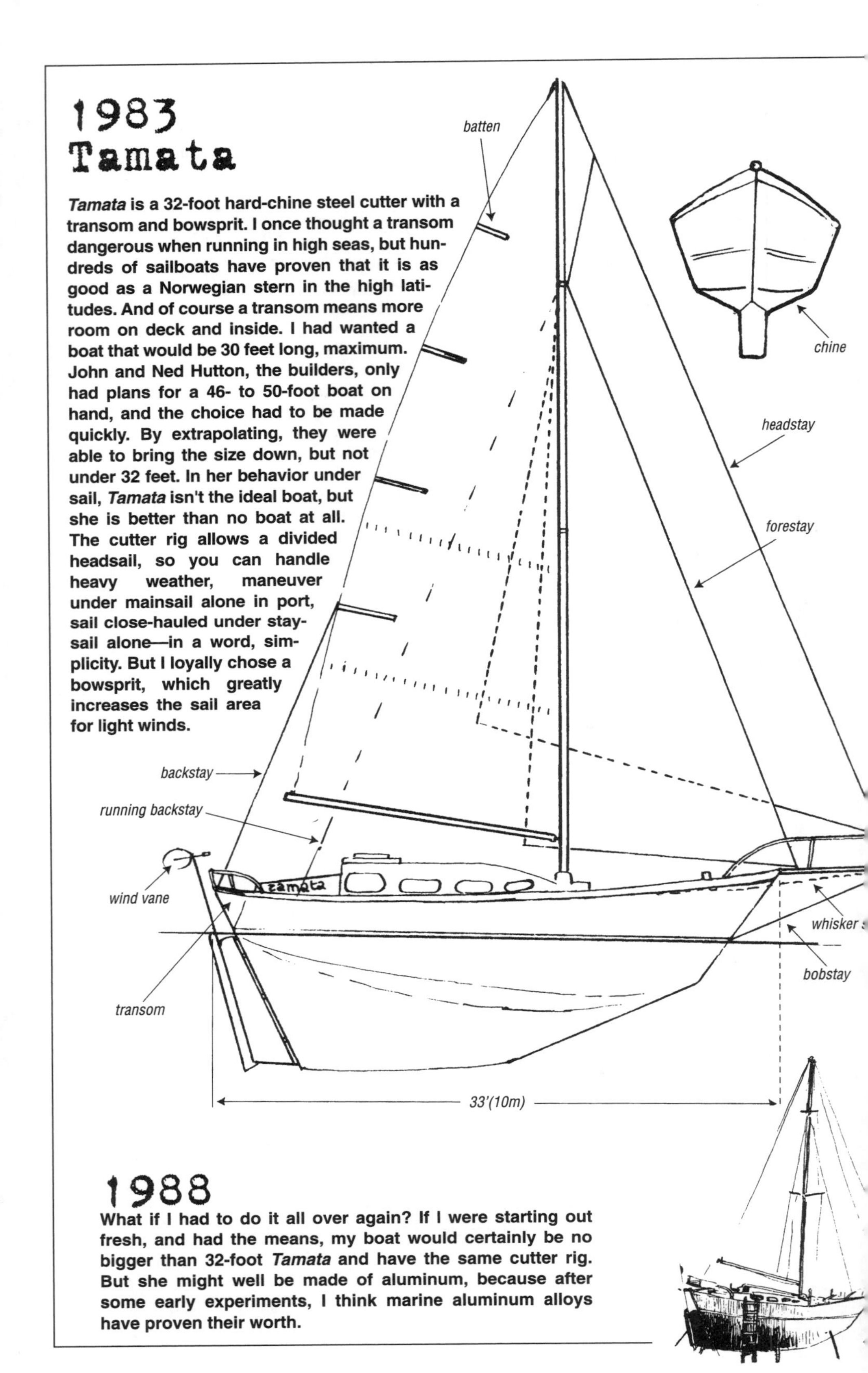

1988

What if I had to do it all over again? If I were starting out fresh, and had the means, my boat would certainly be no bigger than 32-foot *Tamata* and have the same cutter rig. But she might well be made of aluminum, because after some early experiments, I think marine aluminum alloys have proven their worth.

Another advantage of metal construction: a hollow keel with removable ballast, which makes it possible to careen the boat in waters without tides where the harbor lacks a haul-out or crane.

Maintenance

Steel's two enemies are electrolysis and rust. During the 1960s, L. Van de Wiele gave me what I think is the last word on the problems faced by a steel hull destined to cruise in waters around the world. This was his advice:

"Having analyzed the issue, I have to admit that for a boat hull, steel had almost every advantage over wood, except for corrosion risk and the resulting difficulty of maintenance. And I think the day is coming soon when we will come up with a really efficient way to isolate steel from seawater. At that point, there will be no justification for a wooden hull . . . Let's now turn to the disadvantage of steel. There is just one, which isn't all that serious: salt-water corrosion. I'm ignoring electrolysis, because if care is taken during the boat's design and construction, it can be almost completely eliminated . . . You can also have your hull sandblasted and galvanized. That is relatively expensive, but effective, and, in my opinion, currently the best protection against corrosion. Zinc bonds to steel perfectly, and there is no danger of its peeling off . . . It is worth noting, however, that it is as hard to protect zinc as steel, since paints don't adhere to zinc very well either.

"Note that the paint on the inside of the hull doesn't present any problems . . . It is the custom here to completely panel the hull above the cabin soles, but I prefer minimal inner planking, consisting of only a few easily removed laths . . . This lets me keep an eye on the inside of my hull . . . In sum, as you can see, corrosion protection is just a matter of painting, nothing else."

Paints have evolved since the 1960s and continue to evolve, but the principle behind Van de Wiele's advice remains valid: maintenance is simple, provided you don't cut corners in the preliminary base treatment of the steel; avoid design choices that can lead to complications; and always watch out for corrosion problems. Contrary to what you might expect, the biggest corrosion problems occur in the boat's interior, where the hull can't be seen or is hard to reach for maintenance.

Here are a few design errors to avoid:

1) Don't use any angle irons or T-sections. Floor plates, frames, stringers, and rails must all be flat bar, welded on edge. That way, a paintbrush can reach everywhere—which is essential if you don't want to face insoluble problems of interior corrosion. With flat bar, there are no hiding places for rust, and everything is visible. Places that can't be reached (the junctions of the keel with the bow and the sternpost, and under the mast) should be made watertight by welding a sheet of steel over them.

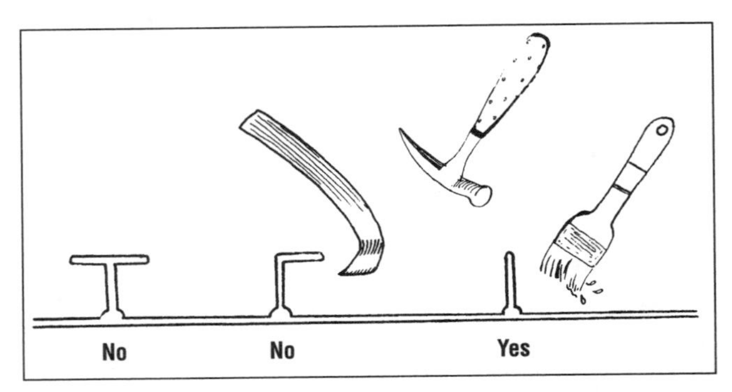

On a steel boat, no corners should be hidden and beyond reach of a paintbrush. Use flat bar, not angle irons or T-sections.

2) Don't use limber holes in the bilge, either. On wooden boats, the frames always have limber holes, so any seawater that leaks in can flow freely the length of the keel, which avoids any risk of rot. A metal boat should not have limber holes; that way, when a wave splashes through the companionway—which happens fairly often—you will only have a small section of the bilge to sponge out and rinse with fresh water, instead of the whole length of the keel. But of course you have to be able to get to all parts of the bilge.

On the other hand, it is best to make regular openings in the stringers to let condensation flow from the deck to the bilge (where it can be mopped up), especially if the interior is paneled, or when sailing in areas with a large temperature difference between outside and inside the boat.

3) Don't screw or bolt any wood onto the deck and cabin top, regardless of the quality of the putty you use

between the two materials. Using wood for bulwarks, hand rails, or hatch rails will almost always create corrosion sites. A pretty varnished hand rail may tempt you, but using a length of galvanized (or stainless steel) pipe makes much more sense. Putty is dangerous stuff, since it is squeezed out in tightening, and good, uniform protection can't be guaranteed.

4) All pieces that must be bolted to the deck (such as plexiglass portholes) should be mounted with flexible joints such as neoprene, which shapes itself to irregularities in the deck and isn't crushed when the bolts are tightened. This prevents humidity from entering between the materials, and avoids damage to the paint on tightening. A silicon joint, if it isn't correctly applied, is not enough; like putty, it squeezes out under pressure, and corrosion can soon begin.

5) Inside the boat, you must also reduce the risk of electrolysis; be sure to insulate the electrical system. And don't ground it to the hull.

Preliminary anticorrosion treatment

Remember that the boat's life span will depend on the quality of this initial treatment, which is done on the bare steel plates when the boat first comes from the yard.

Ideally, you should sand-blast the hull and deck before applying the first coat of paint. If you can also sand-blast the interior, so much the better.

By far the most effective anticorrosion paint I know is Dox Anode, a terrific zinc silicate paint sold in France by the Méta shipyard under the name Metagrip. It acts by cathodic protection against electrolysis (the zinc is destroyed while protecting the steel thanks to their difference in potential) and also protects against rust. So Dox Anode is more than just a paint; it is a kind of cold-dip galvanizing, and it adheres perfectly. It is also somewhat antifouling (this usage may now be outlawed because of toxicity), and can be scrubbed clean before a passage. It must be applied to the plates immediately after sand-blasting. All the other paints go on over it. For her first seven years, JOSHUA sailed with only this zinc silicate paint on her bottom, though I had to dive often to scrape barnacles off.

Another approach is to hot-dip galvanize the boat. This operation involves spraying several layers of molten zinc on the freshly sand-blasted surface. The treatment lasts a lifetime, but the bill can be steep!

Ideally, all small fittings should be stainless steel, provided you paint them carefully where they are welded to the hull to avoid any danger of electrolysis. Lacking stainless steel, galvanized iron (or at least hot-dip galvanized) will greatly reduce the time spent maintaining the boat.

Anticorrosion protection

The first coat of paint to go on next must adhere well to the Dox Anode (to zinc, that is). I first used zinc chromate in France, then Silver Primocon in the United States, which proved excellent and worked better with antifouling paints. But you have to let Dox Anode air for about two weeks before you start painting; this gives the zinc time to slightly oxidize and return to a neutral acid level, which will allow the primer to adhere well. If you don't have the time to wait, swab the sections painted with Dox Anode with a diluted 2 percent solution of phosphoric acid, then rinse with fresh water after a few minutes. You can then apply the primer immediately.

If you can't get Silver Primocon, it's important to find a primer that leaves the zinc surface inert and ready to take the finish paint.

I think it is very important to do a careful paint job (six or seven coats) before the boat is first put in the water, to provide a thick protective layer. I have heard that ships in the French Navy get more than ten coats before being launched.

Protection against electrolysis

The wetted surfaces of a steel boat will remain in perfect condition when protected from electrolysis by zinc anodes. These are either welded to the hull by their mounting brackets or bolted on, which makes them easier to replace when they corrode (you can dive and do it underwater). The "3 Z" anodes made by Zinc et Alliages are currently used by the French Navy, which chooses its equipment carefully.

On JOSHUA, "3 Z" anodes lasted five or six years. On TAMATA, the same anodes had to be replaced after two or three years, especially the ones close to the bow. Why the difference in longevity? It's a mystery. In any case, it's best to weigh anchor with a good supply of anodes in the hold; you can't find them just anywhere in the world. Before attaching the anodes, paint the back sides, which will be in contact with the hull, so they don't erode at the attachment points.

<u>Finish paints</u>

For the bottom: antifouling paint without copper or copper oxide.

For the topsides: various finish paints can be used, ranging from alkyd paint, which is the cheapest but most short-lived, through epoxies and polyurethanes (the latter are better suited for the final coat).

For current maintenance, see "Maintenance and repairs," page 155.

Paints and paint techniques continue to evolve. Someday, we're sure to have a miracle protective product, but the quality of the initial treatment will always be vital. TAMATA, which was built in 1983 in the United States, was given a slightly different treatment from the one described here.

Summary of initial treatment principles before launch (based on my experience with JOSHUA)

STAGE	BOTTOM	HULL AND DECK	INTERIOR
Treatment before launch	Scoured by sand blasting		
	Anti-corrosion protection paint Dox Anode (2 coats)		
Protection and finish	Nothing	Primer Silver Primocon (2 coats)	Zinc chromate primer (2 coats)
	or primer of Silver Primocon type (2 coats) then antifouling without copper or copper oxide (or other metals)	Alkyd or Two-part epoxy or polyurethane (2-3 coats)	Alkyd (2-3 coats)

At the beginning of this section, I said that maintaining a steel boat is simple. If you live aboard, that's true. But I wouldn't recommend this type of construction to a busy person who can only go sailing for a few weeks a year. Such people might wind up spending most of their vacations in port doing basic maintenance chores.

ALUMINUM AND STRONGALL

Steel construction is more than a century old; aluminum construction is still fairly recent, but is starting to prove itself. "If you want an aluminum boat without taking too many chances," a friend once told me, "it's best to buy a second-hand one and get expert advice; if everything is in good shape, you'll improve your chances of finding a decent boat." As I said before, I would be inclined to try aluminum if I needed a new boat and could afford it. But I have no experience in this area, so I'll say no more.

From what I've been able to learn here and there, aluminum won't cause serious electrolysis problems if the electrical system is completely grounded and you avoid long stays in industrial ports, where stray currents are common. My friend Antoine told me how much Americans fear aluminum: "They talk about aluminum sailboats that had spent two or three years at their moorings and were so corroded that it looked as if a giant can opener had split them along their waterlines." Was this the result of stray currents or inadequate (or non-existent) cathodic protection on the hull? Antoine thinks the problem was caused by the two factors combined.

It's worth noting that Antoine's boats VOYAGE and BANANA SPLIT were built by the Méta shipyard using the "Strongall" procedure: extremely heavy aluminum sheets, without ribs; the thicker the aluminum, the stronger the welds.

One final point: it is essential to get an antifouling bottom paint that is truly compatible with aluminum from an electrolysis standpoint. Since launching his first aluminum boat, Antoine had chosen to stick with Dox Anode (Metagrip), which, as I noted earlier, is somewhat antifouling. He has to dive to brush off his hull a little more often, but figures that he is minimizing the risk of electrolysis by only using Metagrip.

FIBERGLASS

Boatyards turn out production boats very quickly and they're almost always lightweight, to keep costs down. Even such basics as rigging, chainplates, and rudder strength have left me shaking my head. Do they enjoy playing Russian roulette? I have far more confidence in good amateur construction, and have seen some excellent examples: heavy, carefully reinforced hulls; numerous chainplates of respectable size; strongly stepped masts; sturdy pillars and rudder blades, with fittings to match; wide, relatively long keels well attached to the hull. These are real boats, made to last. They can face heavy weather with confidence, handle an occasional scrape on a coral reef without splitting open, and require virtually no maintenance.

WOOD

How easy it will be to build your own boat depends on the type of construction you have in mind. The simplest is hard-chine plywood construction, followed by traditional planking, and finally cold-molding, which takes the most time.

Maintenance

The shortcomings of wood are shipworms, leakage, and rot.

Shipworms or teredos and other wood-boring marine worms live in warm, tropical seas, but are also found in the Atlantic and the Mediterranean.

If your hull is easy to inspect, that is, if you can quickly detect the presence of shipworms, there is nothing to get excited about. A boat that is careened regularly—every six or eight months in the tropics—shouldn't have any problems. But beware of coatings that might hide shipworm tunnels.

Rot is also one of the major problems a wooden boat can encounter during its lifetime. Its risk will first depend on the materials used. But rot doesn't spread like wildfire; it goes very slowly. (See "Maintenance and repairs," page 155.)

I worked too quickly, under the* badamier *tree on Mauritius, I rushed the job. I bought cheap boards from the local lumber yard because I wasn't patient enough to wait for a shipment of better ones . . . And there were so many basic steps I didn't know about when I was building* MARIE-THÉRÈSE II*, such as swabbing the planks and ribs with creosote or something like it, to prevent rot.

Traditional plank construction

This is absolutely solid, and such boats can sail for decades without major problems if the construction is well done, with first-class materials. But unless you are very skilled, it's best to leave the work to a reputable shipyard. Or to find a skilled craftsman and work together as much as possible, to learn as many useful things as you can. Either way, you have to be financially very secure to build a good boat using classic plank construction.

Before World War II, and even for a time afterward, those boats were superbly built. The logs would spend eight to twelve years buried in mud to draw out the sap (and keep them out of reach of shipworms, which are found in all climates). Then the logs were allowed to dry very slowly, in the shade. They were cut into sheets and planks that were stored in dry, well-ventilated warehouses to cure for several more years. The shipyards had a large supply, and the wood was really ready, without a trace of sapwood. The humblest fishing boat was built with the same love as a cathedral, because the shipwrights had the time. Those days are gone.

A traditional plank boat with a modern frame of glued laminated wood (bow and stern pieces, bulkheads, floor timbers, ribs, side stringers, struts, deck- and cabin-top beams) will be terrifically strong if you don't skimp on fittings. But unless you're a millionaire, I doubt you'll ever find those wonderful long planks from our grandparents' day to cover that great framework.

Molded wood

Cold-molded construction produces a boat that is very rigid, light, and watertight, if certain joints (cabin to deck, deck to hull, and keel to stem and sternpost) are made with great care. But construction takes much longer than one might expect.

You often see molded wood or plywood hulls covered with fiberglass and polyester resin to protect them against shipworms. I think that is very dangerous, because if the layer cracks—and it will, sooner or later—shipworms will get in without your realizing it.

And from then on, they will quickly chew their way through the thin planking. You may not always realize what is going on, and after a few years the damage will be irreparable.

If you're lucky enough to notice the problem in time, the best thing to do is to haul the boat out for a few months to be sure no teredos or their larvae remain alive and that the water in their tunnels is completely evaporated (you can hasten this by drilling small holes, to be plugged later). I would let everything dry out completely; three or four months wouldn't be too long. Once that's done, I would inject a very fluid epoxy such as Everdur, which is used to "vitrify" wood that has become spongy. But these are just suggestions; others with more experience than I have will be better able to help you solve this admittedly serious problem.

Plywood

Much faster to build with than molded wood, but not as rigid, since you're making a hard-chine boat; also, it is subject to the same shipworm problem. I've often heard it said that the layers of glue in plywood or molded wood are barriers to shipworms. That's absolutely false; I've seen some disasters.

Do you have to be handy with tools?

When you start a job that you don't know how to do, or when you don't know the solution to a problem, you will get it done by starting, by doing it. As a friend used to say, *"The work is teaching you the work."*

V: Do you have to be handy with tools to be a sailor?
B: I can't quite see someone going sailing without being a bit of a handyman. I learned . . . well, I can't say I really learned, I had to do it . . . You don't learn how to do things from books; you learn with friends, you learn by trying to make something and figuring how to make it work.
V: So experience is the main thing?
B: That's right. Experience, and watching how other people go about things.

Size of the boat

Careful, not too big! A small boat has the advantage over a bigger one of costing much less to buy and maintain. If your eyes are bigger than your stomach, you always wind up paying for it in time and worry. A 30- to 33-foot boat can spin out a wonderful wake. Here are a few examples among many. LEGH II: around the world by the three capes. SUHAILI: around the world by the three capes, nonstop. DAMIEN: Greenland, the Amazon, the three capes, and the Adelie Coast. Many smaller boats have sailed around the world by following the trade winds and rounding the Cape of Good Hope. Naturally, a 45-footer is much faster and more comfortable than a 30- or 35-foot boat, but the difference in purchase price (or construction cost, if you build it yourself) and maintenance expenses is enormous.

Sail area and choice of rig

"Easier" and "faster" are often synonymous with "less tiring" and "safer."

People will always have different opinions about picking a rig for a blue-water cruising boat. For me, temperament and habits count almost as much as personal experience in making the choice.

I always bear two points in mind: maximum sail area, and a divided sail plan. Being able to carry a lot of canvas in gentle to moderate airs means you can go quite a bit faster. And a split rig is easier to handle when you're alone or in heavy weather.

As for choosing between split rigs, I made my choice long ago. What I like about a ketch rig is that it is perfectly adaptable to any wind condition. A ketch's sail area is spread over four sails: jib, staysail, main, and mizzen. This gives you great flexibility when handling sail alone. You can jibe smoothly in a fresh wind, with the mizzen blanketing the main. The same applies when putting in a reef, and since the mizzen helps take the pressure off the main, you don't have to come up into the wind. Another advantage is that you can rig a mizzen staysail, which considerably increases your sail area, reduces rolling, and makes the sails as a whole perform better.

Just the same, I have come to prefer a cutter over a ketch rig. It means less weight and windage aloft; a more open deck; better performance close-hauled; the possibility of sailing into a strong wind under staysail alone; and being maneuverable (including coming about) under staysail or mainsail alone when making an anchorage in light airs and a flat sea.

A cutter, unlike a sloop, has double headsails forward. Of course it's easier to handle a staysail or genoa on a sloop's foredeck than out on a cutter's bowsprit. But in my opinion, the advantages of a bowsprit outweigh its drawbacks. A six-foot bowsprit, for example, lets a boat carry much more sail. And if the boat has a mast that is three feet taller, the difference in the amount of sail it can carry in light or moderate wind will be enormous—and so will the difference in speed. In light airs, a boat's speed isn't only a function of the pressure of the wind on the sails, but how regular that pressure is.

Let's take a concrete example.

1) Suppose two boats are sailing between a beam and a broad reach in a fresh wind under somewhat reduced sail toward the same destination.

2) The wind begins to slacken, then drops considerably. Both boats raise all canvas, but the swells are big and the sea fairly choppy. This is when a large total sail area will make all the difference. The boat with more sail (the one with a bowsprit and taller mast) will move much faster than the other one, not only because of the greater pressure of the wind, but also because the boat won't pound into the waves as much at all points of sail between a close reach and running. Moreover, the airflow is much more efficient on sails that are well filled. By carrying a lot of canvas in light or moderate wind on a choppy sea, the boat pounds less and the sails remain more stable, which is all to the good. On the other hand, it will be at a disadvantage vis-a-vis the other boat when close-hauled in a fresh wind, because of its extra windage aloft. So it's a matter of choice. I made mine long ago.

JOSHUA's total sail area was 1,259 square feet, which, for 15 tons of displacement, works out to 84 square feet per ton of displacement. By lacing a 108-square-foot bonnet to the foot of the genoa, I could increase the ratio to 90 square feet per ton. On TAMATA, the total sail surface was 775 square feet for seven tons, or about 110 square feet per ton of displacement.

The rudder: on the keel or the stern?

I much prefer a rudder hanging outboard on the stern.

1) You can add a self-steering trim tab that is extremely simple and virtually indestructible, and which you can make yourself for next to nothing. When I see the prices of the sophisticated and often fragile self-steering rigs on the market, it really makes me wonder.

2) A keel-hung rudder might someday jam on its shaft, whereas a transom-mounted rudder, which is a model of strength and simplicity, will never cause problems. Finally, I think having a keel-hung rudder on

a wooden boat is really asking for trouble. Despite every precaution, shipworms will sooner or later burrow into the sternpost throat, and—which is far more serious—into the rudder trunk.

Buying versus building

Short of building your own boat, I think it's wisest to order a bare hull—hull, deck, cabin top, and rudder-from a good boatyard. The advantage of going this route is that you will have the basics in two or three months. If you choose a metal boat (and I hope you do) and the owner lets you work at the yard, you should build all your own topside fittings: stanchions, bow pulpit, sheet cleats, mooring bitts, hand rails, etc. You can't imagine the number of pieces and hours of work this means. Not only will you get exactly what you want, but it will also cost much less. And working alongside professionals has two further benefits: you will learn plenty of things that will come in handy later, and you'll get to know your boat backward and forward.

Snark

When we went on board, the boat was completely bare; customs had seized her for smuggling. I stepped aboard, crouched down in the empty hold, and in a flash, I knew that my entire life up to that point was over and done with. We were going to go to sea, and of course I said, "All right!" The two of us put everything we had into her . . . Six weeks after I first saw that hulk . . . Snark *was being towed at 10 knots down the Saigon River.*

Marie Thérèse

At Kampot, Xian's father took me in . . . He helped me find a little junk, 30 feet long and 10 feet wide, which I named Marie Thérèse *. . . Four weeks of intense preparation followed . . .*

Marie Thérèse II

Marie Thérèse II *was built by eye, not because I wanted to show off, but because I was so short of money. I had to adapt to the local conditions on Mauritius, where curved lumber used for cross-cut ribs was rare. Having a plan drawn up that was specially suited to the materials available on the island would have cost me a lot . . .*

Building Marie Thérèse II *was slow and peaceful. I did it with a saw and plane, and no power tools . . . She was launched nine months later, and I rigged her as a gaff-rigged ketch.*

Joshua

With the help of the Méta boatyard, building Joshua *took three and a half months. As planned, work began when school started in September . . . My beautiful boat was finished in mid-December. The first cruising-school crew would come aboard on May 1 . . .*

Tamata

John and Ned Hutton built Tamata *in California in record time. Jacques Toujan and I completed the interior in just ten days: no partitions, open interior, no closets; inner-tube strips stretched between the ribs held books and other small things; everything was simple, functional, and fast. Three months after the hurricane that hit* Joshua, *I was painting my new boat's hull.*

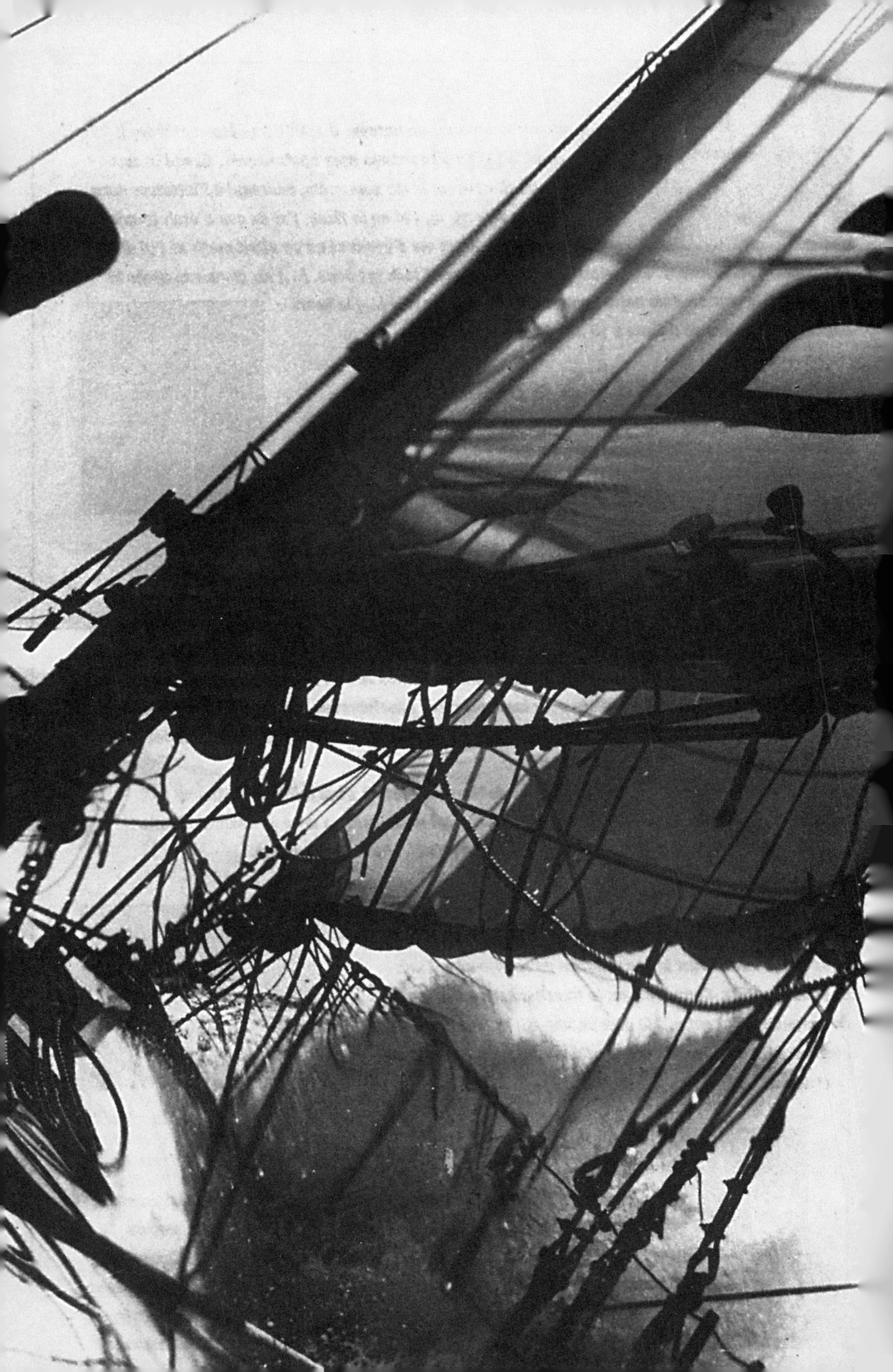

Fitting out

Stick to the basics

It would be stupid not to take advantage of technological progress that makes life easier and sailing more fun. But you can go very far with very little, provided you get under way. The first time I rounded Cape Horn, I didn't have any winches and was using galvanized wire shrouds. But if I could have had winches and stainless steel shrouds, I wouldn't have hesitated to use them.

Remember the mental process that guides us in cruising: if you have to choose between something simple and something complicated, pick what's simple. It will be cheap, faster to make, and can be repaired for next to nothing with whatever you have on board, at sea or in some out-of-the way place, without having to write to Australia or Europe for spare parts. That way, you can sail with peace of mind, and safely come and go as you please.

Let's say you decide to have your boat built by a boatyard. With the bulk of the job finished in just a few months, you might be tempted to think everything is done. But you're on a roll, so stick with it. Get your mast, rigging, sails (second-hand, if need be), a few rolls of line, three anchors, chain, a fresh-water tank (or jerrycans), some pots and pans, a kerosene or propane stove, a bare-bones interior—and it's home sweet home! Not very comfortable? A mere detail, for the moment. You have the basics. You can tinker with the interior arrangements during stopovers. The advantage of doing things in increments is that you will know exactly what you need. It also gives you time to really think through what you want to accomplish, and avoid expensive forays that turn out to be useless in practice. Better to raise anchor with plenty of money in the ship's kitty than to stagger along under a ton of stuff you can live without. During her first five or six years, JOSHUA sailed for miles with a decor that was strictly "bed of nails," and no winches. I'm not saying that a more comfortable cabin and winches wouldn't have been preferable, but we had to choose between hoisting sail before winter started or shivering in the port of Marseille while burning a hole in our savings. Once the bow is pointed toward the open sea, you always manage. Twenty years later, TAMATA left San Francisco with only a few boxes of candles for light. Kerosene lamps, then a solar panel and batteries, came later.

Masts, shrouds, and turnbuckles

A racing mast must be as thin as possible, even if it occasionally breaks, just as blocks have to be as light as possible, even if it means replacing them more often. But when you're cruising, everything has to be strong, and especially the mast.

JOSHUA's masts were solid poles, slightly oval in section, shaped with an adze and a plane. I used telephone poles to save money, although laminated hollow masts would have been lighter and probably just as strong, while putting less of a strain on the standing rigging. TAMATA's mast is hollow.

Of course just because I used telephone poles for masts doesn't mean I think that's the best way to go. But eighteen years ago, it was the obvious choice: the poles only cost five francs a meter! If I'd had enough money, I wouldn't have hesitated to equip JOSHUA with the best that was available—within limits, of course.

The taller the mast, the more sail you can carry, and the better the boat's performance in light airs. You can always shorten sail, but you can't extend the mast when the wind drops. JOSHUA's mainmast stood 49 feet above the deck; on a 39-foot boat, that's a ratio of 1.25. TAMATA's mast is 43 feet tall; she is 33 feet long, which gives a ratio of 1.3.

Lots of chainplates, many shrouds, and oversized turnbuckles are the best combination I know for peace of mind in bad weather. JOSHUA's mainmast survived six or seven serious knockdowns, plus a collision with a freighter. It was supported by six shrouds on each side, plus backstays. TAMATA is rigged the same way. Of course this kind of rigging represents extra weight and windage where you want it least when close-hauled, but to each his own.

Galvanized steel has always been my favorite material, because it is reliable. I have heard that stainless steel can crystallize over time and fail without warning, and that welding stainless steel can cause molecular changes within the alloy. Chainplates are subjected to considerable strain during the life of a blue-water cruising boat, and on a steel boat, they are welded to the hull. That's why I never recommend using stainless steel chainplates on a steel boat; your mast will end up on the deck someday. (If it's for a cabin hatch cover slide or a hand rail, there's no danger.) Production fiberglass boats are usually fitted with stainless steel chainplates, but they are bolted to the hull (or cast in the fiberglass), not welded.

For everything else, I've taken to using stainless steel. TAMATA is rigged with oversized stainless steel 1/2" Wichard turnbuckles (where 3/8" or even 5/16" might theoretically be enough). Remember to put a toggle between the turnbuckle and chainplate to avoid major problems, especially with the jib and staysail stays. For the same diameter, a stainless wire rope shroud will be stronger than galvanized wire. But over time, the successive stretching caused by the working of the mast can crystallize the stainless steel and make it brittle. I think it wise to choose oversize shrouds if you are going to use stainless steel wire. It will mean less stretching, less vibration, and fewer surprises over the long haul. JOSHUA's stainless steel shrouds were 5/16" to 3/8" for the mainmast, and 3/8" for the mizzen, which can't have a forestay or fixed backstays. I prefer not to use a spring stay (a wire joining the two mastheads, sometimes found on ketches), because if one mast comes down, the other always follows suit.

I don't splice my shrouds; I use three cable clamps instead. The lowest one (nearest the thimble) should be tightened moderately, the second more so, and the third all the way. This avoids putting a strain on the cable where it loops around the thimble. I always put the U-shaped part of the clamp against the shroud's standing end; otherwise, it could stress the shroud.

Cable clamps, small and large thimbles

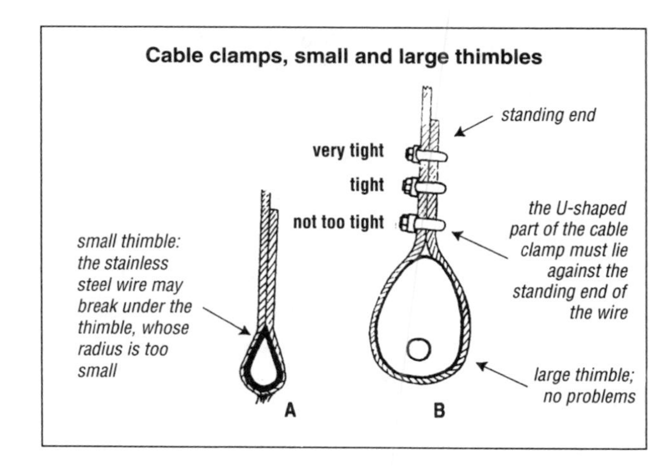

THIMBLES

Whether you use clamps or splices, most thimbles are not designed for stainless steel. Stainless wire is fragile when bent, and most thimbles' radius of curvature is too small. I once saw a new mizzen shroud that had broken right under the thimble, at the point of greatest curvature. With galvanized wire the problem doesn't arise, because galvanized doesn't fatigue and tolerates a much smaller radius than stainless. Good thimbles for stainless steel should be very big: I could easily see them 3 inches wide and 4-5 inches high. And I instinctively mistrust the system used on airplanes, where the shroud is swaged onto the end of the turnbuckle. Sure, it will never slip—but if the shroud should fatigue, it will part right at the swage. With a thimble, you can see what is happening; a few strands beginning to fray under the thimble will give warning, and set you thinking about a remedy. Mine consists in making up the shortened shroud's length with a bit of chain. As for the mast end of the shrouds, no problem up there; on both JOSHUA and TAMATA they go around the mast and rest on wooden chocks called hounds.

Repairing a shroud that has broken at the thimble

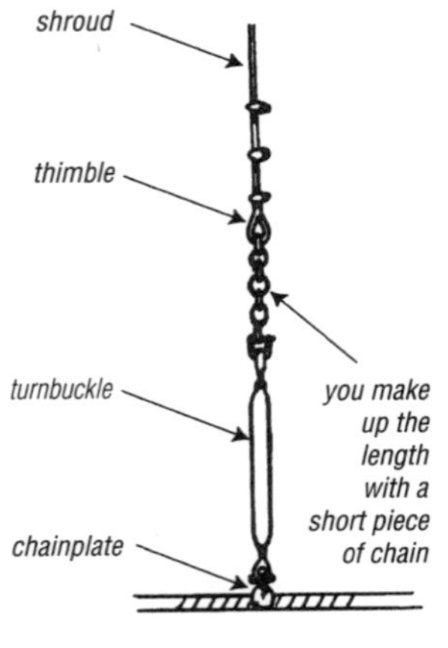

SPREADERS

The spreaders on JOSHUA and TAMATA were mounted with flexibility in mind. On JOSHUA, they weathered a collision before my first rounding of the Cape of Good Hope, then five knockdowns that put the masts in the water, four of which—when I crossed the Indian Ocean and the Pacific the second time—were very serious.

Flexible spreader mounting and looped shrouds

wooden block, slightly countersunk into the mast

a metal strap connects the two spreader bars but lets them rotate around the mast

the loops go around the mast

metal strap

sail track

The wooden block that the sail track is screwed to is open where the spreader strap passes through it. This lets the strap slide back and forth.

If the spreaders had been mounted rigidly, with metal fittings, I am sure that JOSHUA would have stopped before reaching Tahiti, and very probably before first rounding Good Hope, after my collision with the freighter.

Not only is the flexible

mounting safe, but it is easy to install, simple, and cheap.

MAST STEPS AND FALSE SPREADERS

I consider it essential to be able to climb easily to the top of the mast under any conditions to replace a halyard, free a jammed sail slide, look around to pick up a buoy, see a low shore or a reef, etc. I found the stainless steel Seabird Mast Steps from Seabird Marine in California excellent. The halyards can't foul or chafe on them, and the steps can be adapted to any shape mast, whether wood or aluminum.

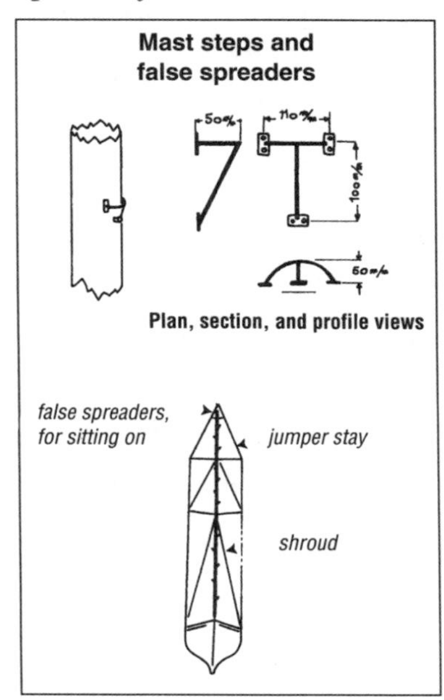

Plan, section, and profile views

A pair of false spreaders located about three feet below the main masthead lets me sit and work comfortably (to replace a block, for example).

Halyards, lines, and chafe

All my halyards are single (by which I mean with no tackles), and without turning blocks.

This means less length of halyard on deck when the sails are raised. Also, the sails go up much faster, which is very welcome when you're maneuvering under sail in a crowded harbor. They can be struck much faster, too. A single halyard gives you mobility when you're raising or lowering sail; you can move about the deck while holding the halyard in your hand.

I use very old-fashioned blocks with nylon sheaves. They can take 9/16" to 5/8" lines without any friction against the wooden cheeks. They are strong, and inexpensive compared to more modern blocks.

The experience of The Long Way

I was satisfied with Lancelin braided Dacron line, which resisted chafe well. A 9/16" line used as a sheet on a 40-foot boat won't break unless it is chafed somewhere. Tallow, grease, oil, or other fatty substances help protect synthetic lines against wear. I have always been careful to vigorously rub grease into lines and halyards where they run through blocks. The prestretched Dacron jib and staysail halyards were deliberately measured about five feet too long. That way, I could cut off a few inches each week, which moved the point bearing on the sheaves. The working parts of those halyards then were always new. Plus grease, of course. I didn't have to replace one halyard during the entire trip. To be on the safe side, I kept a spare jib and staysail halyard in place along the shrouds. I didn't need them, but felt safer knowing they were there.

The jib and mainsail halyards were very flexible 3/16" stainless steel wire running through stainless blocks a pal made for me, with very wide 3" sheaves. It is important that stainless halyards run through very wide diameter blocks, so they aren't bent at too sharp an angle.

As a last word on chafe, I got excellent results from soaking my reefing lines in oil where they passed through the turning blocks at the end of the boom. The lines were only 3/8", and thus are susceptible to a lot of wear where they pass through the leech cringles of the sail, which is in constant movement. Once soaked in oil, the nylon lines were far more wear-resistant. I had to replace the reefing lines twice in ten months; without the oil, I would have had to replace them at least five times. The idea of using oil came from my friend Henry Wakelam, and works for halyards and sheets where they pass through the blocks. I have heard it said that fatty substances reduce the strength of synthetic lines. But a line's breaking strength isn't an issue, compared to the problems of chafe and wear.

Sails

MINIMUM SAIL INVENTORY

A mainsail is out of reach of waves. Once it is furled on its boom in bad weather, nothing can happen to it, except in very unusual circumstances. If it is made of heavy enough material it seldom rips to shreds, and can always be repaired. The mainsail on David Lewis's REHU MOANA, which reached Tahiti after passing the Strait of Magellan and the Patagonian canals, displayed 30 to 50 feet of hand stitching from one bolt rope to the other, sewn between gales.

Headsails, on the other hand, are much more exposed. To be properly prepared, you must have an extra set of headsails, if only in case of damage. And beyond the risk of tearing a jib or staysail, having some light-weather sails means you can make the most of a light wind by raising a genoa and a large staysail.

Not that you can't sail without having spare jibs and staysails. JOSHUA did two years of cruising school with a single set of sails. It just means being a little more cautious so you can survive a squall. And you go slower in light airs while dreaming of a genoa and a big staysail. But those can come later; the main thing is that you can put to sea and go very far with a single set of sails, if you want to.

When I say a single set of sails, it should be understood that every boat must have a storm jib as well. After all, 50 or 70 square feet of sail isn't that expensive, especially since you can cut and sew this heavy-weather sail yourself; the quality of the cut of a storm jib isn't too important. Raised in place of the jib in a fresh wind, a storm jib can add years to the life of the working headsails.

For the 1968-69 circumnavigation I call "The Long Way", I had two complete sets of sails, plus a good number of jibs and staysails. They were all cut from a cloth designed for the America's Cup race by Ferrari, in Lyon. He gave me the sails, with the understanding that I would return them after the voyage, so he could study the cloth in the laboratory, to see how his sails had stood up to this ultimate test. With two complete sets of sails, I wasn't taking any risk, and was happy to try the experiment. Otherwise, I would have never dared set out on such a long voyage with unfamiliar sailcloth.

CHOICE OF MATERIAL, STITCHING, AND PROTECTION

For a racer, a good sail is one that keeps its shape and draws well for a season, even if it is worthless at the end of the year. For us cruisers, a good sail is one whose cloth lasts a decade, even if it loses its shape a little.

It isn't easy to recognize material that suits the needs of cruising. If the sailcloth is very flexible and doesn't crackle at all between your fingers, it should be all right. A sail needle (which is triangular in section) should go through it without the slightest sound as it parts the fibers. But if the material is already somewhat stiff even before being made into a sail, and if you can hear the needle push through, then it probably doesn't meet our requirements, since we put durability well ahead of an extra tenth of a knot on a close reach.

A good sailmaker knows the difference between

racing and cruising, and will have materials designed specifically for each. And I think that the best credential a sailmaker can show is to be a sailor himself. Being in a gale helps you grasp many things about reinforcements; a flat calm with some swell shows where a sail rubs against the shrouds and helps you understand how to protect the stitching from chafing.

From long experience, I am convinced that sails sewn with very heavy thread are much stronger and more durable than those sewn with fine thread. But sewing such sails takes longer (and is therefore more expensive) because you have to change the thread bobbins more often. I've often heard it said that fine thread is less subject to chafe because it embeds itself in the sail instead of lying on the surface. That argument makes no sense at all. Whether the thread is heavy or fine, it still lies on the surface. It was only with old-fashioned cotton sails that the thread sank beneath the surface, and then only if the stitching was done by hand, and not zig-zag stitched on a sewing machine.

For a sail to last a long time, it should be triple-stitched with the heaviest thread available. With only two rows of stitching, occasional flapping and the constant shivering of a sail close-hauled tend to cause the panels to work very slightly. This chafes the thread in the needle holes, because Dacron is a hard, sharp material. With three rows of stitching, the panels are more tightly held together and work less, which prevents or minimizes cutting the thread in the needle holes.

Small triangular (not rectangular) patches sewn where the seams meet the leech add considerably to the sails' durability, by reducing the risk of rips during violent flogging (for example when you're dousing sail in a major squall).

When a sail tears, it's almost always because flogging has split it along a seam, starting from the leech. The higher stitching is always the most exposed, because the upper part of a sail whips around most while you're coming about in a fresh wind, or dropping the sails.

For headsails snapped onto a stay (without a roller), it is very useful to sew a patch at each of the sail snaps. In a calm with some swell, snaps tend to wear through the material. When the wind is fresh, the tension of the snaps on a poorly set sail puts a lot of strain on the area around the eyelets.

Other patches (rectangular, of necessity) sewn along the seams where they rub against the spreaders and the lower shrouds can keep the stitching from chafing at those vital points. Wrapping the shrouds is useful, but it isn't enough over the long haul. The patches protecting the sail from wearing against the shrouds must be long enough so they remain effective when the sail is reefed or roller-furled.

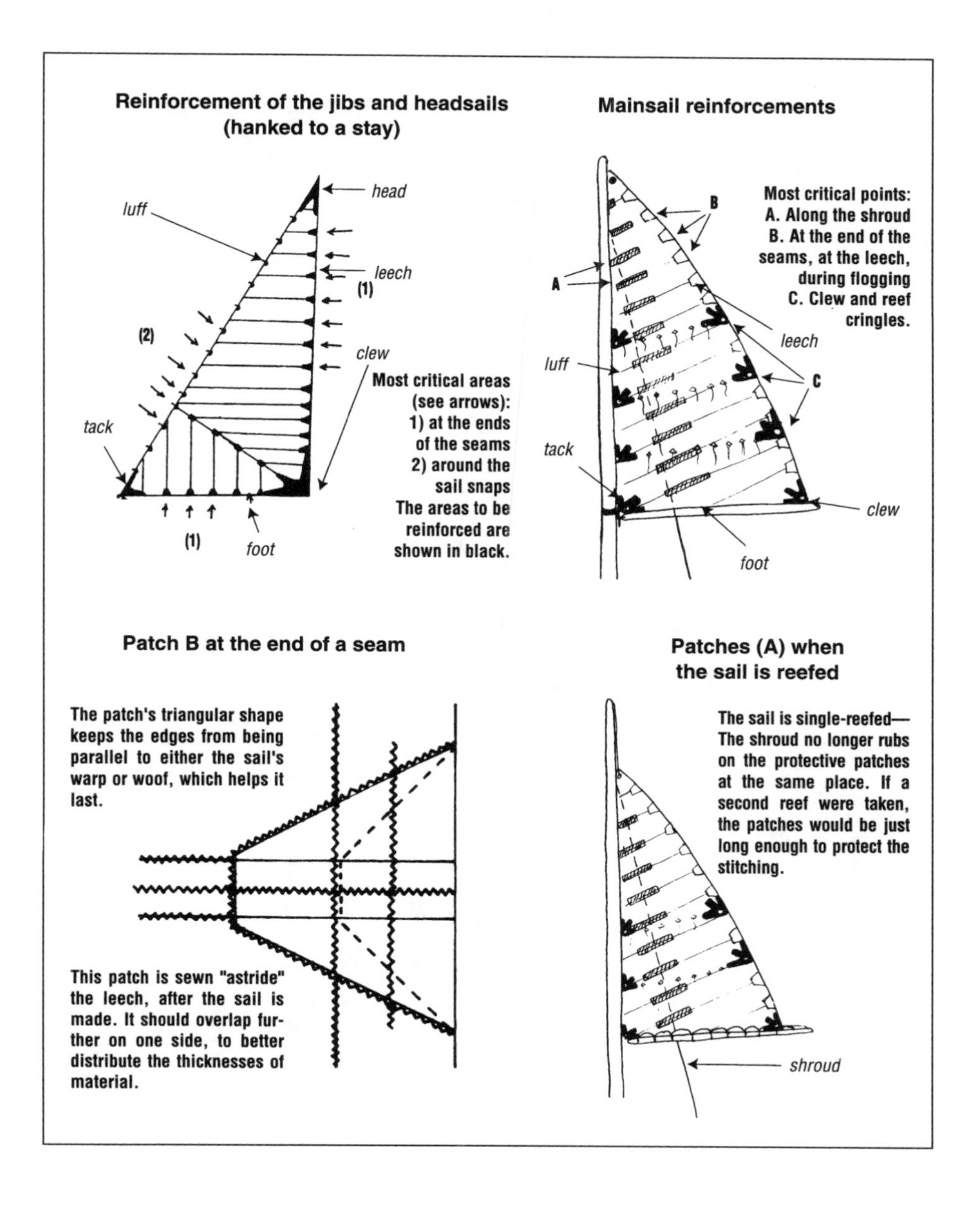

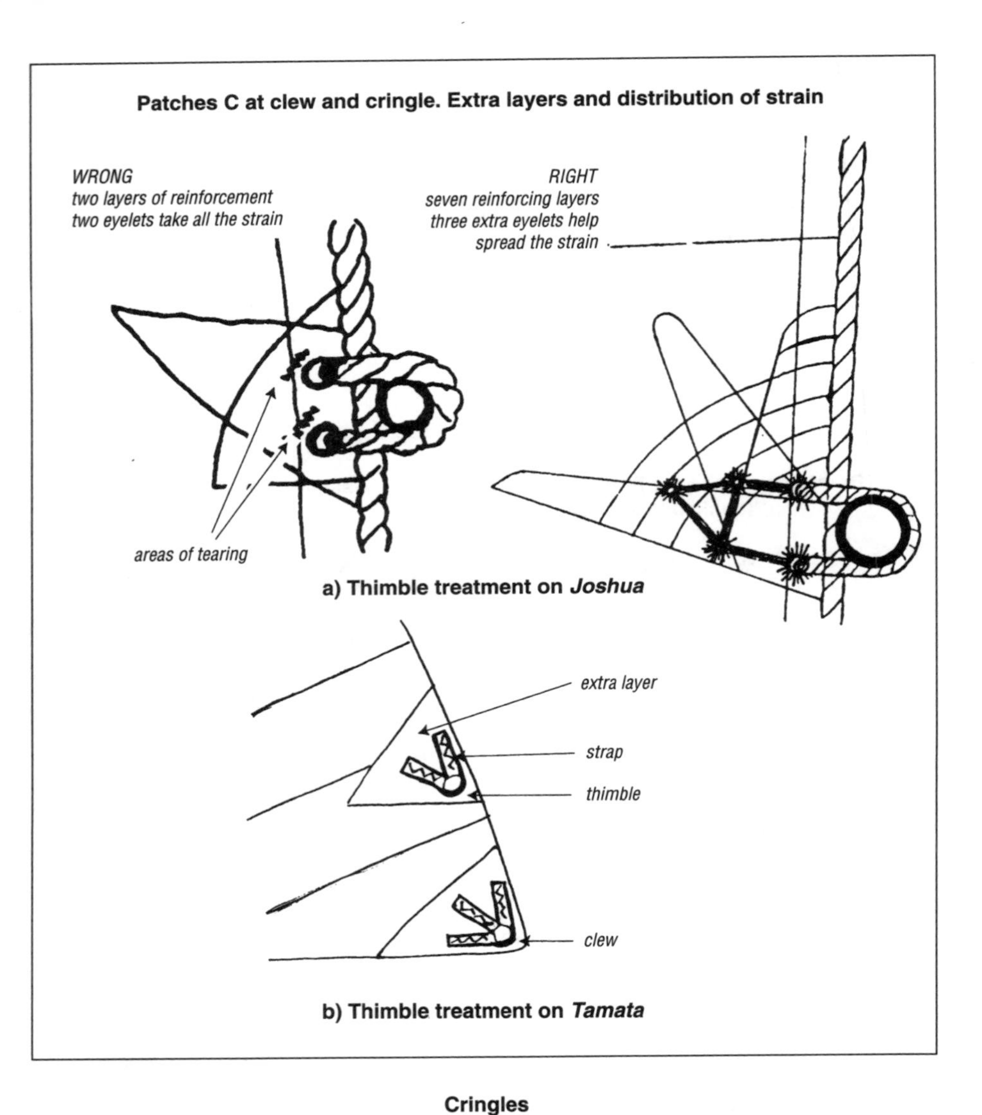

Cringles

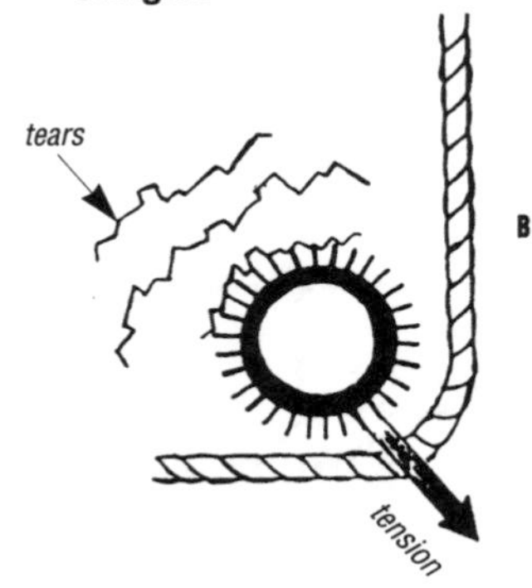

A. RIGHT
The stitching is made along two circles, one of which is quite far from the grommet's edge.

B. WRONG
The stitches are close together and on the same circle, too close to the grommet.

SAIL TRACKS AND SLIDES

Whether you're entering a port or dropping the mainsail in a fresh wind, it's essential that the sail come down smoothly; a well-lubricated sail track will make it easier. I used to use tallow, but it tends to get sticky after a few months. Vaseline gave me excellent results. Two-stroke motor oil will also work, but it doesn't last as long as Vaseline.

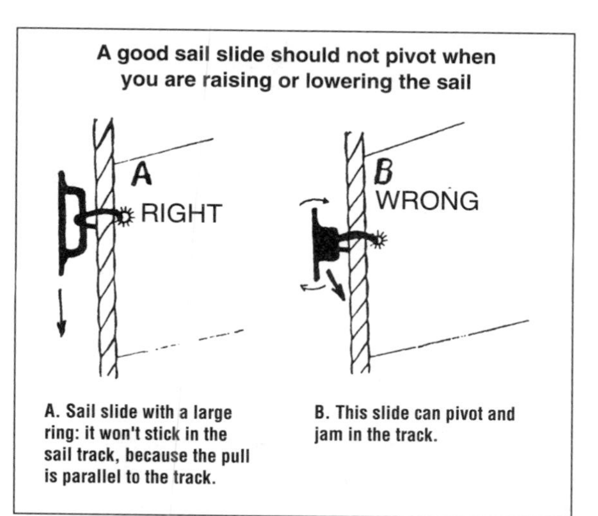

A. Sail slide with a large ring: it won't stick in the sail track, because the pull is parallel to the track.

B. This slide can pivot and jam in the track.

JOSHUA's sail slides had large rings, of the kind shown in the sketch. The kind with a hole in the middle have a bad tendency to get stuck.

FIXED GASKETS

To save time when reefing, I keep gaskets permanently attached to the boom for the mainsail, and to the pulpit for the jib and staysail. I painted them black to make them easier to see at night.

Joshua's sail inventory

Mainsail: 325 square feet with three reef bands.
Small mainsail: 270 square feet with three reef bands.
Mizzen: 215 square feet with three reef bands.
Small mizzen: 150 square feet with three reef bands.
Large staysails: 195 square feet with three reef bands.
Small staysails: 110, 65, and 55 square feet, each with reef bands. These small staysails were cut so that I could also set them on the bowsprit if I chose.
Small genoa: 380 square feet
Large jib: 330 square feet without reef bands.
Small jib: 160 square feet with reef bands.
Storm jibs: 55 and 75 square feet with reef bands.
All those sails were cut in 9-ounce Dacron, which seems to me a reasonable weight, not too heavy. But the 160 square feet jib was light, 5-ounce Dacron. This light jib was so handy that it lasted for six months, before giving out shortly before my second rounding of Good Hope. I was very sorry to lose it, because it was easy to handle, furled very tight, and was easy to carry between the end of the bowsprit and the forepeak when the weather worsened. And when the wind dropped, it stayed full. But it would never have lasted as long as it did without all the reinforcements I mentioned earlier.

Anchors and anchoring

With very few exceptions, I always choose my big anchor over a smaller one. Whether an anchor weighs, say, 50 pounds instead of 35 doesn't make much difference in terms of muscular effort when weighing anchor. But the extra holding power on the bottom will be welcome in case the wind rises while you're at anchor.

Your primary working anchor should be very heavy and able to handle a real blow without any problem.

The second, reserve anchor should be nearly as heavy as the main one. A disassembled CQR plow anchor doesn't take up much room and can often be stored under the cabin sole. The other spare anchors can usually be smaller for easy stowing, but it is important that they be readily available when you want to set a series of anchors on the same rode. (See page 100.)

TYPES OF ANCHORS AND BOTTOMS

I can't recall having the least problem anchoring in sand or mud bottoms with CQR plow, Fob, Britannia, or Tripgrip anchors. For rocky bottoms, I prefer to use my good old stocked Herreshoff; thanks to its diamond-shaped flukes, it rarely fouls the anchor line.

Three kinds of anchors: Fisherman anchor, pivoting-fluke anchor (Danforth), plow anchor (CQR)

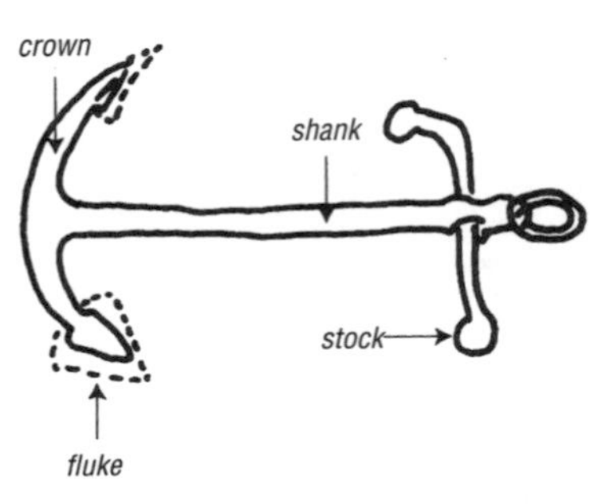

A Fisherman anchor won't let you down. It works on all bottoms, but on one condition. Look at the sketch carefully; it shows a classic Fisherman anchor, and it can fail to hold in bottoms that are covered with sand, soft mud, or sea grass, because its flukes are neither pointed nor wide enough. I tinkered with *Joshua*'s Fisherman anchor by welding a large 5/16" (8 mm) triangle of sheet steel on each fluke; this helps it hold even in sand or soft mud. Thus improved, my anchor really digs in.

A Danforth (pivoting-fluke) anchor requires more length of chain than a stocked anchor because the angle between the shank and the flukes is too acute. The Danforth must work with a horizontal pull, which means that it needs more chain than a Fisherman.
Once dug in, the Danforth holds very well. But it can easily fail if it doesn't dig in, or does so only after sliding along the bottom for a long time.

The CQR anchor: extraordinary holding power in all bottoms, except sea grass, where it can drag without penetrating the mat of vegetation. Putting both a Fisherman and a CQR anchor on the same line provides the safest combination I know of.

When the boat swings more than 180 degrees, the chain tends to slide along the exposed fluke, rather than catch on it.

In my opinion, the CQR is the best anchor there is. Following it, in descending order of preference (still my opinion):
—the Fisherman anchor, because it's an "all-bottom" anchor and doesn't suddenly give way, provided its stock is very long and its flukes are wide and pointed. This is how stocked Chinese anchors are designed, and they hold extremely well. The stock must be longer than the hooks.
—the Colin Tripgrip, whose holding power surprised me, and which I would choose over a Fisherman anchor in tidal waters (where the flukes of a stocked anchor can foul).

CHAIN OR ROPE?

Some people prefer "all chain." Others prefer a combination: 45 to 75 feet of chain shackled to a nylon line. For various reasons—light weight, ease of handling, stretch in the rode—I belong to the latter group.

Combining nylon and chain gives a rode much more stretch than chain alone, but requires a greater length for the same holding power. Moreover, nylon line makes maneuvering much easier in case of a real blow; you can easily row upwind a hundred yards in

Joshua's ground tackle

Anchors

An 85-pound Fisherman anchor with 40 feet of 1/2" chain and 180 feet of 7/8" nylon line. This is our working ground tackle.
A 66-pound Danforth anchor with 25 feet of 3/8" chain. This anchor is secured on deck near the main mast during coastwise cruising.
Two smaller Fisherman anchors, 22 and 44 pounds, and a 35-pound Colin Tripgrip anchor, stowed in the hollow keel. These are mainly used when setting anchors out in series, but the Tripgrip has proven to be superior to the Danforth.
An 88-pound Dial anchor, broken down into three pieces for stowing on the hollow keel ballast.

Chain

35 feet of 1/2" chain on the working anchor.
300 feet of 3/8" chain in several lengths, with a shackle at each end, so they can be linked together without wasting time rummaging through the box of shackles.
180 feet of 1/2" chain.
All this chain, except the working tackle, is stowed in the hollow keel.

Line (all nylon)

180 feet of 7/8" line for the working ground tackle.
300 feet of 5/8" line (wound on a spool).
450 feet of 9/16" line (wound on a spool).
300 feet of 1/2" line. 600 feet of 5/16" line (of which 300 feet are on a spool).
300 feet of 7/32" line.

At Durban, where the bottom was sand and mud,* MARIE-THÉRÈSE II *(4-5 tons) was hit by a fair number of small gales during my yearlong stopover. Four of those blows were so strong I could only get to shore by swimming; my dinghy would have been blown away. The boat was anchored on a 25-pound CQR.

your dinghy to set an anchor if it is rigged with nylon and only 30-45 feet of 3/8" chain. You could even swim out with an anchor buoyed by a couple of jerrycans if the wind is too strong to use the dinghy. On the other hand, nylon is risky on rocky bottoms and must be watched carefully. If there is any risk of a nylon rode getting caught under a rock or coral head, I always rig a float on the line to keep it off the bottom if the wind drops. Of course, if I were spending the winter in port I would anchor on chain alone.

WEIGHTS

Since I use relatively short lengths of chain on my anchors, they may need to be supplemented in a stiff blow by extra weight at the point where the nylon line joins the chain; this allows the anchor to work best, that is, with the tension horizontal.

In a crowded harbor, it is also useful to be able to sink the nylon line a few fathoms, so it doesn't foul another boat's prop or rudder when it is leaving or coming in. Finally, a weight at the nylon-chain juncture can add to the rode's stretch. Nylon alone is usually elastic enough, but having an extra ace up your sleeve is always helpful in a real blow.

TAKEUP SPOOLS

Having a few coils of strong nylon line on board is useful, but only if you can use the line very quickly in an emergency, especially at night. Following Henry Wakelam's example, I built takeup spools that hold 300-foot lengths of line ready for immediate use. Mounted on a stanchion, the spool lets the line reel out automatically, without any tangles or knots, for example when I'm carrying an anchor to shore or out to sea. To bring the line back on board, you just crank it in and stow the spool in the forepeak; the line will stay there for months without getting tangled, ready to use.

Using those spools greatly simplifies maneuvering: changing moorings, moving the boat in harbor, and getting out of a narrow port upwind without a motor when you can't tack in the channel. For getting around a harbor and for quick maneuvers, I use a spool with 300 feet of 5/16" line. For mooring lines, I use a spool with 300 feet of 3/8" line (see sketch).

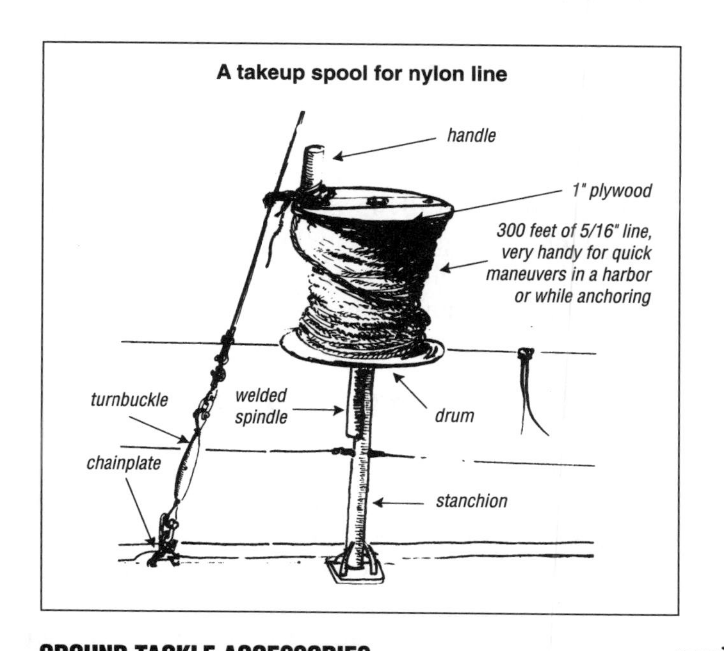

GROUND TACKLE ACCESSORIES

The bow should have a good roller, to reduce the friction of the mooring line against the fairlead.

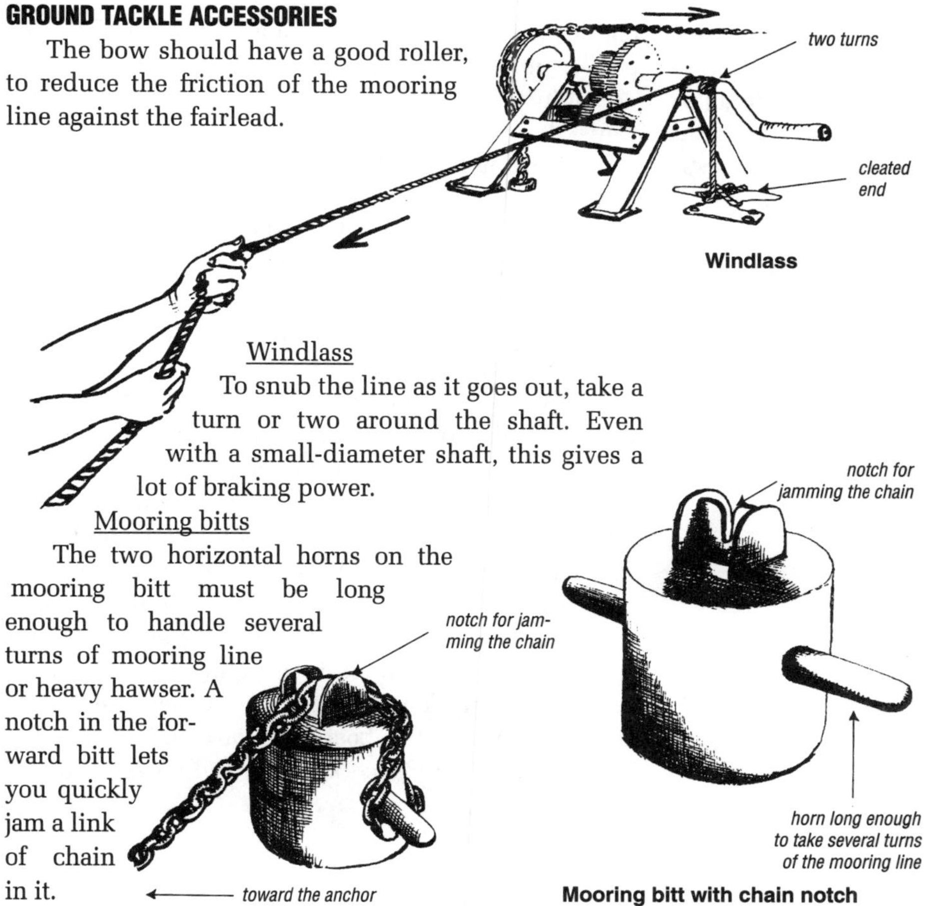

Windlass

To snub the line as it goes out, take a turn or two around the shaft. Even with a small-diameter shaft, this gives a lot of braking power.

Mooring bitts

The two horizontal horns on the mooring bitt must be long enough to handle several turns of mooring line or heavy hawser. A notch in the forward bitt lets you quickly jam a link of chain in it.

Propeller

JOSHUA had a very small two-bladed prop, but its drag still cost me a dozen miles every 24 hours, so I used to remove it (by diving down with a wheel puller) before a long passage. To avoid that annoyance, I outfitted TAMATA with a folding propeller; it is much less efficient, but doesn't slow the boat under sail.

Self-steering gear

In the ten months of my nonstop sail around the world during The Long Way, I steered for an hour off the island of Trinidad, about the same at the entrances to Hobart and Cape Town, and then for the second half of a night following the last capsize in the Pacific; the wind vane broke and I didn't dare go on deck to fix it, so I used the inside wheel. Finally, I steered to take the Papeete pass, and drop anchor.

Using readily available materials, it is easy to build a self-steering rig suitable to any kind of boat, even one with a keel-hung rudder. The main principle comes down to simplicity and strength. The vane is cut from a sheet of 1/8" plywood and mounted on a broomstick. This is the only part that can break, and even that's no big deal: you can rig a new vane in nothing flat. I replaced mine five or six times during The Long Way. The adjustment linkage consists of two sections of galvanized pipe, welded one on top of the other. The broomstick holding the vane runs through one pipe and the shaft with the counterweight through the other. They are adjusted and tightened with wing nuts.

With a keel-hung rudder, the vane acts on the supplemental rudder through a system of connecting rods. The tiller is then lashed amidships and the supplemental rudder adjusts the heading.

With a stern-mounted rudder, as on JOSHUA, the vane controls a trim tab, which in turn acts on the rudder. The tiller is left to move freely.

JOSHUA's system was good but not perfect, because the trim tab extended below the main rudder and could snag things in port, or foul the log or fishing line. (It never caught on seaweed, which floats on the surface.)

When the vane is mounted directly on the head of the trim tab, be sure to locate its pivot point at the junction of the trim tab and rudder axes. Otherwise the system won't work: the boat will yaw and drift off its heading. The last sketch shows a badly designed self-steering rig.

JOSHUA's self-steering gear, and operating principle

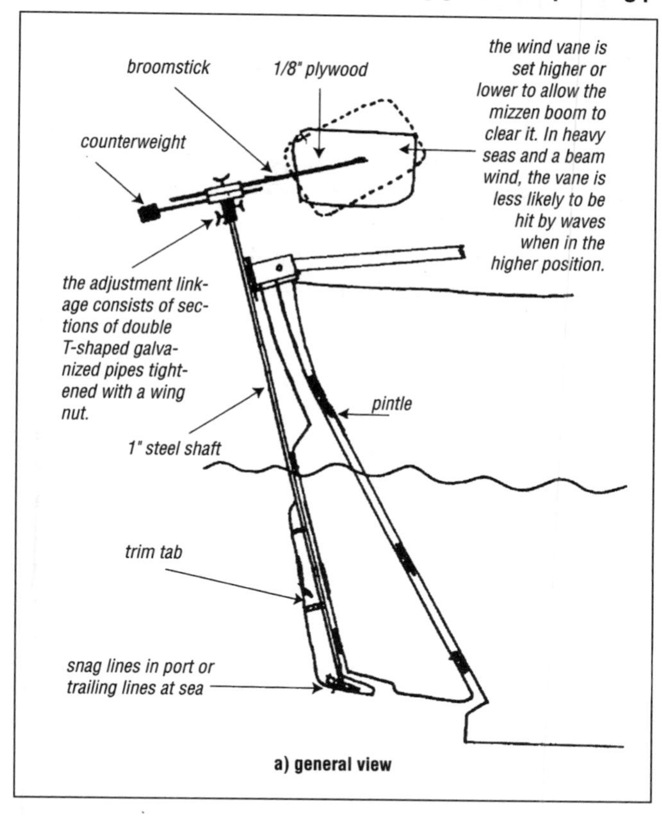

a) general view

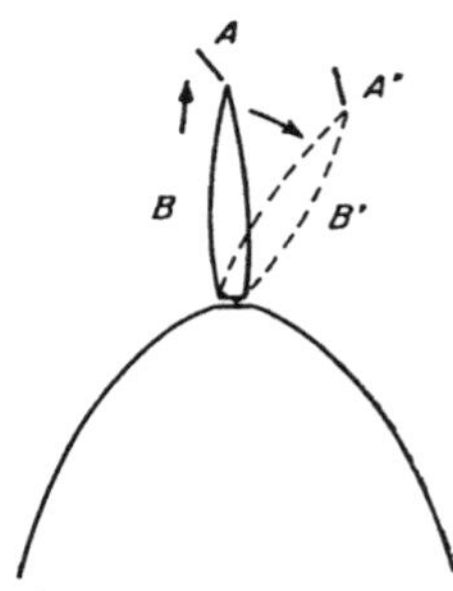

b) operating principle
If the small rudder (A) is no longer parallel with the main rudder (B), the water pressure on A pushes the main rudder blade, which corrects the heading.

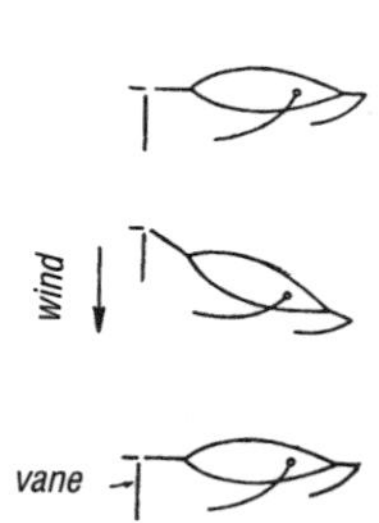

c) From top to bottom
—the boat is sailing on a beam reach
—the boat has drifted from its heading, but the small rudder remains in the same position relative to the wind and acts on the main rudder
—because of the action of the main rudder, the boat regains its heading.

Right

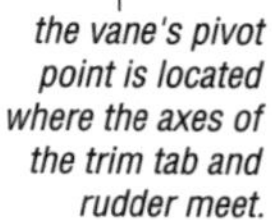

the vane's pivot point is located where the axes of the trim tab and rudder meet.

Wrong

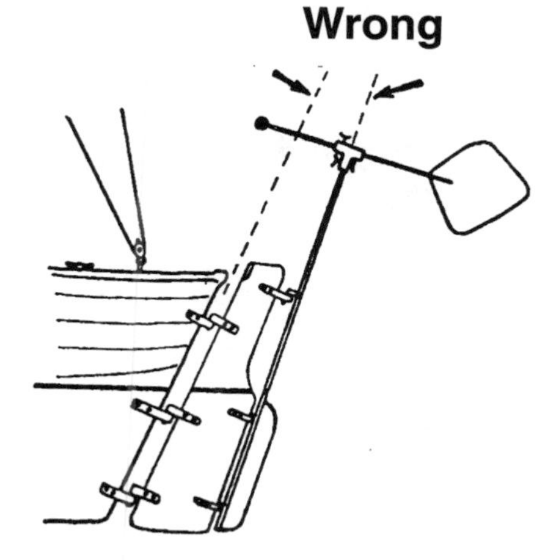

d) locate the vane's axis carefully

Tillers and steering wheels

There are three ways to steer aboard JOSHUA and TAMATA: a tiller, and two steering wheels. Both wheels are of the same diameter, with one in the cockpit and the other inside the cabin; they are mounted on the cockpit's forward bulkhead. The steering wheel system is easily accessible, which makes quick repairs easy. The wheels are connected to the tiller by lines on deck. The wheel can be disconnected from the tiller in a second, which gives great flexibility in how you choose to steer, and a margin of safety in case of a problem, with the tiller lines, for example. This double-wheel system is ideal. Having an inside wheel means you can steer from the cabin, protected from heavy seas. It also lets you get out of the wind or rain when approaching a shore or port, or when you're on watch and the weather isn't too bad.

Triple steering system

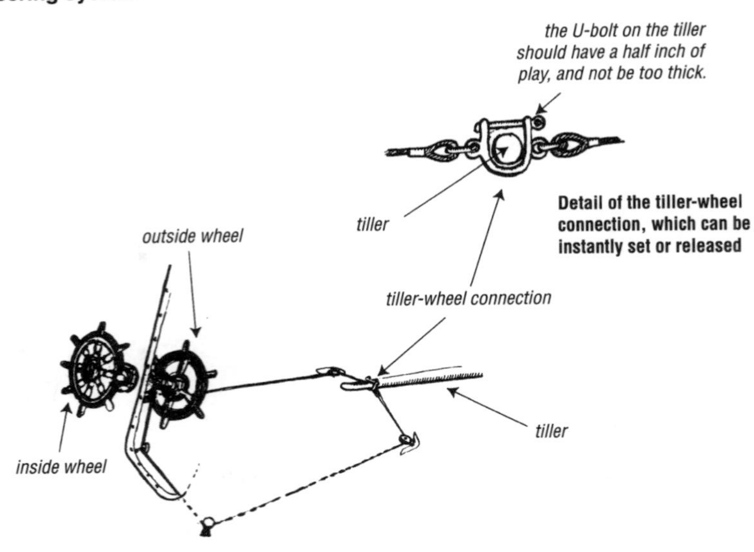

Miscellaneous fittings

BLOCK AND TACKLE

Before JOSHUA had winches, I used a little four-part block and tackle nicknamed "Attila;" it still sees action aboard TAMATA. Attila theoretically multiplies one person's strength by a factor of four, and in practice by slightly less, because of friction. It consists of two 3/8" blocks (that is, with 3/8" between the cheeks); one is a simple block with a becket fitted on the cleat end; the other is a double block, without a becket, on the sheet or halyard end. A braided 5/16" nylon line is used for the running part, and a 3/8" line for the standing part.

"Attila": a multipurpose block and tackle, essential on board

Even after JOSHUA was equipped with winches—which are much quicker and more practical than using a block and tackle—Attila wasn't relegated to some dark corner; it always stayed close at hand, just in case.

A block and tackle can be used for lots of things: hardening halyards and sheets, raising anchors, moving heavy objects on shore, etc.

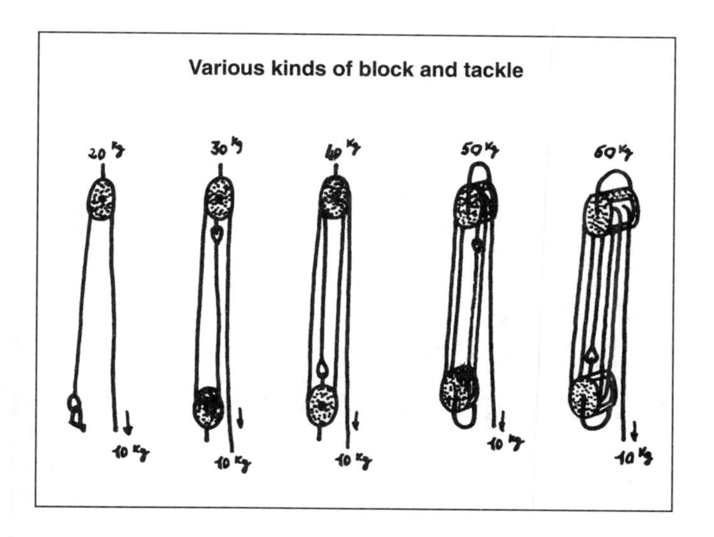

Various kinds of block and tackle

Rolling hitch

For example, to harden a halyard: the block is rigged with one end secured to the halyard with a rolling hitch as high as possible, and the other end to the foot of the mast. When tied correctly, a rolling hitch won't slip, and it doesn't jam when it's hauled on. Few pleasure cruisers know the knot, but merchant sailors use it all the time, for example to haul on a hawser before cleating it to a mooring bitt.

WINCHES, SNAPS, AND SHACKLES

During the circumnavigation, I was entirely satisfied with my Goïot winches and sail snaps and Wichard stainless steel shackles. I took the winches apart after the voyage to look inside: they were like new; the mechanism is simple and sturdy. When mounting winches on a steel boat, it's vital to very carefully isolate their light alloy bases from the boat's hull, to avoid any possibility of corrosion. I used to coat the four anchoring bolts with Bostik, a black rubber-based cement; today, neoprene could be used for the same purpose.

SHEET CLEATS

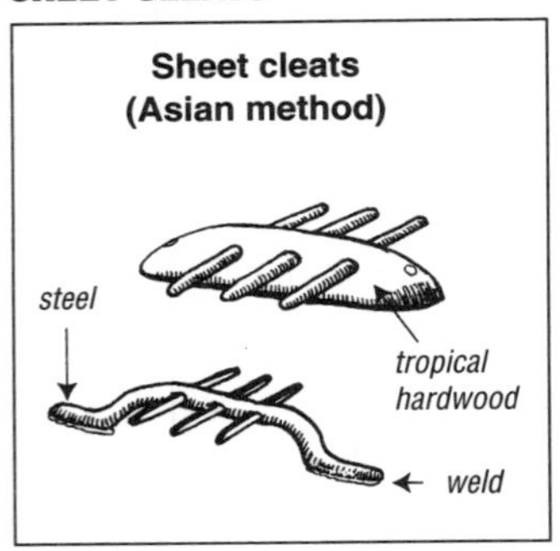

Sheet cleats (Asian method)

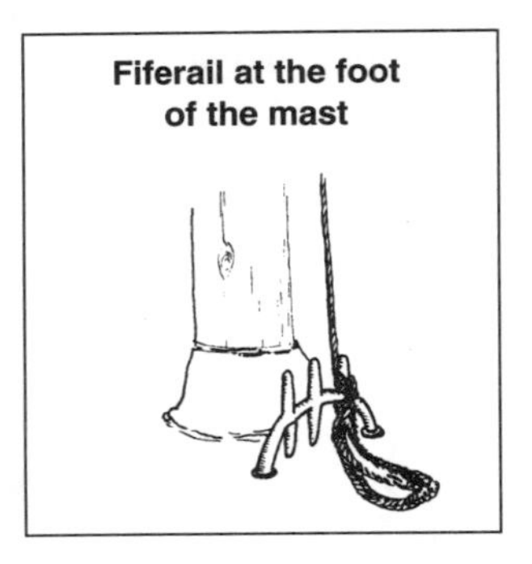
Fiferail at the foot of the mast

Waterproof emergency storage tanks

During The Long Way, I used one of my 100-gallon tanks for water. Besides food, the other three contained extra supplies: linens, blankets, socks, mittens, batteries, a spare radio receiver, a survival suit, and a sleeping bag. If JOSHUA had pitchpoled, had all her portholes smashed in, and half filled with water, I could still have gotten dry clothes and other gear intact from those tanks.

Lights and electric power

In the late 1960s, I used a small lantern with a dioptric glass when I was in the shipping lanes. This was a small kerosene lamp whose glass focuses the wick's light (which would scatter in an ordinary lamp), and it could be seen from much further away than even a large lantern. It used very little kerosene (four tablespoons per night), and never blew out.

In bad weather with a sea running, I used a 250 candle-power pressure lantern, which could be seen from a great distance. It burned a bottle of kerosene per night.

All that belongs to the past, however. Now, I need only flip a switch in TAMATA's cabin, and the masthead lights go on.

WHITE MASTHEAD LIGHT AND RUNNING LIGHTS

In the old days, fish were abundant and there were far fewer fishing boats than there are today. But times have changed. Fishermen now seek their catches in the most unexpected places, and you can encounter them almost anywhere on the open ocean. I carry a white masthead light, visible over 360 degrees. It isn't "regulation," but if I'm asleep, I prefer to be spotted from a long way off.

When entering a port, I use little portable red and green lights, powered by ordinary 1.5 volt batteries. This keeps outside wiring to a minimum and avoids the risk of electrical failure and maintenance problems in general.

Hanging a lantern in the shrouds

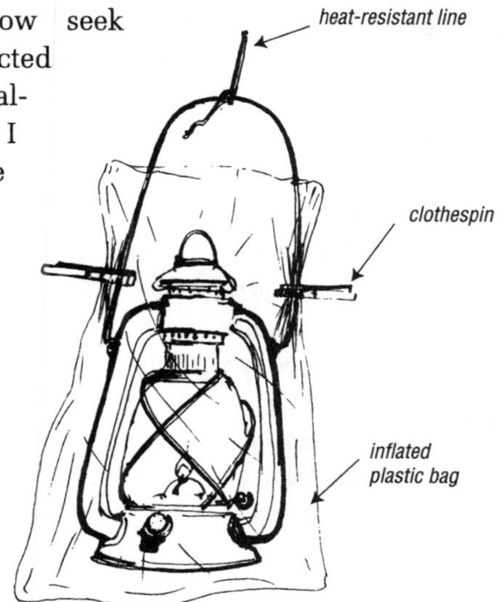

LANTERN

You may have occasion to hang a lantern in the shrouds, while at anchor, for example. I put mine in a transparent plastic bag which I seal with two clothespins; that way, it never gets blown out. Protected from the wind, the flame remains clear and bright and is more visible.

SOLAR PANELS

These are a real marvel, and becoming less expensive as demand and new manufacturing techniques bring their cost down. TAMATA does perfectly well with a solar panel that charges her single 70-amp battery, which in turn powers a ceiling and fluorescent light in the cabin and a white masthead light. The panel is portable, instead of fixed, and I can set it up in full sunlight and correctly oriented. That way, it charges the battery at top efficiency from morning till night. At sea, in bad weather, or when approaching an anchorage, I stow the panel below to keep the deck clear for maneuvering.

Navigation aids

COMPASS

On a steel boat, a compass is strongly influenced by the boat's metal mass. Even if well compensated for a given region, the compass readings can be way off in an area with a different magnetic variation (the difference between magnetic north, as shown by the compass, and true north). Adding or subtracting the degrees of variation isn't enough to straighten things out, because the entire compass compensation must be redone. To make matters worse, heeling throws everything off. So I chose to simplify things. JOSHUA had a compass at the foot of my berth (the heading indicated was wrong, but it still showed course changes), and a Vion hand-bearing compass in the cockpit. Neither was compensated; I had even thrown the magnets away. When I stood in the center of the cockpit, holding the hand-bearing compass as high as possible, it gave a correct reading. I do the same thing aboard TAMATA, standing on the cabin roof. In addition, I frequently check my heading by using sun and star azimuths, especially when nearing land.

The junks of the Gulf of Siam didn't have compasses and I didn't want my cruising-school students in the Mediterranean to use them either. Instead of steering 110° from Porquerolles to Calvi, my crew had to keep the mistral swell very slightly aft of starboard. At night, they kept Polaris one hand's width aft of the port beam. And if there was neither a distinct swell nor a star, we made do with whatever we had. I wanted it that way, because concentrating on a magnetized needle prevents you from participating in the real universe, both visible and invisible, through which a sailboat moves.

I recognize that all this has a do-it-yourself quality, but that's a lot better than relying on a compensated compass aboard a steel boat. Besides, it suits my temperament; I prefer to read my course in the sky and in the signs of the sea rather than from a magnetized needle. If I were to regularly sail in the English Channel, or in some similar place full of fog, rocks, and currents, I would mount my compass on the mast high above the metal masses, with an electronic repeater in the cockpit.

Taking along a radio transmitter would have meant adding a generator, batteries, gasoline—in short, complicating my life to keep all that gear in working order. I wanted to save all my energy for what was essential: sailing my boat to the best of her capabilities, without overreaching, but also without distraction. It was a sort of dance between her and me. Every movement had to be coordinated; our balance could never be threatened. Having a transmitter in the midst of all that, communicating on a fixed schedule—it was impossible. Right away, I would lose my main trump card: my inner peace and tranquility.

SEXTANT

Though you can get good fixes with a vernier sextant, a micrometer drum sextant lets you read a measured altitude more quickly. This is a minor detail when shooting the sun, since a single sight almost always produces a good fix. The enlarging lens increases the sun's apparent diameter and allows you to bring it down to the horizon very precisely, so one sight is enough. But a drum sextant is far better than a vernier sextant at night when shooting the stars. It is better to take three sights of the same star, and get at least two good ones.

TIME: BY RADIO AND CHRONOMETER

A four-second error translates to an error of a mile on a fix. A one-minute error means a 15-mile error in equatorial latitudes and a 12-mile error in temperate ones. I own a waterproof Rolex watch that is very accurate and reliable, and it never leaves my wrist. That is the watch I normally use when taking a fix, since I can use it wherever I happen to be on deck when I take my sight.

A radio lets you check the time. I use station WWV, which broadcasts GMT time every five minutes, 24 hours a day.

Dazed with fatigue, we crumpled into sleep at about 10 in the morning, after a grateful glance at the rising curve of the recording barometer: it had been at 755 mm since 8 o'clock.

BAROMETER

During the Tahiti-Alicante voyage, our recording barometer let us immediately see changes in atmospheric pressure.

RADAR

Another marvel! Although let me say at the outset that radar can play some nasty tricks when you are near atolls, such as the Tuamotus, because it generally doesn't pick up breaking waves. On the screen, you might see land two miles away, for example. But that might be a small island well inside the barrier reef; the reef itself might not give you an echo. But radar can often be an invaluable aid: for watching out for ships and fishing fleets, setting a pre-set alarm, making port at night . . . The list would be a long one, but I'm hardly one to talk, since I have no personal experience with radar sets. If I were planning a long cruise, however, I wouldn't hesitate to install one. Their cost, size, and current drain have all fallen over the years, while their sensitivity and usefulness as an auditory alarm have increased. Some day, radar units will be as small as cracker boxes and be sold in every supermarket.

Thanks to the GPS you know where you are, you can check your position against the sextant, see the difference, note any little errors, gradually correct them, and become almost as good as the GPS itself. Your fixes will be accurate to within a quarter of a mile, which is certainly good enough. But, if your GPS gets a little wet, it's going to conk out; one case of the sniffles and it will die, and you won't be able to repair it.

GLOBAL POSITIONING SYSTEM (GPS)

This too, is amazing. You can find your position to within 500 feet in the middle of the ocean! But remember that in rarely traveled areas, nautical charts can be off by several miles. Remember too, that a broken GPS unit can't usually be fixed with what you have on board. I wouldn't hesitate to buy one, but not before I had outfitted my boat with all the basics. And if I treated myself to a GPS, it would be mainly to help me completely master my sextant.

Thanks to a GPS's extreme precision, you can become a real star-juggler, in intimate contact with the sky; you can then save the electronics as an ally in case of emergency.

ESSENTIAL NAUTICAL DOCUMENTS

Pilot Charts

I can't imagine setting out without Pilot Charts. They are absolutely ingenious. A few inexpensive sets cover all the oceans, providing seasonal data on wind and current patterns. The data are statistical, and reliable for a dozen years. They give information on wind patterns, calms, general direction and strength of currents, gales, and hurricane seasons and tracks. Pilot Charts provide an overview that is essential for long voyages. With one complete set, you can easily plan a trip around the world without really having to dig into any other documents. At a glance, they give you useful information for an overview that greatly simplifies choosing reasonable alternatives. They are published by the Defense Mapping Agency (DMA), Department of Defense, Washington, D.C. In the U.K. Pilot Charts are published by the British Hydrographic Office.

Light List

An essential aid. Each volume covers extensive areas of coastline and ocean islands.

Ephemeris

Miniature electronic calculators programmed for ten or twenty years are very handy and fast, but a few drops of seawater can do them in. I would never sail without an ephemeris, which is a table of star positions. I find the American editions handier—more rugged and compact—than the French ones. Moreover, they cost much less; in 1993, ship chandlers in California were selling them for about $15.

The English ephemerides in the *Nautical Almanac* are laid out like the American ones. One page gives all the elements needed to calculate the hour angle for all useable celestial bodies (sun, planets, moon, stars). The facing page indicates the altitude corrections to be made to the sextant readings.

Tables

I originally used the Dieumegarde and Bataille tables, but sailors I met said they felt that the American HO 214 or English HD 486 tables were quicker to use than Dieumegarde and Bataille, since they provide height-azimuth values in a single step, without your having to enter as much data.

Later, I used the HO 249 Sight Reduction Tables, but they can prove quite dangerous if you rely on them blindly when taking star sights, because they give a very limited selection of stars for any given time. The tables were originally designed for use by airplanes, which fly high enough that most of the stars are visible at the same time. This isn't the case for us sailors when the sky is overcast, with only occasional breaks in the cloud cover. Since being unpleasantly misled by HO 249, I have used HO 229, with its wider selection of stars.

These tables are published by the Defense Mapping Agency. In the U.K. the equivalent tables are published by H.M.S.O. Calculators also exist that replace the calculation tables.

Star Finder

This is a set of ten eight-inch plastic disks that show the night sky as seen from any latitude. The *Star Finder* lets you identify all the stars used in celestial navigation and predict their approximate altitudes and azimuths. This allows you to pre-set the sextant and look in the right direction. Also, under an overcast sky, you can quickly record the altitude of a bright star that appears in a brief break in the clouds, without worrying what star it is. You can then ask the *Star Finder*, "Which star has an altitude of 31°33' and an azimuth of 306 degrees?" And the *Star Finder* will tell you, "At this hour, only Vega would be 31 degrees above the horizon on azimuth 306."

"His voyage struck us as having a planetary dimension, so we gave him a globe. In JOSHUA's cabin it became a companion, maybe a confidante, during his ten months at sea." Gérard Janichon

Nautical charts

They are incredibly expensive everywhere. But many freighters (especially tankers) carry sets of out-of-date charts that they haven't disposed of yet. The charts may be useless for a ship drawing 15 to 30 feet, but they are valuable for us. They can often be yours for the asking; with a little luck, you can walk down a gangplank with a big roll of charts under your arm.

But the line of the little DAMIEN globe has again become longer. We are almost half-way between Good Hope and Tasmania.

BINOCULARS

A pair of powerful, high-quality binoculars can make sailing much safer. But don't get a pair with more than 7 x 50 magnification if you want good luminosity, which is essential when sailing at night.

The galley

I use a kerosene Primus stove with gimbals (I also have a spare stove, without gimbals). If yours doesn't have gimbals, you can easily fashion a little chain (attached to a shock cord) with pliers and a length of wire to secure the pots to the stove top.

Keeping pots on the stove without gimbals

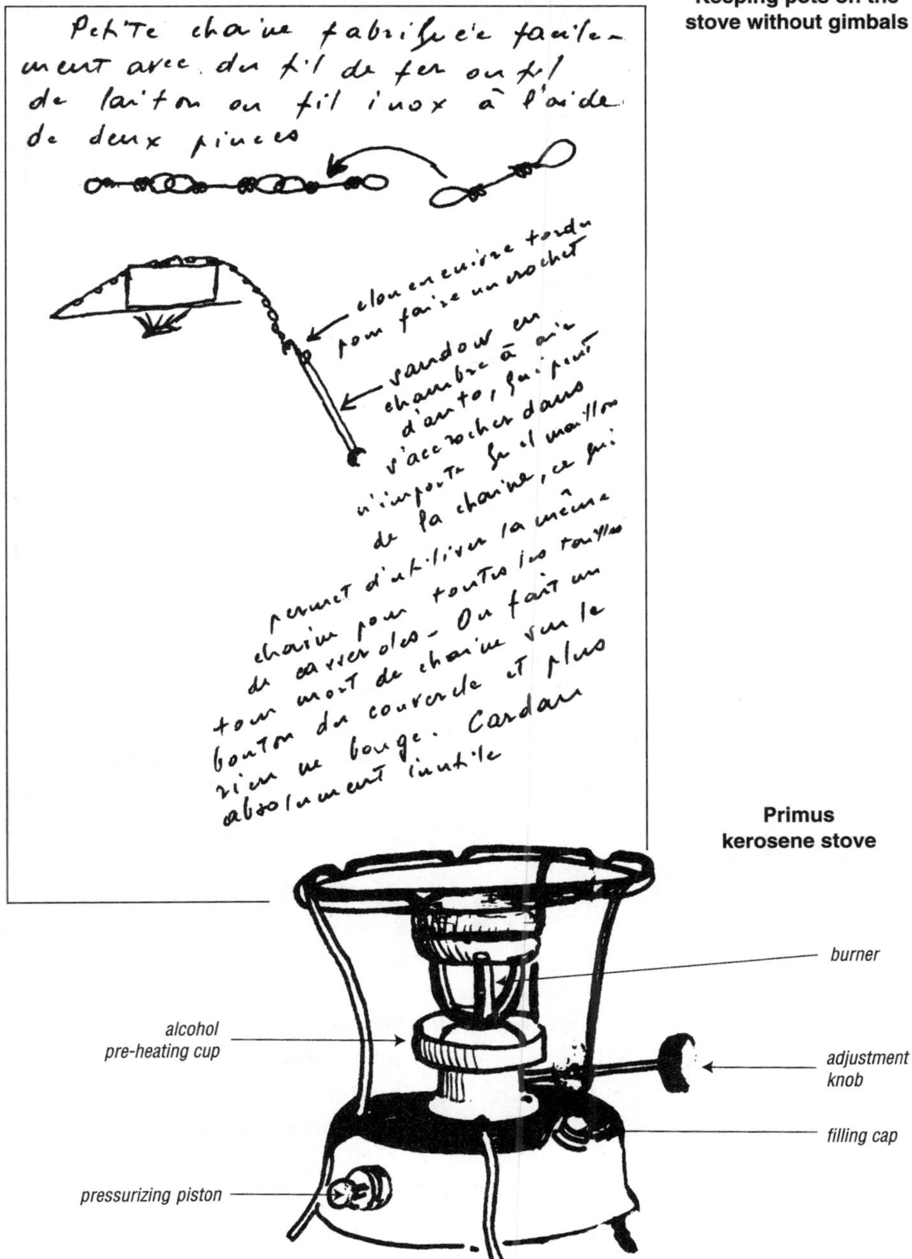

Primus kerosene stove

Sewing

A sewing machine is not a luxury on a boat. Henry Wakelam's WANDA had a tiny cabin, but he wouldn't have been without a sewing machine. Ours did yeoman service on JOSHUA's sails, because worn Dacron is hard to sew by hand.

Dinghy

Inner-tube dinghy, or "Monkey Zodiac"

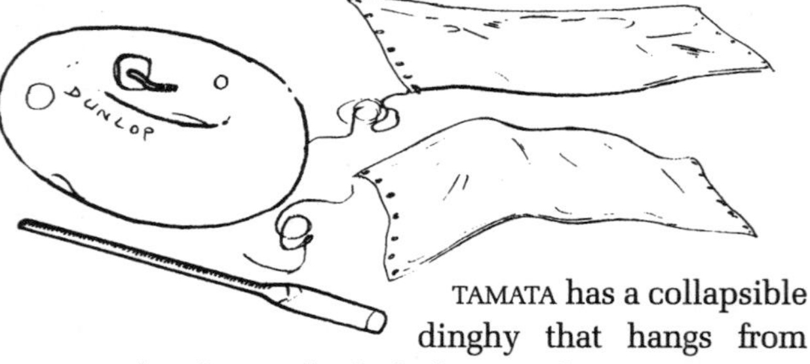

scull forward

direction of travel

TAMATA has a collapsible dinghy that hangs from the forepeak deck beams during passages. JOSHUA's main dinghy was a Bardiaux inflatable.

When there are several people aboard a boat, having a second dinghy is like having a bicycle when you're out in the countryside with a single car: the bike represents freedom for the person lounging by the fire when the other is out driving around. Our dinghy-bicycle was a big tractor inner tube (13.00-24/14.00-24) in a heavy canvas sleeve. A set of carefully tensioned straps gave it an oval shape and a longer waterline. It was very light and could carry two adults, be used to go set an anchor, and be deflated and stored in the forepeak. To paddle it, you crouch facing the direction you are headed and scull, the way the "basket boats" in Vietnam are paddled.

COME-HITHER SYSTEM

When the boat is anchored close to a dock and moored to the shore, it is very handy to rig a system to ferry the dinghy back and forth, especially when there are several people aboard. To avoid the dinghy's dragging on the rocks, bumping against the dock, or being holed by sea urchins, I use a sounding lead to add some counterweight to the line, so it automatically pulls the dinghy back to the boat.

distant shores

The choice

Will you be able turn your dream into reality?

Before heading out to sea, it's essential that you really know your boat and how she behaves: how much way she needs before coming about, whether she jibes well (some long-keel boats need a lot of room), how much leeway she makes. You need to know how she behaves:

1) under mainsail alone, in light breeze, in light breeze with a few waves, in light breeze and a swell, in a fresh wind, a stronger wind, etc.;

2) under staysail alone, at various wind and sea strengths;

3) under bare poles with the tiller down in very light air, in a fresh breeze, a strong wind, etc.

Getting to know your boat requires real commitment. It means hours of patient effort spent during the short period of your first sailing vacation. Meanwhile, your crew may be muttering; they want to cover miles, and usually aren't interested in spending time on experiments. But knowing your boat well can pay off handsomely; it's much more rewarding than all the books and articles you read at home in the evening.

To get to know your boat intimately, it's best not to invite any crew along, except maybe one carefully chosen, trustworthy person. Your boat has lots of things to tell you, and it is only when you are calm that you can understand what she is trying to say.

But the real problem lay elsewhere: the captain would never put to sea . . . because he didn't really want to. Mounier was living SNARK's voyage in his head, in front of his charts, dreaming of horizons and atolls he would never see.

Choosing the moment to leave

In a little Indonesian port, I watched as a Chinese junk prepared to carry a shipment to Jakarta by way of the reef-strewn Thousand Islands archipelago. The taïcong *waited for three days after the loading was finished, squatting without a word, without a gesture, contemplating the sea and the sky, in communion with immaterial forces. Then the junk weighed anchor in a nice beam breeze, with neither chart nor compass. I felt she was protected by the gods of Asia and by the big eye carved on each side of her bow.*

I've always followed these steps, which I learned in Asia:

1) Set sail and then go anchor a little way off, in order to renew your contact with the sea and the boat. Then set out when you feel the time is right.

2) If the weather is good, calculate the approximate length of the passage, and time your departure so the moon is full when you make your eventual landfall.

3) If you don't feel very confident, take short hops at first, then work up to your final departure.

4) I always prefer to leave in good weather, if possible with a complete weather forecast.

Weighing anchor

Setting out when sailing solo is much easier if you do it in calm weather. If you must weigh anchor when the wind is blowing, it's easier if you get far away from other boats and obstacles before raising the mainsail.

Before I had a motor, I usually took advantage of the calm at dawn to get clear of other boats. Using my dinghy, I would tow the boat a few hundred yards out, then anchor and wait for wind. A boat of even several tons displacement can easily be moved in a flat calm by sculling a dinghy.

I used another method when the wind was blowing toward the dock where I was moored. Using the dinghy, I carried a small anchor (on line, not chain) far to windward, then hauled myself out to it. By repeating this several times, I could get well upwind of a crowded dock.

Here are the general rules that apply to most of my departures:

1) Know exactly which way the wind blows in the different areas of the harbor. Contrary to what you might think, that direction often varies depending on where the boat is in the harbor. To be forewarned, observe flags, smoke, dust, etc. in the area you are heading for. This precaution can avoid lots of small problems, such as a botched tack.

2) If the wind is blowing toward any obstacles (anchored boats, jetties, dock, etc.), clear them under bare poles.

3) Always keep an anchor ready to drop in an emergency. Have the sails ready to raise at a moment's notice (sails shaken out, halyards and sheets clear), and rig the tiller so it can be lashed to one side or the other with a line or shock cord.

4) Always keep a boathook close at hand.

5) In case of a major screw-up, loosen the main sheet all the way.

Get underway under mainsail alone, then raise the staysail as soon as the boat has some way on and you know you won't have to come about before you have time to harden the staysail halyard and trim the sheet. A cruising boat under mainsail alone is like a car that can't accelerate; add a staysail, and she comes alive, tacks normally, and makes less leeway. In light airs, it's almost always a mistake to wait too long before raising the headsails.

If I leave port in good weather, I usually also encounter good weather out at sea, at least in the beginning. My most pressing goal is to put as many miles as possible between me and land before sunset, unless all the current weather reports indicate that the good weather will hold for several days.

My second goal is to avoid wasting precious energy, any way I can. You usually feel pretty good when you set out, but that can change well before nightfall if you have to steer for a long time in the hot sun. I deliberately work at taking it easy: I fiddle with the sheets and the tiller line or the wind vane until the boat stays on her heading while I go eat a snack in the cool of the cabin. Spending hours in the cockpit or on deck can drain your energy, especially at the start of a trip.

Stupefaction. Amazement. Now it was my turn to play in total freedom. Yet I felt an insidious fear, the fear of the unknown. From one day to the next the Great Adventure lay before me, as intimidating as a question from the gods: "Will you be able turn your dream into reality?"

Once you've cast off,

and you're at sea

Blue-water cruising requires a lot of patience. Crossing an ocean is a decisive, fabulous step, rich with the discovery of a new rhythm of living. When you're out of sight of land, that's the time to become one with your boat, work on navigation, and study weather signs in the sky and sea. This is when you gradually learn to give your boat the power she needs to perform at her best without risk of mishap. Take care of the boat, watch for wear and tear, find your own tempo of activity and rest, choose your route, make adjustments, adapt to the elements. Sailing is a never-ending apprenticeship.

I say "we," because there were two of us: MARIE-THÉRÈSE and me. In reality, we were one, just as the body and soul are one. This joining of man and boat had happened gradually, by stages. When we first met, I simply fell in love with a beautiful junk. But for man and boat to really merge into a single entity required the Indian Ocean monsoon. We had innocently wandered out "to see if it was real," as if to play. It was real all right; the monsoon didn't fool around.

Route and seasons

AROUND THE WORLD BY THE THREE CAPES

For the 1968-69 circumnavigation I call The Long Way, a route from west to east was chosen because of the prevailing westerlies in the vicinity of the 40th parallel. It's possible to encounter east winds there, but they are rare and seldom last, as they represent an anomaly in the general wind pattern.

In the southern hemisphere, summer lasts from about mid-November to mid-February. December-January is midsummer, the time of year when the days are long, temperatures warmest, and gales least frequent (if sometimes more severe than in winter). It is the best period—or the least bad, if you prefer.

For JOSHUA, it was a good period. But there are some very bad summers. Old-time clipper captains figured they could expect one bad summer out of three.

When making preparations, yachts of moderate size should think of the season as always bad. As I said, December-January is midsummer, but it was in December that the Smeetons' TZU HANG pitchpoled in the South Pacific. In December, too, JOSHUA encountered the most dangerous gale of her career, during the earlier Tahiti-Alicante voyage. It was in January that W.A. Robinson's 70-ton VARUA surfed over incredible distances while trailing warps, bowsprit in the water. So midsummer can occasionally be very hard.

To complicate matters further, a boat leaving Europe for a voyage around the three capes is forced to round the Cape of Good Hope too soon in the season if it doesn't want to reach the waters around Cape Horn very late. And the smaller the boat, the earlier in the season it must face Good Hope, since it goes slower than a bigger one. Thus, Robin Knox-Johnston's SUHAILI had to leave England in June so as not to reach the Cape Horn area too late; this meant rounding Good Hope in early spring, when the gales are fierce, and then continuing across the Indian Ocean in a less than ideal season. But Knox-Johnston had no choice, as his boat was smaller and slower than JOSHUA.

Is it better to round Good Hope too soon or Cape Horn too late? Vito Dumas chose late May or early June to round the Horn from west to east. Francis Chichester rounded it in March, as did Alec Rose a year later on his 33-foot LIVELY LADY. Aboard the trimaran VICTRESS, Nigel Tetley rounded the Horn on March 18 or 19. JOSHUA did it on January 16 during Tahiti-Alicante and February 5 during the circumnavigation. My friends aboard DAMIEN tacked around the Horn from east to west on March 4, headed off to the South Shetland islands, South Georgia, then across the South Atlantic to Cape Town. Knox-Johnston rounded Cape Horn in January, a few weeks before JOSHUA.

I feel that Good Hope is more dangerous than the Horn because of the convergence of the warm Indian Ocean current with the cold Antarctic current. But it's anybody's guess. Loïck Fougeron's CAPTAIN BROWNE and Bill King's GALWAY BLAZER II more or less pitchpoled in late October in the South Atlantic around the 40th parallel before reaching Good Hope. By that time, Knox-

Johnston was nearing Tasmania, having rounded Good Hope and crossed the Indian Ocean much earlier in the season under very difficult conditions (capsize, self-steering out of commission, and leaks). And while CAPTAIN BROWNE and GALWAY BLAZER II were being hammered by fierce weather in the South Atlantic, JOSHUA had already rounded Good Hope and was sailing with a nice force 5 to 6 wind in the Indian Ocean, making a little northing. She then encountered calms and light airs until Australia's Cape Leeuwin, with only one westerly gale for the entire Indian Ocean crossing. A matter of luck. How would JOSHUA have fared, compared to CAPTAIN BROWNE and GALWAY BLAZER II, in the gale that put those two boats out of action? Nobody can tell. In the high latitudes, you're in the hands of God.

We were beginning to discover a rhythm of life that people who haven't sailed in the tropics find hard to imagine; the rhythm of the trade winds where you do nothing for days . . . And yet, those days are as full of life as a wake shining with phosphorescence.

In the Indian Ocean, I opted for the calmer zone between the 37th and 39th parallels, so as to be in good physical shape on entering the Pacific. Knox-Johnston, on the other hand, tore along south of the 40th parallel, so as not to be late rounding the Horn. He was racing against time and the seasons, not against other boats. A sailor is always racing in those parts.

Whatever the size of the boat, high-latitude sailing is always dangerous. Those who have tried it know the high latitudes can be very hard on equipment, and consider technical preparation for the trip to be of prime importance.

THE TRADE WIND ROUTE

Most boats coming from Europe make a shakedown run to the Canary Islands; then they set out across the Atlantic, following the northeast trade winds to the Caribbean, which they usually reach in December. They visit the West Indies during good weather, then continue on their way to Panama before the hurricane season, which usually starts in May or June. Once through the Panama Canal, they enter the Pacific Ocean, head for the Galápagos, and swing through the Marquesas and Polynesia, this time with the southeast trades.

The usual route from France to Tahiti goes by way of the Torres Strait and the Cape of Good Hope, or by Torres and the Red Sea. For small sailboats like ours, this is the classic route.

Running in the trade winds

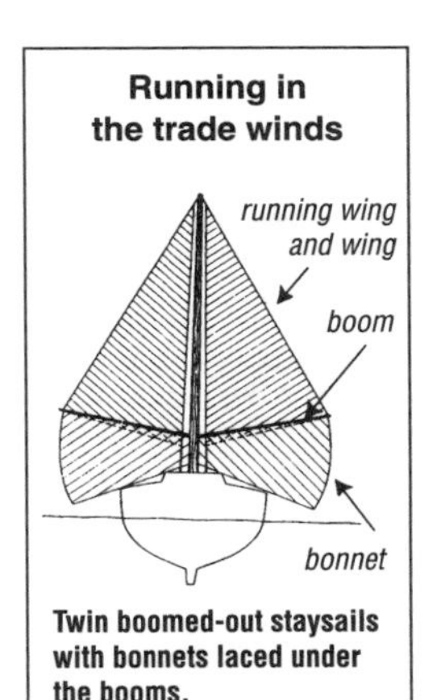

Twin boomed-out staysails with bonnets laced under the booms.

Weather forecasting

LOWS IN NON-TROPICAL ZONES

Forecasts based on direct observation

I heartily recommend Alan Watts' little book *Instant Weather Forecasting*, which taught me how to predict weather changes in minutes.

It's terrific: all you do is compare the lower, or surface (cumulus) wind direction with the upper, or high-altitude (cirrus) wind direction and apply the "crosswind rule." A very clear diagram in Watts' book shows how to do it. On land, you can always find a fixed point (a tree, post, or house roof) to observe the slow movement of the cirrus. At sea, when the moon is up, you can easily see the cirrus moving across the lunar disk. And for the sun, I use the sextant's filters (dark glasses aren't enough to cut the sun's intense glare).

Predicting the weather around a low

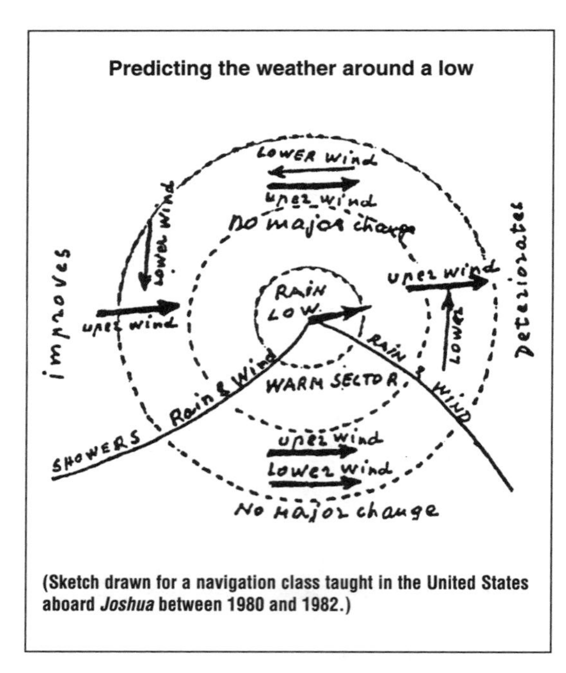

(Sketch drawn for a navigation class taught in the United States aboard *Joshua* between 1980 and 1982.)

Principles of "instant" weather forecasting

This works in non-tropical zones (above or below 30° latitude).

Northern hemisphere

As you face the lower wind (cumulus):

1) If the upper wind (cirrus) is blowing from the left, the weather will improve;

2) If the lower and upper winds are blowing the same way, or are parallel but from opposite directions, expect no major change;

3) If the upper wind is blowing from the right, the weather will worsen.

Southern hemisphere

As you face the lower wind (cumulus):

1) If the upper wind (cirrus) is blowing from the left, the weather will worsen;

2) If the lower and upper winds are blowing the same way, or are parallel but from opposite directions, expect no major change;

3) If the upper wind is blowing from the right, the weather will improve.

A halo around the sun or moon indicates the presence of cirro-stratus clouds and announces a change in the weather. The halo is always 22° across, and should not be confused with the "crown," which is always much smaller, and doesn't portend anything bad. Cirrus clouds also indicate the proximity of unsettled weather.

There seemed to be a lot of cirrus and cirrocumulus, and the sky was overcast again. All those high clouds were moving at right angles to the surface wind, and they were coming from the left as I faced the wind. It was a sign that a depression was approaching from the west or southwest. Besides, there had been a 22° halo around the sun at noon. But the barometer still hadn't changed.

Maneuvers when a low is approaching

See "Pacific Ocean knockdowns," page 132.

HURRICANES IN TROPICAL REGIONS

In my opinion, hurricanes are the only real danger of a trade wind passage. Hurricanes, which are also called cyclones, are unknown in the South Atlantic but occur everywhere else above latitude 10° north and south during the hurricane season.

Main hurricane warning signs

1) Abnormally large swell, usually from a direction different from the trade wind. This swell may be felt as far as 500 miles from the hurricane's center, or eye;

2) Black clouds that looks like bats' wings, scudding under an overcast sky;

3) A drop in barometric pressure, though this really only becomes apparent within 100 miles of the eye, when it is too late to take evasive action.

Secondary signs

1) Good weather with abrupt barometric changes;

2) A strengthening of the wind, with a change of direction;

3) Lots of cirrus clouds, which can be seen more than 600 miles from the eye. Very red sky at sunrise and sunset;

4) A halo around the sun and moon. This indicates the presence of cirro-stratus coming from the eye and spreading very far out from it;

5) Greatly increased humidity. The weather becomes heavy, hot, and uncomfortable.

During the hurricane season, read the *Sailing Directions* carefully, and listen to weather reports on station WWV.

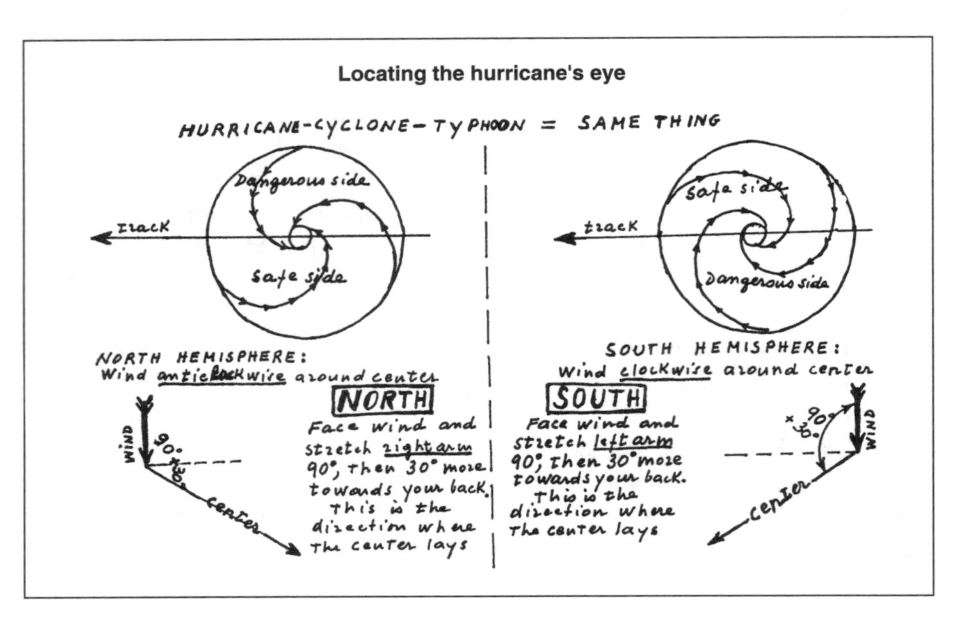

Locating the hurricane's eye

Finding the eye of the hurricane

In the northern hemisphere, the wind blows counter-clockwise around the eye. Face into the wind and stretch your right arm 90° to it, then bring the arm back another 30°; you will be pointing at the eye of the hurricane.

In the southern hemisphere, the wind blows clockwise around the eye. Face into the wind and stretch your left arm 90° to it, then bring the arm back another 30°; you will be pointing at the eye of the hurricane.

Three levels of danger are commonly recognized:

—tropical depression: wind above 34 knots;

—tropical storm: wind from 34 to 63 knots;

—hurricane: sustained wind above 64 knots.

Table showing hurricane risk

REGION	NORMAL SEASON	OCCASIONAL OCCURRENCES
Northeast Pacific	June to October	May and November
Southeast Pacific and Australia	December to April	May, June, November
South Indian Ocean	December to March	April, October, November
Northwest Pacific	April to December	All months
North Indian Ocean	May to July and September to December	April and August
North Atlantic	August to October	June, July, November

Tracking of a hurricane

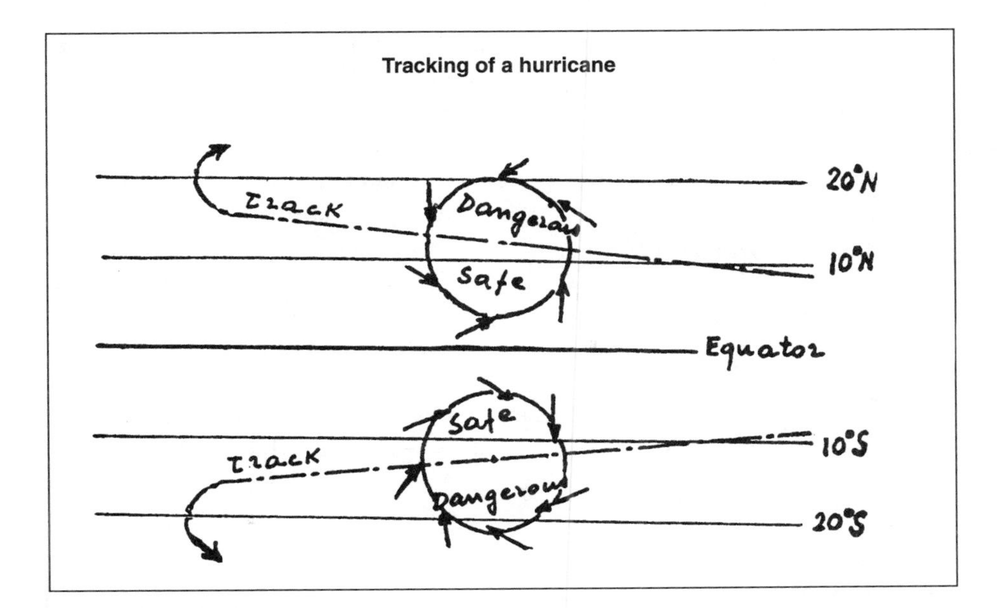

Maneuvering in a hurricane

In dealing with a hurricane, the two primary considerations are to avoid the eye (because of the strong winds surrounding it) and the side of the hurricane where its movement over the water adds to local wind speed. On that side (called the "dangerous half-circle"), the wind speed may be 30 mph stronger than on the other side (called the "navigable half-circle"). In the northern hemisphere, the strongest winds will be on the right side of the hurricane's path; in the southern hemisphere they will be on the left side.

Preventive heaving to, for observation

1) Heave to as soon as you suspect a hurricane may be coming;

Watch for wind shifts

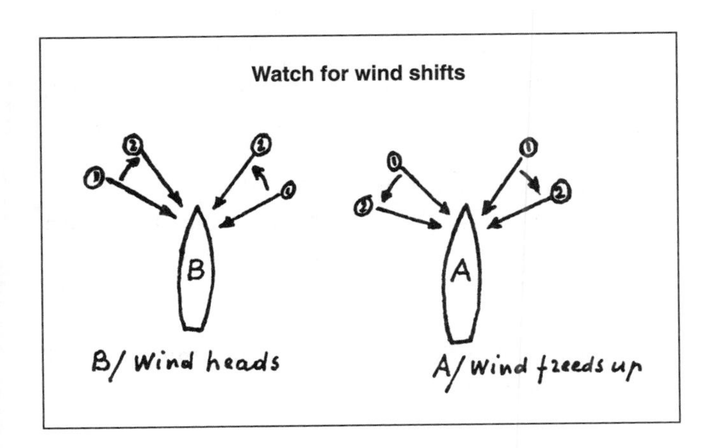

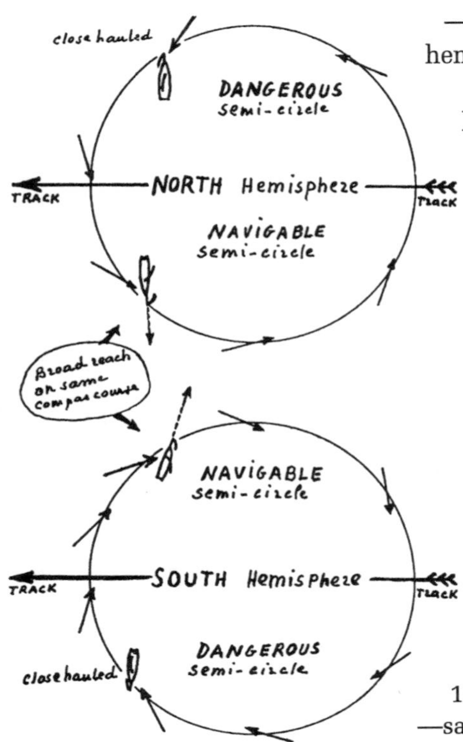

Maneuvering in a hurrricane

—on the starboard tack in the northern hemisphere;

—on the port tack in the southern hemisphere.

2) Remain hove to for at least three hours and carefully watch for wind shifts.

—in either hemisphere, if the wind is veering, you are in the dangerous half-circle;

—if the wind is backing you are in the navigable half-circle;

—if the wind doesn't change direction and the barometer plummets, you're in the monster's path.

Above all, move away from the eye

The idea is to stay as far as possible from the eye. Beyond 200 miles, the wind shouldn't blow harder than force 7.

1) If you are in the dangerous half-circle:

—sail close-hauled, as fast and as long as you can, on the same tack (starboard tack in the northern hemisphere, port tack in the southern hemisphere). This will move you away from the eye;

—when the sea becomes too rough to make headway close-hauled, heave to on the same tack, and remain hove to, whatever happens.

2) If you are in the navigable half-circle:

—sail on a broad reach on the same tack (starboard in the northern hemisphere, port in the southern hemisphere);

—maintain the same course. The wind will gradually head up, until you are sailing close-hauled. When you can no longer stay on the same tack close-hauled, heave to on the other tack and wait for the hurricane to pass.

3) If you are in the hurricane's path:

—sail on a broad reach on the same tack (starboard in the northern hemisphere, port in the southern hemisphere), and maintain your course. That will bring you into the navigable half-circle.

Never run with the hurricane's wind from astern; it will bring you into the eye.

RADIO WEATHER REPORTS

Station WWV, which gives time signals, also broadcasts weather forecasts every hour between minutes 45 and 51 on 5, 10, and 15 khz. The forecast is given in English, and covers these zones: North Atlantic, North Pacific, Eastern Pacific, Western Pacific, and South Pacific. This last report is given at 51 minutes after the hour, and is invaluable during the hurricane season.

Here are a few rules I used aboard JOSHUA when listening to weather broadcasts:

1) Tape the forecasts.

2) For coastal forecasts, use tracing paper to copy the general small-scale chart and pencil in the details of the forecast, using symbols (e.g., "F.W." for fair weather, a shaded arrow to show wind strength and direction).

Weather forecasting tips

Twinkling stars announce wind

"One beautiful night, a *taï-cong* fisherman told me why the stars announce the wind when they twinkle strongly.

"It is because there is wind up there, and it blows on the little flames of the stars, the same way you blow on a candle. So the stars flicker. The wind then blows with all its might, but can't blow them out. So it gets angry and comes down to the sea seeking revenge for not being able to blow out even a single star, even the lowest ones close to the horizon. There, the stars couldn't resist the wind, which can blow very hard when it gets really angry. But there is a god close to the horizon to protect the low stars.

"If it weren't for the horizon god, the wind would blow them out one after the other. Then it would wait for the high stars to sink close to earth, to blow them out in turn. And people couldn't go on living, because there would be no more stars.

"Years later, I learned that low stars always twinkle more than high ones because their light penetrates a thicker layer of air than at the zenith, making for greater light refraction.

"I believe that science may someday permit people to reach the stars with spaceships. I believe above all in old Asia, which lets me go there anytime I like with a candle and some wind."

The hygrometric rag

"That rag, which I hadn't washed since the Atlantic doldrums, helped me predict weather changes. When it was nice and stiff, it meant the air was dry and I could expect continuing southwesterly winds with pretty good weather except for the cirrus clouds. When it was less stiff with a southwest wind blowing, it was almost always a sign the wind would soon become westerly, as the air was no longer so dry. And when my rag hung all sticky and limp, as if it had wiped up all the world's sins, I could expect winds from the north, loaded with humidity."

Sky color at dawn

"In the high latitudes, dawn tells what the weather will be. When the sun rises red, it's a bad sign. Dawn should be a bit milky. It's the contrary from the trade winds, where a red sunrise announces a beautiful day, with better weather than usual."

3) Pencil in the date.

4) Lay tracings from subsequent broadcasts over the first one; this will help you better visualize changing weather patterns.

It is very useful to listen to radio stations broadcasting news from the countries where you are headed as soon as you can pick them up. They are often followed by weather reports, which will give a general idea of the climate. When we were still anchored at Suvorov and getting ready for the passage to New Zealand, we listened to daily news broadcasts from New Zealand, which proved very helpful.

Maneuvers

ENCOUNTERS AT SEA AND RISKS OF COLLISION

"Technique" consists of caution and common sense, not acrobatics. When we reread the stories told by the greatest sailors, we will find that they had plenty of close calls, but that they usually managed to see them coming a long way off, and took care not to get too overwhelmed by them.

If it collides with a large ship, a sailboat will almost certainly sink in a few seconds, with no time to put out a dinghy or even to send up a distress flare to alert the ship, which is steaming on, unaware of the drama unfolding in its wake.

I have twice nearly been run down in broad daylight, once on MARIE-THÉRÈSE II, between Cape Town and Saint Helena, the second time on JOSHUA in the Atlantic half a day from Gibraltar. The era of Slocum, Voss, and Gerbault is long past; these days, constant vigilance is called for.

Freighters aren't very maneuverable; at cruising speed, a turn of the wheel to right or left produces only a very gradual, curving course change. So if our boat's path crosses that of one of these steel monsters, common sense dictates passing astern or very far ahead of it, and sailing at right angles across its course.

AVOIDING COLLISIONS AT NIGHT

The tactics I use at night in the shipping lanes depend on whether I'm asleep, with my boat sailing or hove to; or whether I'm awake and under way, and therefore can maneuver.

When you can't maneuver

I consider my boat non-maneuverable in three situations: when she is under way with the tiller lashed or under self-steering and I am asleep; when she is hove to; or when the wind is so light that I can't maneuver when I want to.

During the 1960s, I used to hang a 250-candlepower Aladdin or Optimus pressure lantern in the windward shrouds. Nowadays, I need only flip a switch in TAMATA's cabin to turn on my masthead light, which is white and can be seen over 360°.

This is where having a well-tuned radar unit with an alarm would prove a valuable aid when resting, whether day or night. But in general, I never quite sleep when in the shipping lanes; I just stretch out in the cockpit to rest from time to time.

When you can maneuver

At sea, when my boat is under way and I am awake, I don't show any outside lights. I remain in control of any maneuvers, since freighters always steam in a straight line.

You never see a blind person bumping into a pedestrian walking the other way, because the pedestrian gets out of the way. But we have all been amused by the sight of two pedestrians who collide because each was trying to avoid the other.

At sea, where the other "pedestrian" weighs 100,000 tons, I prefer to safeguard my health by remaining in control of the situation. In fact, this is made very easy by the two white lights that all ships carry; they are high above the water, and very bright.

The rule of constant bearings

A classic rule says that a collision at sea can only occur if two ships see each other on a constant bearing. Every ship carries two white lights, which are visible from very far away, mounted at different heights and on separate vertical axes. The lower light is always forward of the higher one. That way, you can tell the ship's approximate course at a glance.

1) If you see two white lights, one above the other and in the same line, the ship is heading straight for you. As you head off at a right angle to either right or left, you will see the two white lights gradually move apart, a sign that you have gotten out of the ship's path.

2) If you see the lower white light to the left of the upper one, the ship is heading to your left.

3) If the lower light is to the right of the upper one, the ship is heading to your right.

4) The spacing of the white lights (and how it changes) lets you estimate the ship's course. If the two lights are gradually getting closer together, the ship's course will intersect yours. If you come about in the correct direction (or significantly change your heading), you will see the two lights gradually move apart, or at least not get any closer together.

5) In addition to its two white masthead lights, a ship also carries position lights: a green one to the right and a red one at the left, just as sailboats do.

If the lights' bearing remains constant, a collision will occur. To avoid that, change your heading or speed (by heaving to when under sail, for example).

This rule of constant bearings is mathematically exact, but it still presents dangers for a small sailboat.

1) A ship's speed is constant; a sailboat's is less so, since the situation can change if the wind drops or shifts direction.

2) Relying on constant bearings will allow the sailboat to cross behind the ship (which would be perfect)

Avoiding a collision, or how to cross a freighter's path by passing astern

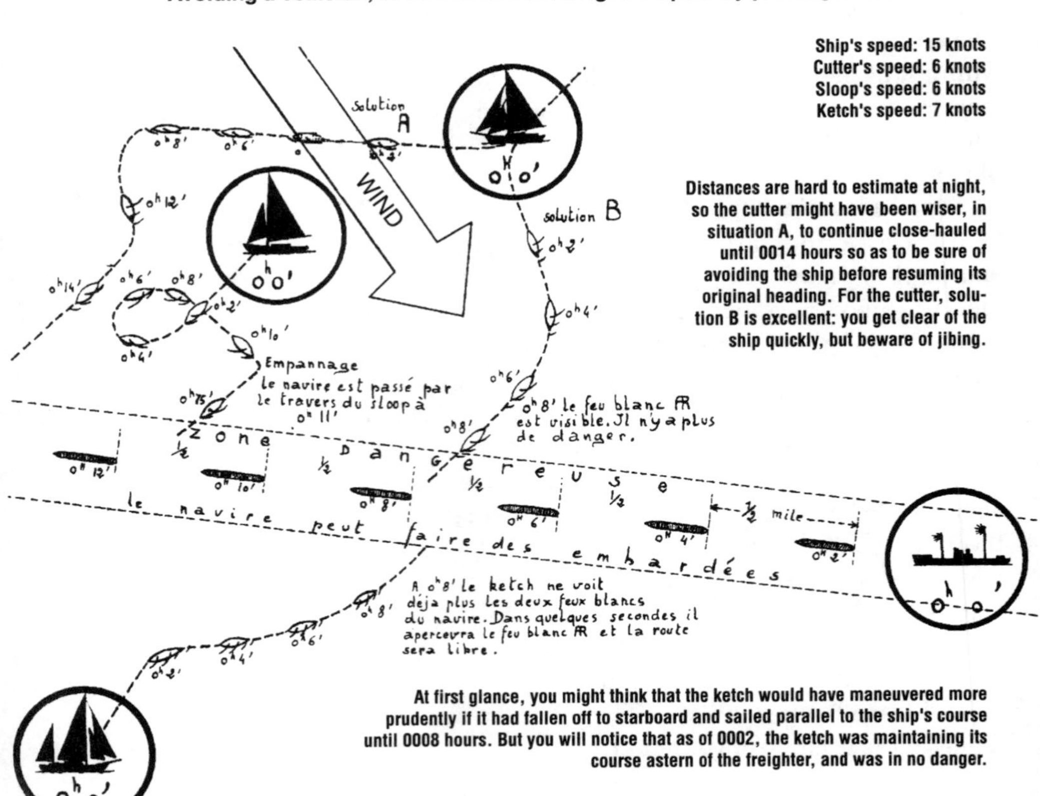

or ahead of it, which can be quite dangerous if the wind direction or strength changes. If I spot a ship's lights 7 or 8 miles away and find myself more or less in its path, I prefer to pass well astern or very far ahead of it, crossing its course at right angles. That may be less mathematical, but it doesn't give you so many grey hairs.

Attracting a ship's attention

In a flat calm, if you don't have a motor, it is good to have a high-quality, powerful waterproof flashlight close at hand. But it is pointless to shine it on your sails; your masthead light is enough to help a ship locate you. Better to shine the flashlight directly at the ship, if it refuses to change course.

Shining a flashlight on your sails doesn't really make them visible to lookouts on other boats, and tends to blind the person shining the light. By the time the freighter sees you, it will be too close to your sailboat to change course. It's much better to shine the light directly at the freighter. By resting the flashlight against your cheek, you can aim the light at the ship very accurately without blinding yourself.

HEAVING TO

Heaving to is a heavy-weather tactic that lets the boat fend for itself when the sea is very rough. There are various ways to heave to. For example, you can drop all the sails, lash the tiller alee, and go to sleep. The boat will gently bob along, without making any way, while you wait for the bad weather to clear.

But it can be dangerous not to carry any canvas while hove to, so you carry reduced sail. The boat makes some leeway and creates a kind of protective eddy to windward. This slick calms the sea like a sheet of oil, or at least keeps it from breaking.

How do you heave to? Here is my formula:

1) I bring the boat to a close reach, while keeping enough way for coming about, which I will do in a moment.

2) When the time is right, I come about without touching the jib or staysail sheets.

3) Once I have come about, I push the tiller all the way down to leeward, and lash it. To keep the tiller down, I usually tie it with lines on either side—though using strong shock cords (or inner-tube strips) in-

Joshua hove to

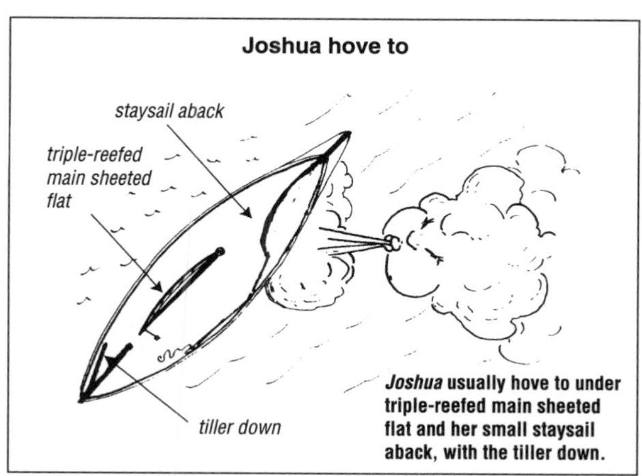

Joshua **usually hove to under triple-reefed main sheeted flat and her small staysail aback, with the tiller down.**

stead will give the helm some play, and reduce the twisting force between the rudder blade and the pintles. How far down to lash the tiller depends on the boat and the state of the sea.

If the boat absolutely refused to come about, I would jibe, if I could do it without risk to the rigging.

For a ketch, there are variations: staysail aback, mainsail sheeted in, and tiller alee; or jib and mizzen aback, for example, instead of the staysail and main.

PREVENTIVE HEAVING TO

Heaving to isn't useful only in bad weather. It's also a simple way to minimize rolling and pitching without danger to boat or rigging. You can heave to when you want to reef a sail in peace, or change or reef the jib in a fresh wind. A hove to boat is a boat asleep, almost motionless, and doesn't require anyone at the helm.

When sailing solo, I often heave to in order to facilitate certain tasks that are delicate (such as reefing the main) or dangerous: changing a jib at the end of the bowsprit, and especially, reefing a jib when the boat is tearing along close-hauled. (My jib always has a reef band; it's much less expensive than a heavy-weather jib.)

HEAVING TO IN FAIR WEATHER

Music has its rhythm, and so does vastness. At sea, everything becomes clear. That's when you have time to see what is true and what isn't.

This is exactly the same maneuver as heaving to in general, but it isn't for heavy weather. I use it when I want to rest and give myself time to figure things out. To heave to, sheet all the sails flat, then come about (or jibe, if you prefer) without touching the sheets, and lash the tiller down when you have come about. The boat will then drift along very slowly, and the sea will seem quite calm. This gives you time to rest or think, without risking a hasty or stupid decision. Here are a few examples:

After a crossing during which I had been slammed around for three days, I finally sighted land. I was hungry and exhausted, and hadn't picked up a single light before dawn. I felt drained, sailing along like a blind man, my frozen neurons dead and useless. What could I do? Simple: heave to! Suddenly the boat quieted down, my neurons started firing again (jump-started by a hot cup of coffee and some soup and crackers). A twenty-minute nap did the rest. After that, a good breakfast and all was well again.

I was sailing through the Tuamotus, with its many small, low atolls. It was night and the weather wasn't very good. Even with a GPS, I wouldn't have been sure of my position since the atolls aren't perfectly charted. So I hove to from time to time, listening to be sure I didn't hear swells breaking on some barrier reef hidden in the darkness. Heaving to is especially valuable for listening. (See page 171.)

Sail areas adapted to the weather, on JOSHUA

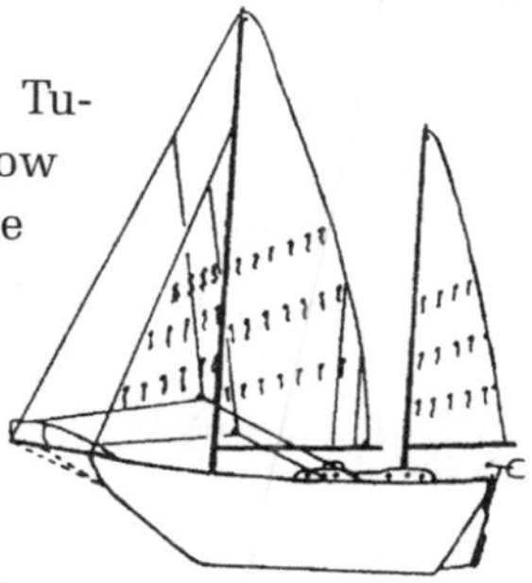

In the trade winds
Main: 375 sq ft with 3 reef bands
Mizzen: 215 sq ft with 3 reef bands
Staysail: 195 sq ft with 3 reef bands
Big jib: 235 sq ft or small genoa: 375 sq ft

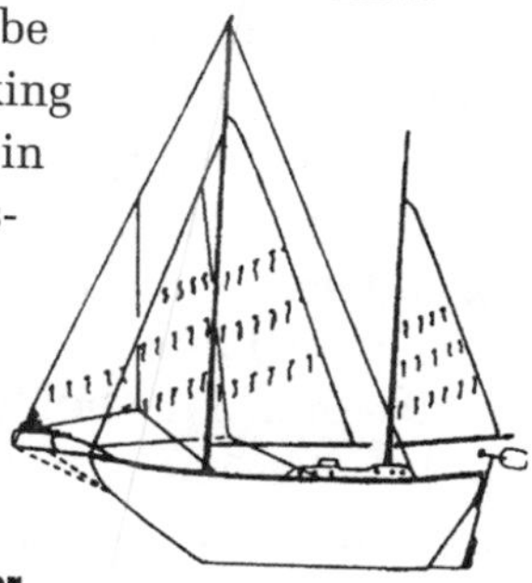

High latitudes (fair weather)
Small mainsail: 270 sq ft with 3 reef bands
Small mizzen: 150 sq ft with 3 reef bands
Small jib: 160 sq ft, light Dacron
Large staysail: 195 sq ft.
The storm jib is furled tightly on the bowsprit.

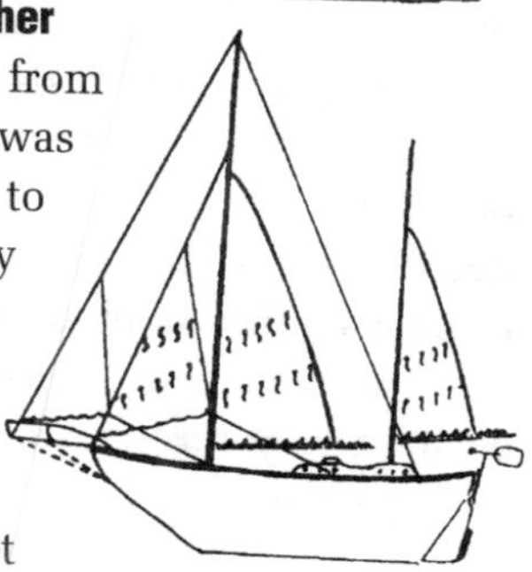

High latitudes (fresh wind)
Single-reefed mainsail: 195 sq ft
Single-reefed mizzen: 130 sq ft
Single-reefed staysail: 140 sq ft
Single-reefed jib. But I later chose to reef the 160 sq ft jib and wait until the wind rose; I then replaced it with the storm jib.

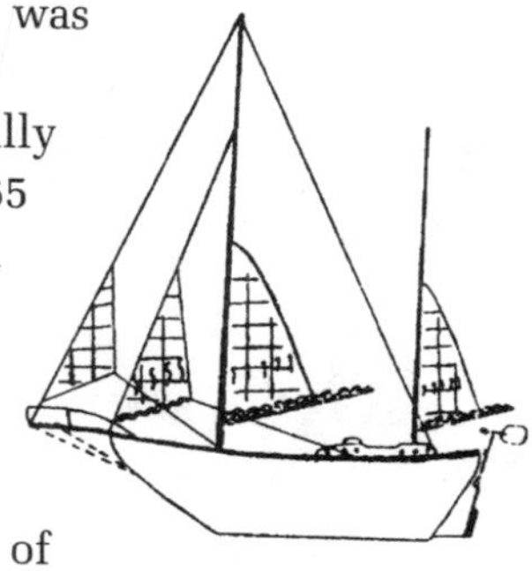

High latitudes (strong wind or moderate gale with probable improvement)
Double-reefed mainsail: 130 sq ft
Double-reefed mizzen: 85 sq ft
Double-reefed staysail: 65 sq ft
Storm jib: 55 sq ft

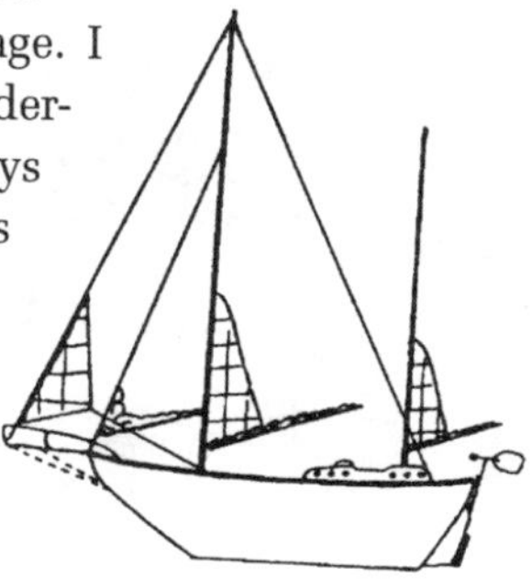

High latitudes (very strong wind or gale with heavy seas)
Triple-reefed (fully reefed) mainsail: 65 sq ft
Fully reefed mizzen: 55 sq ft
Storm jib: 55 sq ft
I strike the staysail, because putting in its third reef is too complicated. I often replace it with a small 75 sq ft staysail with reef band.

REDUCING AND CHANGING SAIL

Sail areas adapted to the weather

The great lesson I learned from the Tahiti-Alicante passage was the necessity of being able to adjust my sail area in any weather. During Tahiti-Alicante, JOSHUA wasn't really prepared on that score; its smallest sail (the storm jib) was 85 square feet and the triple-reefed main was 195 square feet.

For The Long Way, the fully reefed main measured 65 square feet, the fully reefed mizzen 55 square feet, and I had a wide selection of headsails when I needed them, with tiny sail areas. This let me sail with peace of mind during the whole voyage. I was never over- and rarely under-canvased, and I could always adapt the sail area to changes in the weather.

The sketches here illustrate the importance of this set of small sails and the many adaptations made possible by having many reef bands, the last of which were very high.

I prefer to reef the large staysail instead of changing it. It's much less complicated, in my opinion. And when the weather improves, it's easy to shake out a reef. Or put one back.

Reefing the mainsail

In reefing the mainsail and the mizzen, I use a "jiffy-reef" system with running reefing lines, which lets me reef without having to secure the line at the boom end. With this system, it is easier to haul on the leech line, then take care of the luff line. Without running reefing lines, it's the other way around: you have to take care of the luff line first.

It took me no more than a minute at most to reef the mizzen, and two to reef the main. No need to luff up; it was easy, even with the wind aft, since the mizzen blanketed the main. Because my lines worked both ways, to either port or starboard, I could always stand on the windward side of the boom, which makes reefing much easier. This detail is very important. All it takes is a cleat on either side of the boom for each line (i.e. for each reef band). The line runs from its port cleat, is rove through the port cheek block screwed to the boom directly under the appropriate reef cringle, runs up to that cringle, goes through it and down the other side, is rove through the starboard cheek block, and runs back along the boom to its starboard cleat. You can therefore haul on either the port or the starboard end of the line, while always standing to windward of the boom. This is a good idea in foul weather: you can see breaking seas coming and won't be caught by a sudden roll, which, if you were to leeward of the boom, might send you overboard. You should be wearing a safety harness, of course, but there's no reason to take chances.

Jiffy-reef system ready for action

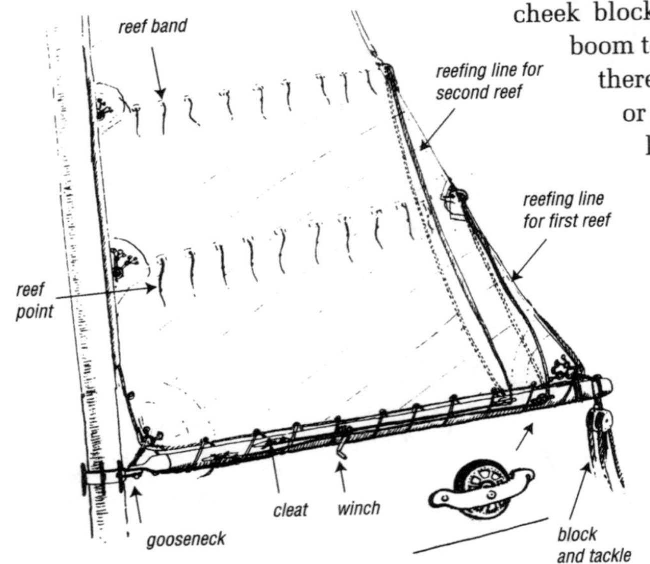

A small winch on either side of the main boom makes the leech line easy to haul taut, which saves time. The last inches are important, since they spell the difference between a well-set sail and a bag. No need for a winch on the luff line, as the halyard will be hauled taut after reefing. Nor do you need a winch for the mizzen reefing lines; one good pull will get them tight.

Note that reef bands should angle slightly upward toward the leech, so as to raise the boom end. The stronger the wind, the heavier the seas; so the boom end has to be higher than in fair weather, to keep it from hitting the water during a roll, when running.

Reefing shackles

Beware of using reefing shackles or other metal systems. With a shackle, it's either "yes" or "no," but when it's "no," it's really "no." Using a 5/16" nylon line lashing is a lot more reliable. You're always sure to get a "yes" and it holds without risk of chafing the sail or the bolt rope. And making the attachment is often much faster than with a shackle, however well-designed it may be.

Reef points

The reef points of the second and third reef bands are longer than those of the first, because they have to tie up more material. The knots on either side of the sail, which keep the points in their eyelets, should be about six inches apart, so you'll always have enough length to tie them.

I use different colors for each reef band, so as not to get them mixed up, especially at night.

With the wind aft, once I have reefed the main, I sheet it in so I can tie the reef points without having to lean out. In a strong wind, I first tie every other point, then go back and tie the ones in between. I use a square knot, not a slip knot. It may seem hard to loosen a tightened square knot, but it's actually very easy (see sketch).

Loosening a square knot in a small diameter line

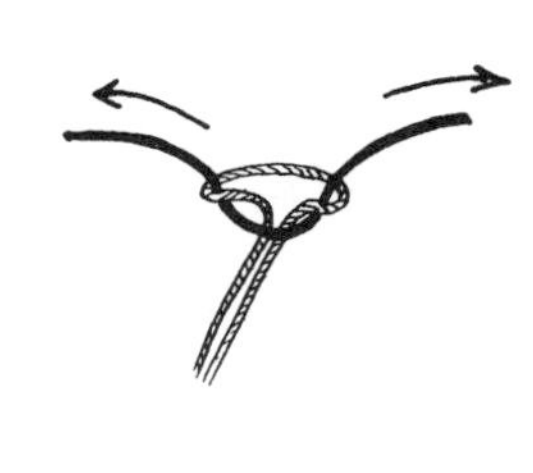

A square knot won't come loose in heavy weather, whereas a slip knot often will. Using a square knot is especially appropriate for the staysail reef points; if they are hit by seas at night and come untied, the bundle of freed material will hang down like a big pocket and can wreak havoc with the sail. I also tie an extra knot very close to and on either side of the square knot; that way, there is no chance the reef point will work free.

Reefing the jib in a fresh wind

To change a jib or reef it, especially when close-hauled in a fresh wind, a solo sailor will heave to for safety. So will a small crew, to reef a jib on the bowsprit, for example. The boat is hove to, the mainsail sheeted flat, and the tiller put down. (On a ketch, the main and mizzen would be sheeted flat and the tiller down.) The boat meets seas a little further forward than when hove to under staysail. Rolling is practically eliminated because of the wind resistance of the mainsail's relatively large sail surface, even when reefed. But the boat pitches a little, since the waves hit a little ahead of amidships. Still, with speed down to practically zero, the boat jogs along quietly, and changing the jib becomes easy for a person alone, even out on the bowsprit.

With a crew, here is the maneuver:

1) Come about without touching the sheets, then put the tiller alee. The boat is hove to, beam pretty much to the wind, with jib and staysail aback.

2) One sailor eases the jib halyard (the jib will remain sheeted during the whole operation) while another, sitting astride the end of the bowsprit—with his feet and knees wedged against the bobstay and the whisker stays—hauls on the jib bolt rope to bring the new tack down to the level of the first. He then lashes the line and tugs on the bolt rope to further lower the jib to make it easier to reach the clew. Note that the jib, which is still sheeted, doesn't flog.

3) The sailor who eased the halyard now cleats it temporarily so it doesn't get tangled around the spreaders. He then ties the sheets to the new clew thimble.

4) The job is nearly done. All that remains is to tie the reef points before hardening the reefed jib's halyard.

You then get under way and put the jib and staysail over, unless you prefer to jibe. Jibing may seem less technical than coming about into the wind, but I often prefer it to avoid the extra effort involved in bringing the staysail and jib sheets over in a crosswind. Marking my halyards so I can find the point at which to cleat the halyard that was eased for reefing saves me a lot of time. Marking a halyard this way avoids having to ease it again if you haven't given it enough slack. This is especially valuable for the headsails, and will often reduce the number of trips between the tack and the foot of the mast.

Changing the jib on the bowsprit

Here is a simple system to change the jib on the bowsprit without too much pain. Stretch a taut 1/8" steel cable between one of the mainmast shrouds and the jib's tack shackle. You can then hank all the new jib's snaps onto the cable and slide the whole sail out to the end of the bowsprit (or vice versa) without the wind or sea being able to tear it out of your hands.

JIBING A KETCH IN A FRESH WIND

1) Begin by sheeting the main flat.

2) Set the wind vane for wind full from astern.

3) Ease the mizzen sheet out all the way; the mizzen then blankets the mainsail.

4) Set the wind vane to jibe. The main passes smoothly to the other side because it is blanketed by the mizzen and is still sheeted flat, for the time being.

5) Bring the mizzen over (this isn't difficult, considering its relatively small area).

6) Bring the jib and staysail over (which are aback following the jibe) and trim the mainsheet for the new tack.

SLOWING THE BOAT

You can slow the boat with wide sweeps of the tiller, and by pushing the sails aback.

To be ready to brake the boat while maintaining steerage way in a following wind, drop and raise the jib, drop it again and raise it part way, while using the rudder, if needed.

CONTROLLING LEEWAY IN MODERATE DEPTHS

In the Gulf of Siam, where depths range between 45 and 60 feet, fishing boats ride out bad weather under bare poles by facing into the wind and dragging 50-pound ballast stones on coconut-fiber hawsers along the bottom. It's simple and efficient, and the drag can be controlled or even abandoned (by cutting the hawser) if the wind starts blowing toward shore.

BACKING

I used to back-up JOSHUA by pushing the backed mizzen well over, from side to side, while steering with the rudder. To help the boat keep a straighter course, I hung an anchor on a length of chain from the bow, without letting it touch bottom. (That way, I also was really ready to drop anchor.)

ANCHORING

Preparing to anchor is a ceremony.

Every boat will wind up in bad anchorages during her lifetime, regardless of her skipper's caution or good sailing sense.

Whenever possible, I avoid anchoring in water deeper than I can dive, in case I need to swim down to free the anchor.

Choosing the makeup of your ground tackle

Advantages of "all chain"

1) If you are moored stern to in a crowded harbor, chain doesn't risk being cut by other boats' propellers. Also, because of its weight, chain will almost always hang below them.

2) In a harbor protected from swell, a boat anchored on chain will hold better than an identical boat anchored on a chain and nylon line of the same length. For the same wind force, the latter will have to put out a longer length of line.

3) A chain can't be cut by rock or coral in an unprotected anchorage, or by another boat's chain if you are moored stern to a dock.

Drawbacks of "all chain"

In shallow water (10 to 12 feet), with moderate swell, chain can undergo violent shocks, and lengthening the rode won't change the situation much. A chain rode's "give" depends on the chain's weight and its catenary curve between the boat and the bottom. If

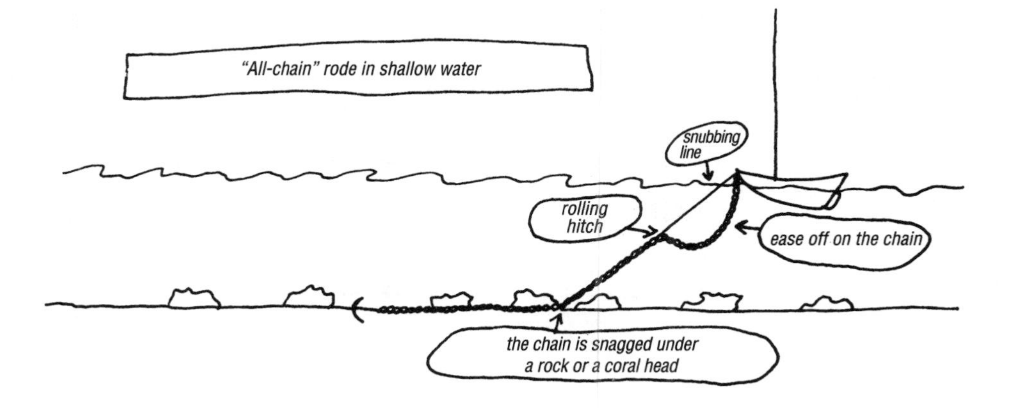

"All-chain" rode in shallow water

there is too little depth for a chain to make an adequate catenary, it will lie in an almost straight line, despite its weight. As a result, the rode will jerk as the boat pitches, which can snap the chain or damage the mooring bitt or windlass.

In moderate depths (25 to 45 feet), a snagged chain will also pull in a straight line when the boat pitches, with the same risk of damage.

There are two excellent ways to avoid this problem: using a spring-based shock-absorbing system (expensive), or a length of nylon as a snubbing line tied to the chain with a rolling hitch (simple, very efficient, requires no extra room).

On the other hand, I don't see any way to avoid two other "all-chain" drawbacks:

1) Chain is heavy, which makes a windlass essential, and windlasses are slow.

2) In a stiff blow, if you want to set out a second anchor in series on the same rode, the operation isn't easy with all-chain; at night with a stiff chop (especially with a collapsible dinghy), it can be impossible.

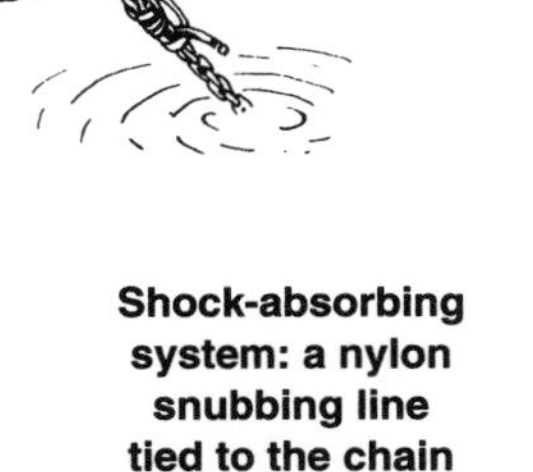

Shock-absorbing system: a nylon snubbing line tied to the chain with a rolling hitch

<u>Drawbacks of a nylon and chain rode</u>

1) The line can chafe or be cut by the fairlead or bobstay, so vigilance and chafing gear are called for.

2) The rode can be cut if it snags under a rock or coral head. This is why you always need 30 to 45 feet

Mixed "chain and nylon" rode: using a float to keep the line away from rocks

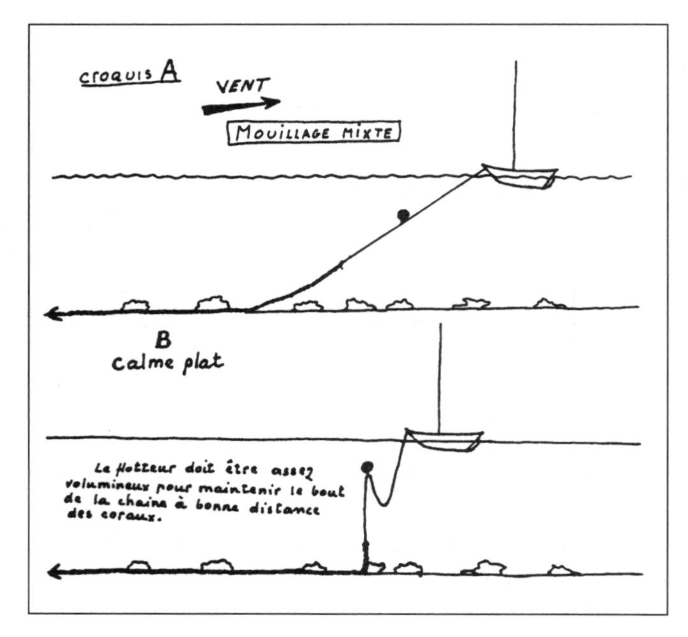

of chain between the anchor and the nylon line. But that short length of chain won't completely protect the nylon in certain cases (in particular, an anchorage that is subject to alternating tidal currents).

In part because of this danger, JOSHUA's main nylon anchor line was grossly oversized: I used 7/8" line, which has a breaking strength of ten tons. This gave me time to notice if the line was abrading on a rocky or coral bottom, and to take action before the wear endangered the safety of the anchorage.

Just the same, beware of chafe of the nylon line at the bow, and especially on rocky or coral bottoms. (This is easy to avoid by tying on floats to keep the nylon line off the bottom.)

<u>Advantages of a nylon rode</u>

Great mobility for the crew in case of a stiff blow.

—You can lay out an anchor a hundred yards or more away, by rowing out in the dinghy while the line unreels all by itself from a spool.

—If the sea and wind make that maneuver impossible in a dinghy, you can easily swim the anchor out, after lashing it underneath a jerrycan (preferably a plastic one).

Any swimmer, even a weak one, can cover a hundred yards while pushing a jerrycan with an anchor hanging from it. A few tricks will make the operation easier: carry a knife, so you can quickly "untie" the anchor from the jerrycan's line. If you aren't a strong swimmer, wear fins, mask, snorkel, or even water wings. You can push the jerrycan or tow it, while doing the crawl, breast stroke, or backstroke.

If the anchor and the short length of chain weigh more than 35 to 40 pounds, you will need several jerrycans, tightly lashed together. Cut the chain and anchor free at the same time. If the anchor is supported by a single jerrycan, it will sink immediately; if only the chain is cut free, it will drag the anchor down, still tied to its jerrycan.

One night in the Spanish port of San Feliu de Guíxols, I was aboard JOSHUA when we had to put out a third anchor on 300 feet of nylon line in a real gale. Attempting the operation with my inflatable dinghy was out of the question, at least for me. But by swimming, it was much easier, even with the wind and chop; there was no windage, and no risk of overshooting or capsizing.

Protecting the rode

MARIE-THÉRÈSE II had been anchored at Saint Helena for a week when she suddenly started to drift for no apparent reason. It was daytime, and I was on board. The nylon anchor line was slack, and when I pulled it in, there wasn't anything at the end: the anchor and chain lay on the bottom in 60 to 80 feet of water. I stared in astonishment at the shackle that had connected the line to the chain. It was still threaded through the thimble, but its screw pin was missing, as if to prove what the problem was. Yet I had a mental image of what I had done the evening before I came into port: I had greased the threads of the pin, tightened it all the way with a shackle wrench, spread the chain out on deck, and coiled the line. So what had happened? The slow vertical oscillations of the rode had gradually unscrewed the pin. Ever since, I've been careful to run a wire through the pins of all my "important" shackles.

Elasticity of the rode

Flexibility and elasticity spell a stronger anchorage and better holding for the anchor because the shocks are absorbed and spread out over a longer period of time.

Here are a few stories that illustrate the importance of having a rode with some "give."

In Durban, WANDA was anchored on chain, with her stern moored to the jetty with 12 or 15 feet of strong manila line. The swell came up and Henry thought the mooring line would snap or break something. So he tied a 30-pound weight to the line and eased off on the rode. WANDA began to ride easily again.

I was crewing for Jean Fricaud aboard SAINTE-MARTHE. We were moored stern to the dock when the swell came up. You don't rip out a mooring bitt on a steel boat the way you pull a tooth. One of the two mooring lines snapped, and the other was about to. It was a 3/4" hemp hawser, not new, but not rotten either. We quickly grabbed a big 40-pound rock from the beach and hung it from the line; that fixed everything.

JOSHUA was anchored in the lee of Fuerteventura, in the Canary Islands. The stiff offshore trade wind funneled through the valleys and came down the mountainsides, blowing a gale for minutes on end. It would ease up, and then start gusting so hard it made the storm jib tremble in its sail bag. It was a lousy anchorage, but the beauty of the long, completely deserted fine sand beaches more than made up for it. We were about 70 yards from the beach, held by the Colin Tripgrip toward the shore (in six feet of water, with 30 feet of chain and the rest nylon line), and by the 50-pound CQR plow on the seaward side. The gusts peaked during the afternoon. The Tripgrip was holding well, but the 5/16" nylon line was under terrific strain. Would the anchor drag? Would the line break? Amazing, what nylon can handle . . . Suddenly JOSHUA took off in a gust, accelerated to a good three knots, then abruptly stopped dead after 30 or 40 yards. This time, I was convinced it was all over. I hunkered down and made myself as small a target as possible, because when a nylon line breaks, it can whip back and take your eye out. Slowly, I raised my head to survey the damage. Everything seemed to have settled down. The anchor had suddenly grabbed when it reached the lava bottom. The line had held, but it was so stretched by the extra tension, it looked like one of those homemade lines Henry and I used to wind with a hand drill in the Cape Town yacht club yard.

Reinforcing the anchor in bad weather

For an anchored boat in bad weather, there are two kinds of situations to consider:

—a port without any swell, or in which the swell is greatly moderated;

—an unprotected anchorage where you can expect every dirty trick imaginable the moment the wind shifts in the wrong direction and stays there. That's when you think longingly of being comfortably hove to, well offshore . . . But it's too late now; the escape hatch is blocked by a howling wind, and you have to take action.

In port (where the swell doesn't enter, or is greatly weakened by a breakwater)

If you've acquired the wise habit of instinctively anchoring upwind of big pleasure boats, the problem will involve far fewer worrisome unknowns.

What I usually do is to lay out my second anchor—a very strong one—as quickly as I can with the dinghy. I use just 30 or 40 feet of chain, and nylon line for the rest. I row out as far as I can with the anchor, in line with the first rode. Handling the dinghy isn't too hard, thanks to the relatively small weight of chain, but it's smart to drop the anchor really far from the boat, so as to get a good horizontal pull on the anchor.

Rowing out with a second anchor when bad weather comes up

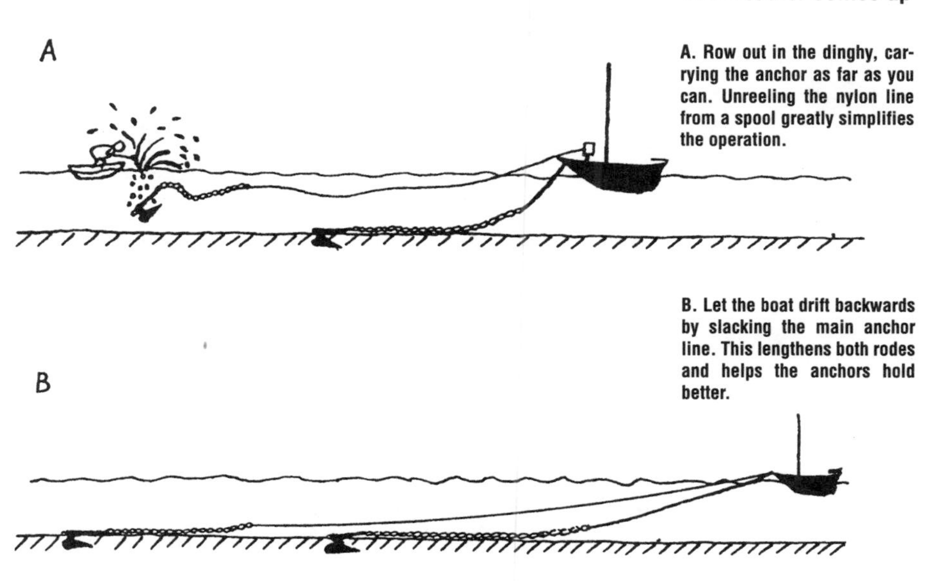

A. Row out in the dinghy, carrying the anchor as far as you can. Unreeling the nylon line from a spool greatly simplifies the operation.

B. Let the boat drift backwards by slacking the main anchor line. This lengthens both rodes and helps the anchors hold better.

In this kind of operation, half-measures often spell extra work later on. It's better to row out with the biggest spare anchor immediately, while the weather is still manageable and you can use the dinghy. That way, when a gale hits, you will be riding on two solid anchor cables.

In port, with two good anchors set well out, on a line that isn't too light, it would take a hurricane to drag the anchors, especially CQRs. But it would also be wise to hang weights on the mooring lines and rig chafing gear—and to check it from time to time.

In an unprotected anchorage

I almost always set out anchors in series when in an unprotected anchorage as soon as the weather starts to look worrisome.

Rigging anchors in series on one cable

When the boat's survival is at stake, setting out anchors in series is safer than other anchoring methods I have used, including using a good pair of anchors set at an angle.

This consists in laying out two or more anchors one after the other on the same rode, so they reinforce each other's holding power. When I have used this procedure—which results in the chain being practically buried once you have hung everything but the kitchen sink on it—it has always produced incredible holding power in heavy weather.

The classic rule has it that two anchors in series, of 20 and 40 pounds for example, should hold as well as one anchor of the same weight (60 pounds, in this example). But over time, I have become convinced that for the same total weight, several anchors in series hold far better than a single one. Because weight isn't everything: the number of "teeth" is what counts.

For example, 65 feet of 3/8" chain (1.5 lbs per foot) that weighs 100 pounds offers more drag resistance than 45 feet of 9/16" chain (2.2 lbs per foot) that also weighs 100 pounds. The reason is simple: 65 feet of chain produces more friction than 45 feet, despite the difference in the size of the links. Weight is essential, of course: only weight will break through a layer of sea grass or a crust of hard sand or broken shells. But weight isn't everything; the anchors have to dig in, as well.

Considerations when setting anchors in series

Whatever the final arrangement of the two, three, or four anchors that will be in series on the mother cable, the primary goal is to "root" the chain into the bottom. Your goal is to plan and execute an anchor rode that can take enormous stress, while remaining elastic.

A. The start of bad weather

Let's suppose that JOSHUA is lying to a 55-pound CQR anchor and 3/8" chain, and 300 feet of 7/8" nylon line.

1) I lay out on deck a good spare anchor (the Colin Tripgrip, say) with about 30 feet of chain.

2) Using the windlass (taking two or three turns of the anchor line around the gypsy), I warp the boat as close as I can to the CQR anchor without breaking it out. I then tie the second anchor line (Tripgrip with 30 feet of chain) with 10 or 12 feet of 9/16" nylon line to the main 7/8" nylon line, using a rolling hitch. (Note that the second anchor line must be the same length as the distance to the CQR anchor; otherwise the Tripgrip will hook only after the CQR has dragged nearly 45 feet.)

3) I then gradually pay out line until the deck is clear. So JOSHUA is now lying to two anchors, one of which is a 55-pound CQR on 3/8" chain and a Tripgrip connected to the 7/8" line with 15 or 20 feet of 9/16" line. (I tie a float to the cable at the rolling hitch, and a second small float in the middle of the 9/16" line, so it doesn't get caught under a rock.) I have put down roots now, and it will take an unusual wind or a very bad bottom for the anchors to drag.

B. The weather gets worse, with much more swell than expected

If the weather continues to worsen, better get ready to give it all you have; you will now be glad you invested in good ground tackle. By now, the situation has changed. The initial anchor arrangement has worked well enough so far, but must now be backed up with a second, virtually bombproof one.

1) I get my largest Fisherman anchor from the forepeak and shackle it to about 100 feet of the 1/2" chain (which weighs 2.8 lbs. per foot) I save for real blows. I then tie the remaining anchors in series one after the other with a few yards of 3/8" chain between each one. The last anchor (the one that will be furthest from the boat) is the 45-pound Danforth, and it gets nearly all the remaining 3/8" chain.

2) Using the windlass, I warp the boat as close as I can to the original chain—again, without breaking it out—then lower the second series' anchor cable while paying out the first.

3) I extend the 7/8" line with a 9/16" line from a spool; I loop it through an eye splice and protect the end of the line with a length of rubber hose. The second rode gets the small 5/8" line, which is also on a 300-foot spool.

JOSHUA is now anchored on two independent series of anchors. One consists of a very heavy anchor, chain, and a single 5/8" nylon rode; the other of lighter anchors, chain, and a doubled nylon rode of 7/8" and 9/16" line. Since they are 300 feet long, the rodes are extremely elastic. Catastrophe can now only come from chafe at the fairleads, and that can be avoided with plenty of chafing gear and constant vigilance.

Why not use two bow anchors at an angle?

I wouldn't use double bow anchors on separate rodes in heavy weather except in some very special cases, such as the absolute necessity to keep the boat within a specific swinging arc. The problem is that at the least wind shift, that is, during most strong gusts, one of the rodes gets all the strain while the other goes slack. In other words, for angled bow anchors to be truly reliable, each of the two cables would have to be rigged with anchors in series. Rigging such an anchor arrangement would be a real circus, and a major problem would still remain: whatever you do, one of the two rodes will have to handle everything during gusts. In a nice little gale that can turn into a hurricane if it has a mind to, a boat will ride much more securely on two cables pulling simultaneously—especially if a third anchor has been laid out on deck, with jerrycans, mask, and fins at the ready in case you can't use the dinghy.

Use the longest possible scope

All the books say that the scope should be long enough so that the pull on the anchor occurs at the best angle, that is, horizontally. What I've never understood, though, is that sacrosanct motto, "Scope three times the depth and it will hold." Three times the depth may be plenty of scope for a boat anchored in a harbor in fair weather, but it can be completely inadequate for a boat moored stern to a dock in a crosswind. For the same wind, the pressure on the anchor on a boat tied fore-and-aft will be much stronger than for a boat that can swing freely. The chain will be pulled at an angle, losing the benefit of friction on the bottom. The anchor, which has to take all the tension, can begin to drag, particularly as the pull becomes less horizontal. To understand the foregoing, just consider the way you harden a halyard by hauling on it at an angle.

It is always wise to figure that the little force 2 breeze blowing from the dock can become a force 5, 6, or 7 crosswind in the course of the night.

I prefer to anchor on an extra-long rode when stern to a dock for the following reasons:

—My anchor will be further out than other boats' anchors. That makes weighing anchor under sail safer when the wind is blowing toward the dock; I will have more room to maneuver if I reach my anchor well beyond the row of other bows and chains.

—If a boat setting out snags my rode, my anchor will have a good chance of holding even with nobody aboard JOSHUA to temporarily slack her cable to facilitate the other boat's leaving.

The power of lateral tension

wind

When you are moored stern to a dock, the tension on the bow anchor is much greater than for a boat that can swing freely. You apply this principle each time you swig a halyard taut.

In a crowded anchorage

Remember to always slack your cable to make it easier for a boat whose chain you have crossed to get under way. Otherwise, both parties suffer: the other skipper will break your anchor out at the same time as his, then drop it again. Your anchor can wind up in a bad position, usually to leeward of where you want it, and in any case closer to shore than before, which is a nuisance (see sketch).

Moving the anchor without moving the boat

When anchored in 10 to 15 feet of water in warm, clear waters such as the Mediterranean, it is often possible to move the anchor further out without moving the boat or using the dinghy. You might do this when you are moored stern to a dock and decide that the anchor rode is too short, or when you plan to spend the night off a beach and want to move further out.

In those situations, here is what I did during cruising-school classes aboard JOSHUA.

1) One of us puts on a swim mask and walks out underwater

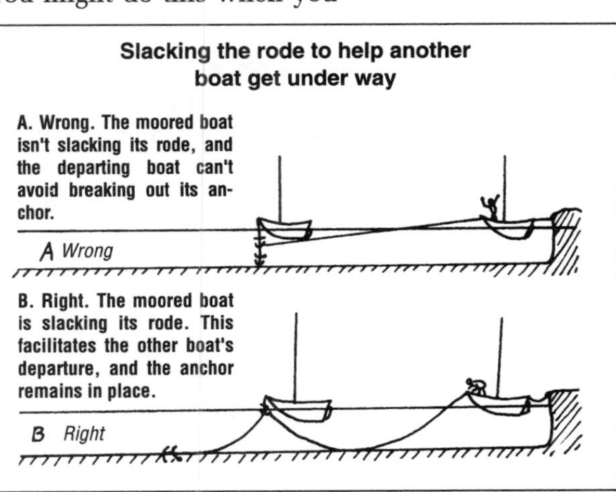

Slacking the rode to help another boat get under way

A. Wrong. The moored boat isn't slacking its rode, and the departing boat can't avoid breaking out its anchor.

B. Right. The moored boat is slacking its rode. This facilitates the other boat's departure, and the anchor remains in place.

along the bottom, carrying a small anchor in his arms or on his shoulder, leaning forward. The anchor is on a hundred feet of line, which unreels from a spool. This is quite easy if you have taken two precautions:

a) Be sure the spool is ready to unreel all the line needed.

b) Breathe deeply for two or three minutes before diving. (Hyperventilating puts extra oxygen in the blood and lets the diver stay underwater longer.)

2) Once the small anchor is set, repeat the operation with the main one. Slack the rode, dive down to the anchor, pick it up, and carry it further out. This is much harder to do, because the anchor is linked to 80 or 100 pounds of chain dragging on the bottom. Here is a technique that can help:

a) Holding 10 or 15 feet of floating line, dive down and tie one end of it to the anchor. The line will float vertically in the water, making the anchor easy to find in murky water.

b) Once you have caught your breath, swim back down to the chain, grab it one-third of the way from the end that is shackled to the line, and carry it out as far as possible. Then surface. (You can expect the anchor and chain to now be hidden in a dense cloud of mud or fine sand.)

c) Again following the floating line, dive down to the anchor again, pick it up, and carry it out until the chain straightens and begins to drag.

Repeat these operations several times: first carry the chain (by picking it up as high as possible so it doesn't drag on the bottom), then move the anchor, which is now free of the chain's drag. In this way, even an average swimmer can accomplish a task that at first glance seems impossible: moving a 25-pound anchor and cable a distance of 30 to 50 yards in 15 feet of water.

Moving out into a bay where you plan to spend the night

It's nice to anchor close to a beach during the day, but it can be risky not to move away from shore if you plan to spend the night in an unprotected anchorage. And it's wise to always approach anchoring situations as if you won't have the use of your motor. On JOSHUA, when we wanted to anchor further out from a beach, it was usually easiest to row out with a small anchor at the end of a hundred yards of 5/16" line stored on the

Moving the anchor without moving the boat

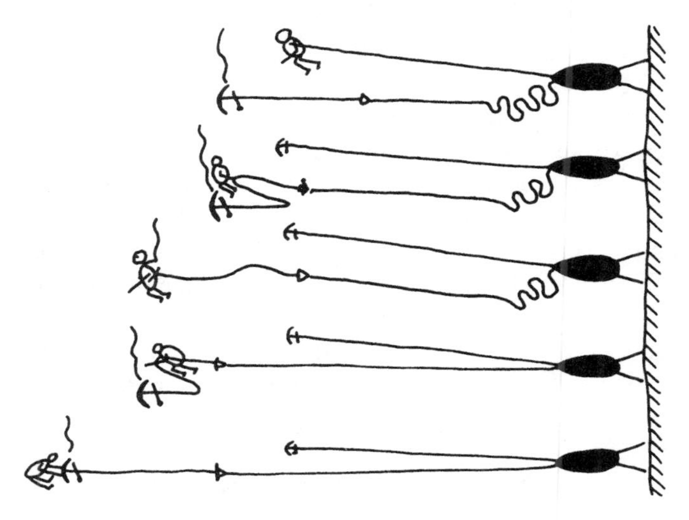

1) Carry the small anchor while walking along the bottom, then slack the main rode.

2) Grab the main anchor chain a third of the way along and drag it toward the anchor, walking on the bottom.

3) Carry the anchor in your arms or on your shoulder, and carry it further out, walking on the bottom.

4) Repeat step 2.

5) Repeat step 3.
NB: Tying a length of floating line to the main anchor makes the operation much easier.

"harbor maneuver spool." We then broke the main anchor loose, hauled the boat out to the small anchor, and dropped the big hook again.

An extreme situation: anchoring in very deep water

Peter Tangvald once had to anchor in the Galápagos in 500 to 600 feet of water, which presented him with two problems: the anchor had to reach the bottom and catch—which called for enough chain to make the rode heavy enough; and he had to later be able to haul in his thousand feet of cable without dying from the effort. Here is the clever trick he came up with. First, he anchored on a light anchor, with just a few yards of chain and a small-diameter line 300 to 450 feet long. He then added enough chain to weigh down the line so it didn't hang at too sharp an angle, while remaining light enough that he could haul it in by hand.

With this setup, when Tangvald was ready to leave he didn't have to lift the weight of the anchor at the same time as the weight of the chain. A weight halfway between the anchor and the boat is less effective than the same weight located close to the anchor. But in this very special case, the most important consideration was for Tangvald to be able to weigh anchor without too much fatigue. Moreover, the connection between the anchor and the upper chain consisted of a short, much weaker length of line. If the anchor snagged under a rock, that line would part and he would lose the anchor, but the rest of his precious cable would go back to the forepeak. As it turned out, everything worked perfectly.

Buoying a line with floats

To keep a non-floating line (such as nylon) from sinking, you need only tie small floats to it at reasonable intervals. The float closest to the anchor should be no closer than the depth of the water. The second float should be no further from the first one than double the distance from the first float to the anchor. Needless to say, the floats' role is simply to keep the line from sinking, not to put a strong vertical pull on the rode, which would hurt the set of the anchor.

Leaving an unprotected anchorage in bad weather

The best array of anchors set out in a series isn't as good as being hove to offshore, or anchored on a little CQR deep in some cove completely sheltered from the swell.

It's easy to understand why it's important to stay alert in an unprotected anchorage. The most obvious danger is a change in wind direction. If the wind starts blowing from offshore, you may have to get underway quickly without screwing up, either to head out to sea, or to find a safer anchorage in the same bay. But you must have originally anchored far enough from shore so you can weigh anchor under sail in less than ideal circumstances.

It's best to get ready to weigh anchor if you notice a long swell beginning to break harder on the beach, even if nothing in the sky suggests an upcoming wind shift. When the ocean swell starts to build, it's a sure sign that something nasty is happening somewhere out there. Deliberately ignoring such a tip-off, especially before nightfall, could be very costly if the wind starts blowing in from the same direction as the warning swell. And of course the seas could rise to the point of turning the bay white, or even become breaking waves if things get really ugly and the barometer stays low. If the primary threat is wind, you can always work things out; it's a matter of having enough anchors and chain on hand and watching out for chafe. But when a big wind-driven swell starts coming in from the wrong direction, things can get much more serious.

I'm convinced that even a half-rotten boat like our old SNARK is in no real danger when out at sea, because the only really serious things that can happen to a boat is to sink or have her hull damaged. And that doesn't happen to a good tight boat (with a reliable bilge pump) under bare poles or hove to, as long as she stays offshore.

At anchor, however, it's a different story. You can find yourself with your back to the wall, unable to either retreat, change anchorage, or head out to sea.

Weighing anchor solo without a windlass

"Give me a long enough lever and a place to stand, and I will move the earth," said Archimedes. Now is the time to bring major force to bear, by applying the principle of the lever. Rig a block and tackle with one end tied to the rode and the other to the fiferail on the mainmast or to some other absolutely sturdy fitting, as far astern as possible. (Be sure to use a rolling hitch; any other knot could slip or jam tight.) That way, you can haul in the greatest possible length of rode with each setting. This in turn saves valuable time, because once the boat is directly above the anchor, you won't want to hang around in a crosswind. With the block and tackle, a solo sailor can bring the same force to bear as four perfectly coordinated people.

If one block and tackle isn't enough, you will have to rig a second block (a four-part one, if possible), to pull on the standing part of the first one. This again produces the strength of four people, and multiplies by four the first block's tension on the rode. When you have the strength of sixteen men hauling as one, you really start to get results. (Obviously, the first block and tackle should have very strong sheaves.)

When the chain reaches the foredeck, there will be much less weight remaining to be raised. You can then dispense with the second block, which will speed the rest of the job.

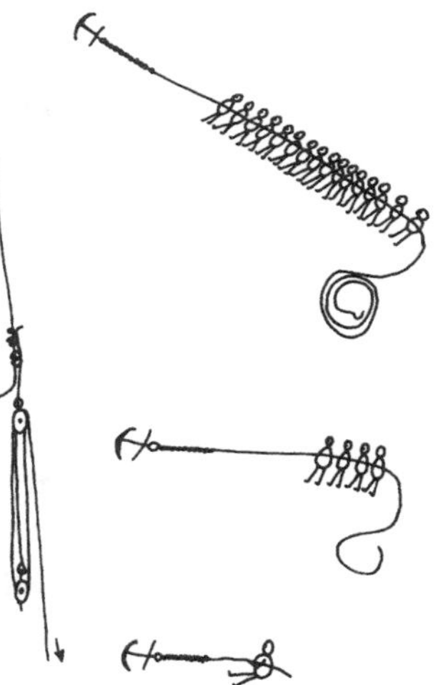

Weighing anchor solo without a windlass
Two blocks and tackle replace 16 crew members.

Freeing snagged ground tackle

On the way back to Indochina, we passed through the Anambas Islands and anchored in the lee of an island, on a coral bottom. But when we prepared to leave, the anchor refused to budge, even when we tried using the swell; all it did was to pull the bow down. The lead line showed we were in 35 feet of water. Deshumeurs dove underwater, and surfaced thirty sec-

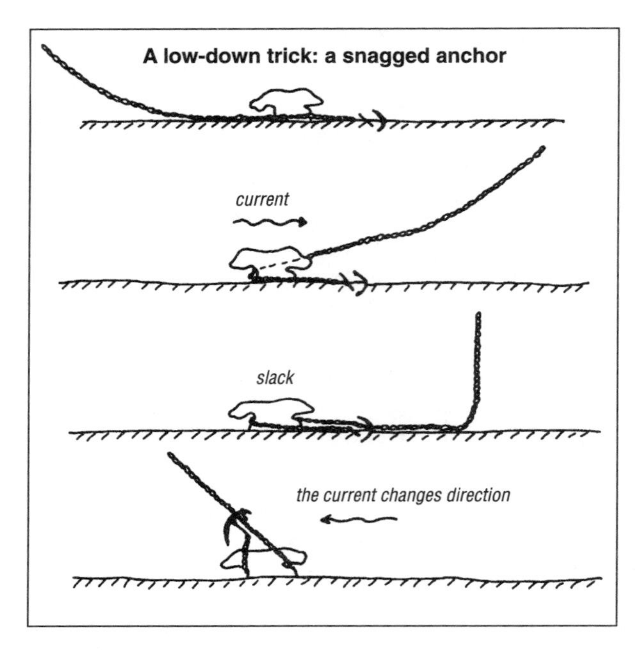

onds later. "Bernard, it's amazing," he said. "You better take a look yourself. Nobody is going to believe this."

I couldn't believe my eyes. The chain was wrapped *under* an enormous coral head, and the fouled anchor was dangling six feet above the bottom. No windlass could ever have raised it, but it wasn't too hard for a diver to free it. Once he was in position, the diver gave the chain a good yank. When the man on deck felt the yank, he quickly paid out ten feet of cable, counted to five, then hauled in the slack, fast. In those five seconds, the diver quickly freed the chain and anchor.

Measuring the boat's distance from obstacles

Here is an easy way to check how far the boat is from underwater obstacles. First swim the length of the boat, counting the number of your strokes. Then swim to the reef, again counting strokes, to see if the boat is a safe distance away. Repeat the operation all around the anchor.

FREEING A GROUNDED BOAT

Here is how LA GAZELLE's skipper freed his gunboat when she ran aground at speed on a Mekong River mud flat. With the engine running full speed astern, he had the whole crew (120 men) run from one side to the other to rock the boat. We got off just fine.

On JOSHUA, we used to do something similar.

1) Set out an anchor and crank the nylon line drum-tight.

2) Rock the boat. With the tension on the line pulling like a giant rubber band, the keel slides along the bottom and breaks free.

We once freed MAYLIS this way as well, using the motor and having the crew run from one side to an-

Measuring the distance from an anchorage's dangers

other to rock her. Rocking the boat allows the keel to gradually break coral or rock (if it isn't too hard), or to loosen sand or mud.

NIGHT MANEUVERS

To be able to see at night, you shouldn't have any lights on deck, or even in the cabin.

The color black

On JOSHUA, the cleats, stanchions, handrails, mooring bitts, and the inside of the bulwark were painted black, and foot-square black flags replaced the usual telltales. Why black? Because at sea at night, black is much easier to see than white. Hard to believe, but true.

Navigation

FINDING YOUR POSITION

When sailing along a coast, you can accurately plot your position by taking compass bearings on landmarks (lights, mountains, headlands) shown on a chart. When you're out of sight of land, you can navigate by dead reckoning, using the boat's estimated speed, heading, leeway, and any known currents. But the longer the passage, the more you will need to correct your dead reckoning.

The mere thought of taking sights at sea can rattle most yachtsmen. But veteran sailors know that the sea is calmer off shore than near the coast. The ocean offers the safety of great open stretches of water, and the won-

I had picked a star to steer by that was closest to my heading. As it gradually slipped to the left across the sky, I adjusted my course a finger's-breadth to the right from time to time. That was what Phuoc's father had taught me, when I went out with him during the fishing season.

derful gift of room to move about in, since we can heave to or run without fear of hitting the land.

That familiar shore, which is now in our wake astern, will appear again when we make our landfall in a few days or weeks, right before the bow. It will be different, and often threatening, because it is unknown.

When out of sight of land, the goal of celestial navigation is to draw two lines on the chart which cross at the boat's position. This is called "taking a fix."

Our first real landing came four or five days later. Can you imagine what that was like for guys like us, who had never seen a real horizon? In the Gulf of Siam, I had always been within sight of land of some sort, an island maybe. And all at once, here we were at sea, it was a total trip—life-size, larger than life. We had a sextant, but no idea how to use it. We used a compass, and that was it.

A number of books explain how to calculate a fix in simple, practical terms. I have used *La navigation astronomique à la portée de tous* by Maurice Olivier and *Navigation en haute mer* by Olivier Stern-Veyrin. There are also a number of good books available in English.

To get you started, here are a few notions of cosmography that helped me understand how to calculate my latitude. Later I'll give the basics of calculating longitude, with a few examples.

Notions of latitude and declination

The earth rotates on its axis once every 24 hours, while orbiting the sun in a year (in 365 1/4 days, to be exact). That axis, which is like a knitting needle stuck through an orange, is inclined by 23° 27' from the plane of the earth's orbit around the sun (which explains why we have seasons). It points to a specific point in space, infinitely distant.

Each day of the year, the sun will pass vertically above a different latitude located between 23° 27' north and 23° 27' south. When I say that the sun passes vertically above such-and-such latitude, I mean that at noon, a pole stuck in the ground at that latitude won't cast any shadow. Navigation tables give the latitude directly over which the sun will pass around noon for each day of the year. This is called the sun's declination.

On December 21, 1991, the sun's declination was 23° 27' south. In other words, on December 21, 1991, a vertical pole at latitude 23° 27' S would cast no shadow at noon, because the sun on that day passed directly above latitude 23° 27' S, that is, it was 90 degrees above the horizon.

Three months later, on March 21, 1992, the sun's declination was 0° 06' north. So on that day, the sun passed vertically above latitude 0° 06' north, or 90 degrees above the horizon at noon.

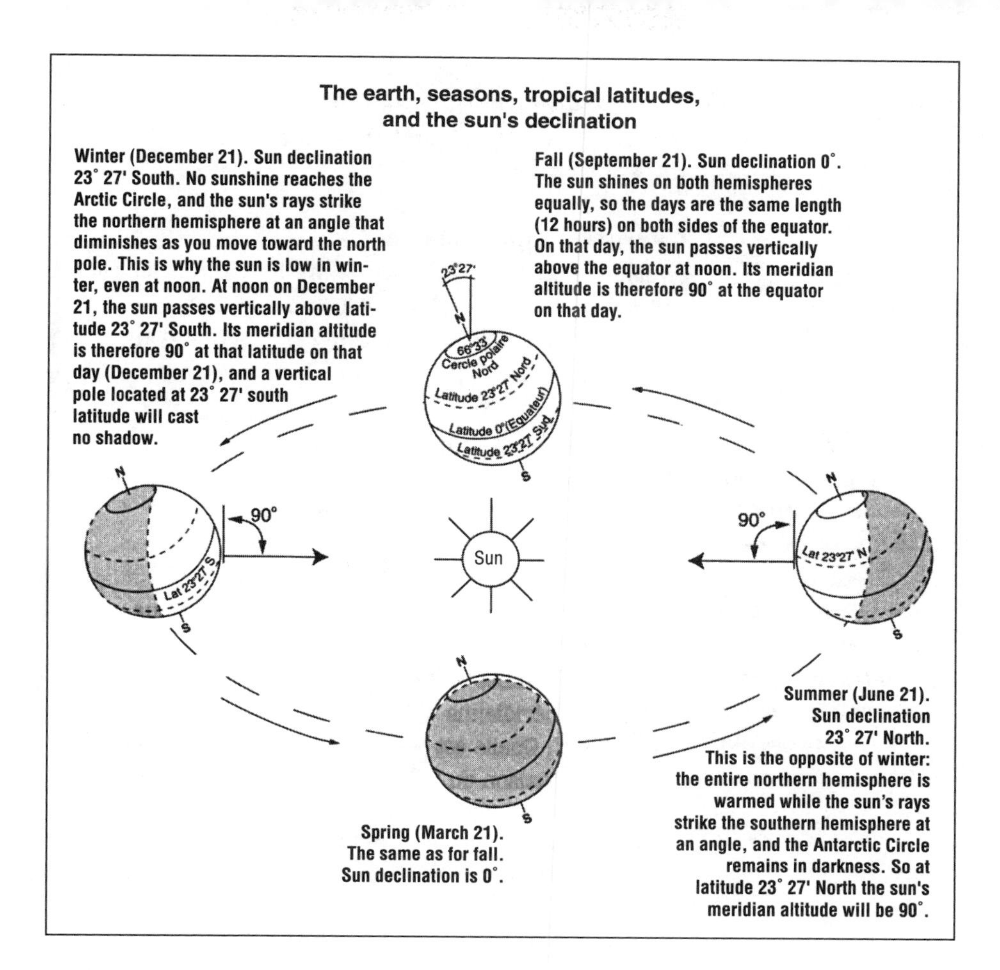

The earth, seasons, tropical latitudes, and the sun's declination

Sun altitude and meridian

When the sun reaches its greatest height for the day (at true noon), we say that it "passes the meridian." The angle formed between the observer's eye and the horizon is the "meridian altitude." So what we call the "sun's altitude" actually refers to the angle formed by the intersection of two lines: a horizontal one, between the eye and the horizon, and another one, from the eye to the sun. This "altitude" (which is actually an angle) is called "meridian altitude" when it is measured (with a sextant) at the exact instant when the sun is at the highest point in its arc that day, at true noon.

The sun's meridian altitude reaches 90 degrees (that is, with the sun directly overhead) twice a year for every point on earth located in the tropics (between 23° 27' north and 23° 27' south), but is always less than 90 degrees outside the tropics. At the Arctic and Antarctic circles, which are located at 66° 33' latitude north and south, respectively, the sun's meridian altitude is never greater than 23° 27', and it reaches that altitude only once a year.

Calculating latitude at noon

Now that you understand the foregoing, let's work out a very simple latitude exercise together.

1) We are at sea on March 21, 1993, and the sun's meridian altitude, as measured with the sextant, is 90 degrees. What is our latitude?

And now, aboard MARIE-THÉRÈSE, *I was becoming a real Old Salt because I had learned to use a sextant to get my noon latitude and I knew the name of that mountain without having to go anchor in some cove to ask a fisherman what it was called.*

The sun's declination for March 21, 1993 is 0 degrees. This means that the sun, at the moment it reaches the meridian, on that day passes vertically above latitude 0° (on the equator).

If we were also located at latitude 0°, the sun would pass directly above us at noon, and a vertical pole would cast no shadow. So the sun's maximum altitude (its meridian altitude), as measured by the sextant, would be 90 degrees.

Since the sextant's sun sight shows a meridian altitude of 90 degrees, we must be located at latitude 0° (position A on the sketch).

2) Sun declination 0°, meridian altitude 60°. What is our latitude, considering that we faced south (away from the North Pole) when we shot the meridian altitude?

Given a sun declination of 0°, the sextant would show a meridian altitude of 90° if we were at latitude 0° (on the equator). Instead, the sextant shows an altitude of 60°.

Since the sun was south of us at noon, we are therefore 90°—60°=30° further north than latitude 0°. So we are at latitude 30° north (at point B).

3) Sun declination 20° south, meridian altitude 78°. What is our latitude, considering that we faced away from the North Pole when we shot the meridian altitude?

Since the declination of the sun is 20° south, the sextant would show a meridian altitude of 90° if we were at latitude 20° south. Instead, the sextant shows a meridian altitude of 78°, and we were facing south when we took the sight.

We are therefore 90°—78°=12° further north than latitude 20° south, in other words at latitude 8° south (at point D).

What is our latitude?

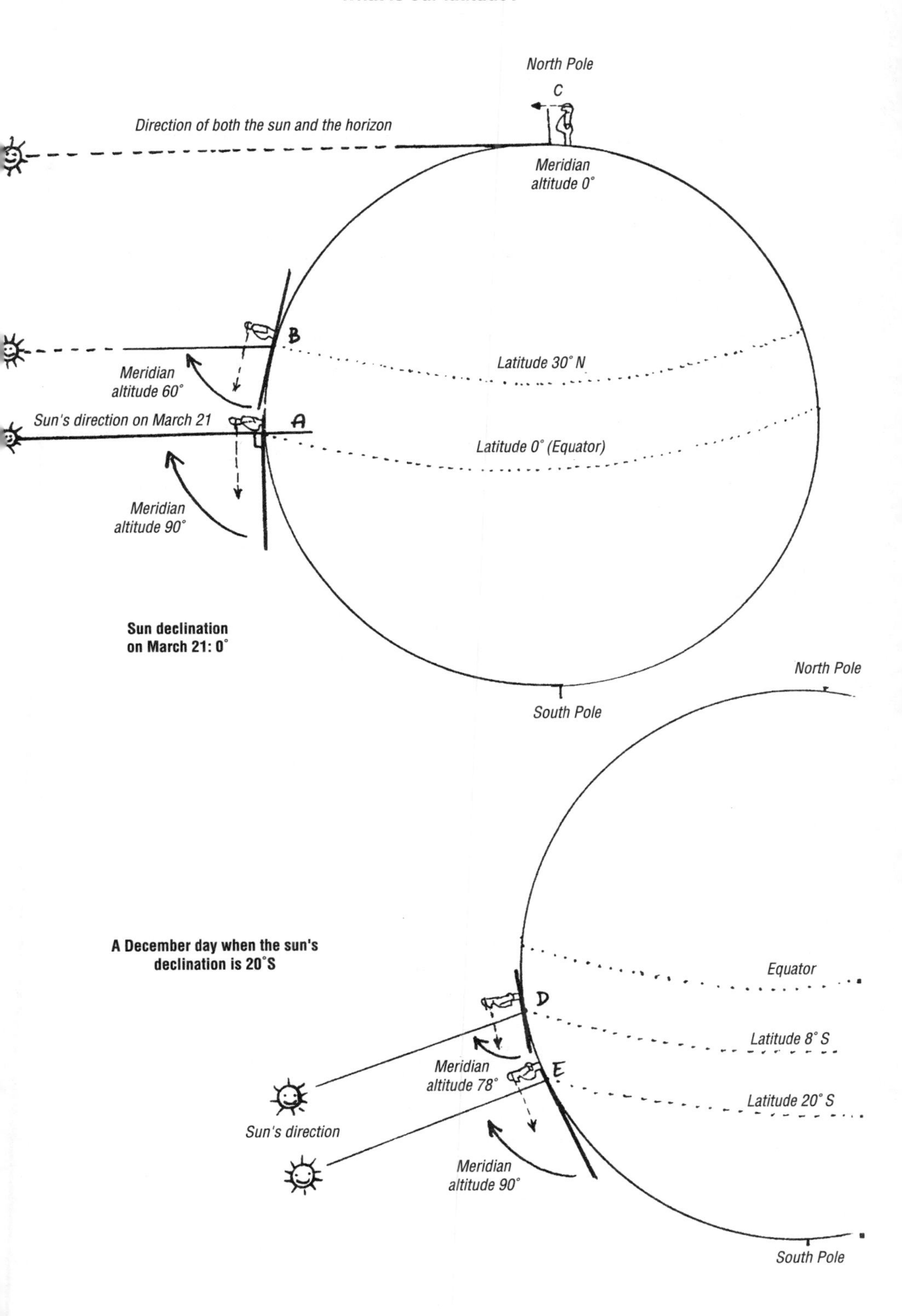

These three examples illustrate the basics. I hope they have helped you understand—by reasoning, rather than memorization—the principle of calculating your noon latitude.

To calculate your latitude, all you need is a sextant for the sun's altitude, a table showing the declination, and the sun, visible at its zenith. You don't even need a watch. But latitude alone isn't enough.

For the last two weeks, MARIE-THÉRÈSE had been running due west in the trade wind along the eighth parallel south. But I couldn't even estimate her speed by timing the foam as it passed the length of the boat anymore; my sweep-second alarm clock had conked out long ago. So my dead reckoning was becoming more uncertain as the wake lengthened. Aside from knowing my exact latitude, thanks to a daily sextant fix at noon, I didn't know where I was in all that vastness.

Calculating longitude using two position lines before and after noon

Let's imagine that you and I are aboard a sailboat somewhere at sea, with a sextant and a good watch set (thanks to radio station WWV's time ticks) to Greenwich Mean Time.

It will soon be (local) noon, and one of us is standing on deck, sextant in hand, to measure the sun's meridian altitude, which we need to figure our latitude.

The person holding the sextant (you, let's say) shouts, "Mark!" at the instant the sun reaches its meridian altitude.

When I hear you shout "Mark!" I note the time shown by the watch (in GMT, or Universal Time). Let's say it shows exactly 1400 hours.

What is our longitude?

At the moment you shouted "Mark!" it was exactly 12 noon where the boat was, since the sun reached its meridian altitude at that instant. Moreover it was exactly 1400 hours at the longitude (or meridian) of Greenwich, as shown by the watch. So our boat was located directly below the sun (since it was the exact moment of the meridian altitude), and west of the Greenwich meridian. The watch showed that it was 1400 hours at Greenwich, which proves that the sun, as it traveled west, had already moved two hours beyond the Greenwich meridian.

The boat's longitude is represented by the difference between Greenwich time (1400 hours) and the time at which the sun reached the meridian at the boat's location (12 noon). Since the sun passes over the earth at a rate of 15 degrees per hour, being two hours to the west of the Greenwich meridian means that we are 30° west of Greenwich, or at 30° West.

Now that you understand the principle behind calculating longitude, let's apply it in practice.

This differs in two ways from the earlier situation.

1) The time shown by the watch is mean time. As its name suggests, "GMT" stands for Greenwich Mean Time. Because the actual length of the day varies, GMT must be corrected, by adding or subtracting a few minutes and seconds, depending on the season, to get true time (technically, "apparent solar time"). The figure (in minutes and seconds) that must be added to or subtracted from GMT to get true time is called the equation of time; it is listed in the tables of the *Nautical Almanac*.

On January 10, 1991, for example, you had to subtract 12 minutes and 36 seconds from the time shown

What is our longitude?

Boats c, c', and c" are all at the same longitude, because all three of them are directly below the sun at the same time (true noon = 1400 hours Greenwich Mean, or Universal Time), though at different latitudes. The sun was directly above Greenwich (longitude 0°) two hours earlier. They are therefore at longitude 30° West.

Boats b and b' are on the Greenwich meridian, and therefore at longitude 0°. True noon = 1200 GMT.

Boats a and a' are east of Greenwich, since they saw the sun reach its zenith at 0800 GMT, earlier than at Greenwich. True noon = 0800 GMT = longitude 60° East.

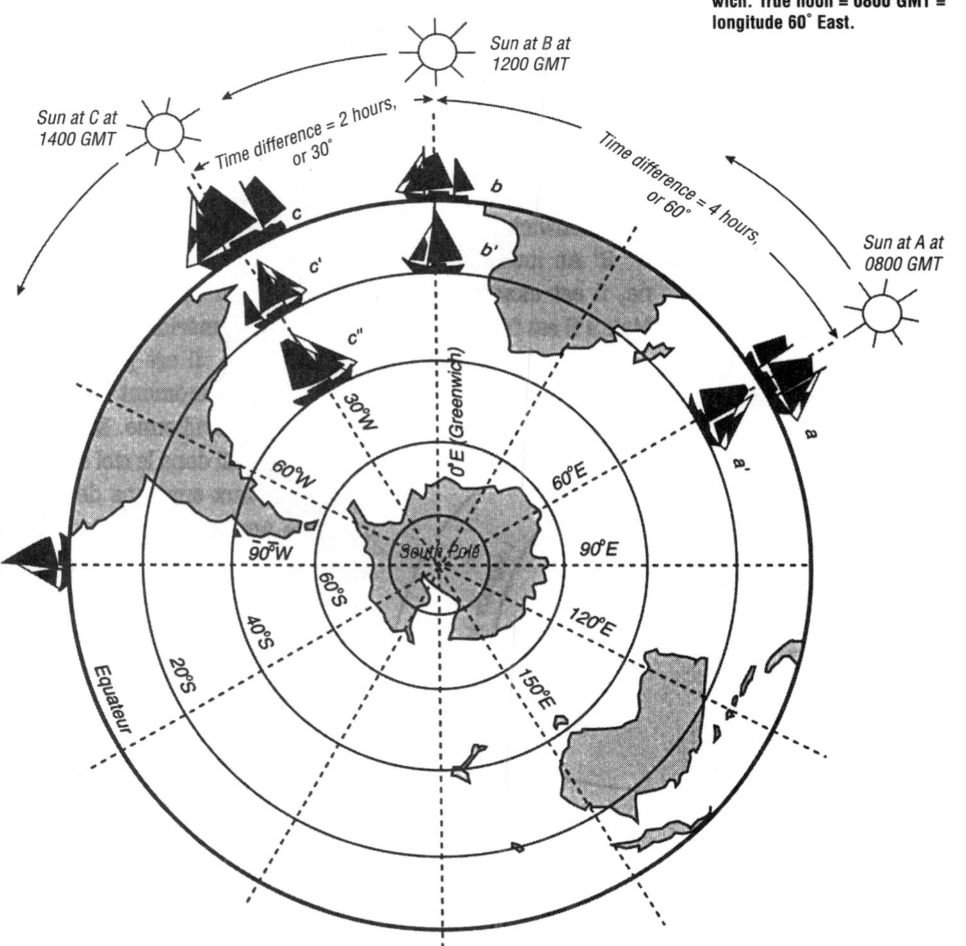

ELAPSED TIME	ARC
24 hours	360°
1 hour	15°
1 minute	15'
4 minutes	1°

by the chronometer (GMT) to get true time. You must use this true time to calculate longitude, because the "noon" you get at the instant of the meridian is true noon. You can't subtract that true noon (1200 hours) from the time shown by the watch (GMT) without first correcting the latter by the equation of time, thereby converting Greenwich Mean Time into the apparent time at Greenwich.

2) The moment the sun reaches its meridian altitude is exactly true noon at the observer's location. But while it is easy to measure with total accuracy the meridian altitude with a sextant, it is impossible to say at what precise instant the sun reaches its highest position. Toward noon, the sun rises so slowly in the sky that there can be a period of five to ten minutes during which you can't be sure whether the sun is still climbing a little or if it has already started to decline. In fact, you can consider that once the sun has reached its maximum height for the day (meridian altitude), it is still moving horizontally westward for several minutes. And a minute of time corresponds to 15 minutes of arc, or 15 nautical miles (at the equator); ten minutes would amount to 150 miles!

On the other hand, the sun climbs and drops fairly quickly twenty to thirty minutes before and after the time it passes the meridian. So to figure the exact time of the meridian passage, you can use the sextant to measure two equal altitudes (with the same sextant angle), one before noon and the other after noon, while noting the watch's time for each altitude. The average of those two times will give the exact GMT time of the meridian passage, to within several seconds. You then use the equation of time correction, which varies with the day of the year, to obtain true time.

What is our longitude?

We will now work on a longitude exercise together, using the method of equal altitudes before and after noon.

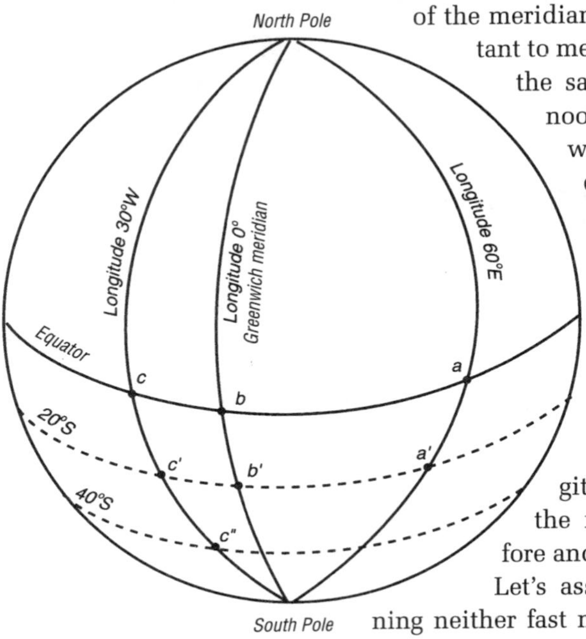

Let's assume that your watch is running neither fast nor slow. On January 10, 1991, the times shown by the watch at the moments of the two altitude observations were:

A. First altitude, before noon (GMT)	13 h	52 m	41s
B. Second altitude, after noon (GMT)	14 h	48 m	27s
C. Total of the two times	27 h	100 m	68s
D. Divide by two; this gives 13h 80m 34s			
E. Time (GMT) when the sun passed the meridian: 13h 80m 34s, which equals	14 h	20 m	34s
F. Subtract the equation of time from GMT	–	12 m	36s
G. True time of noon:	14 h	7 m	58s

So it was 14 hours 7 minutes 58 seconds at Greenwich (true time) when it was true noon (1200 hours) at the moment when the sun passed the meridian where our boat was located.

Since longitude can be expressed by the difference between Greenwich true time (14h 7m 58s) and the true time where our boat was (12 noon), all we have to do is subtract 12 hours from the time at Greenwich to get our longitude

	12 h		
WEST LONGITUDE	2 h	7m	58s

Conversion of longitude expressed in time to longitude expressed in arc:

2h = 30°; 7m = 1° 45'; 58s = 14'30"

So 2h 7m 58s corresponds to a west longitude of 31° 59' 30".

As you see, calculating longitude by this method requires only a sextant, a watch set to GMT, and tables showing the sun's declination and the equation of time.

You are now ready to calculate your latitude and longitude, and a few attempts at sea will provide practice. But you will soon realize that while calculating longitude using two equal altitudes is easy, it's inconvenient. You have to stay on deck for a long time, waiting for the exact instant when the sun, having begun its descent, will again touch the horizon through the sextant's telescope. And a cloud could hide it just then, making the observation impossible. The next time, you will be careful to take several sights before noon, noting the chronometer time for each one, and noting the number of degrees and minutes shown by the sextant.

Note the time

Once we reached the high latitudes, instead of shouting "Mark!" I used to give three kicks with my heel on the aft cabin roof (I usually stand with my back against the mizzen mast). Hearing that, Françoise noted the time on the chronometer, starting with the seconds, the way all sailors do. If you try to "photograph" at a glance the entire time shown on the chronometer, you risk making a mistake. And a mistake of one minute translates to an error of about 15 miles in your longitude.

That way, if a cloud appears during the sun's descent, you should still have a few useable altitudes.

Position line

Note the altitude

A useful trick we used on JOSHUA was to move the blocks in the sextant box so we didn't have to re-set the sextant to zero in order to stow it. That way, if calculating the position line produced an unusual result, we could check the sextant and notice, for example, that we had read 55° 38' instead of 55° 08'.

A noon sight can only be taken at noon, obviously. To calculate your position at any time of day, there is a method that lets you draw a position line whenever you can see the sun or a known star. That line, which is perpendicular to the sun or star's bearing (azimuth), is drawn some distance from the dead-reckoning, or assumed, position and is called an "intercept." These two elements, the azimuth and the intercept, are determined by calculation. The line, called a "position line," can be intersected several hours later by a second line based on another sight. You advance the first line the appropriate number of miles sailed between the two sights; the intersection of the lines gives the boat's exact position.

You will now have reached the stage of quickly getting a fix using position lines. And this is where the tables come into play; I use HO 249. To learn this method, I suggest you consult one of the books mentioned earlier.

It's worth noting that to draw a position line, you can begin your calculation using an assumed position that is way off; the position line will still determine the boat's correct location. In case the intercept is too far off, you can redo the calculations, using a new assumed position. For fun, I sometimes deliberately chose an assumed position 600 miles in error. In two calculations, the boat took its true place on the chart.

Star sights

Since navigation problems in the open ocean are simple, I only took three star sights during The Long Way; shooting the sun was enough. I was satisfied with a sun-sight position line in the morning and a meridian at noon, except when I was near a coast, in which case I also drew a few lines of position in the afternoon. It's worth remembering that afternoon lines of position can be off, because of the greater refraction, especially in warm seas. With the stars, there is no refraction, and star fixes can be incredibly accurate (to less than a half mile, sometimes a quarter mile). That is valuable when approaching a low coast or an atoll, when night fixes

Calculations: three position lines and a meridian (log excerpt)

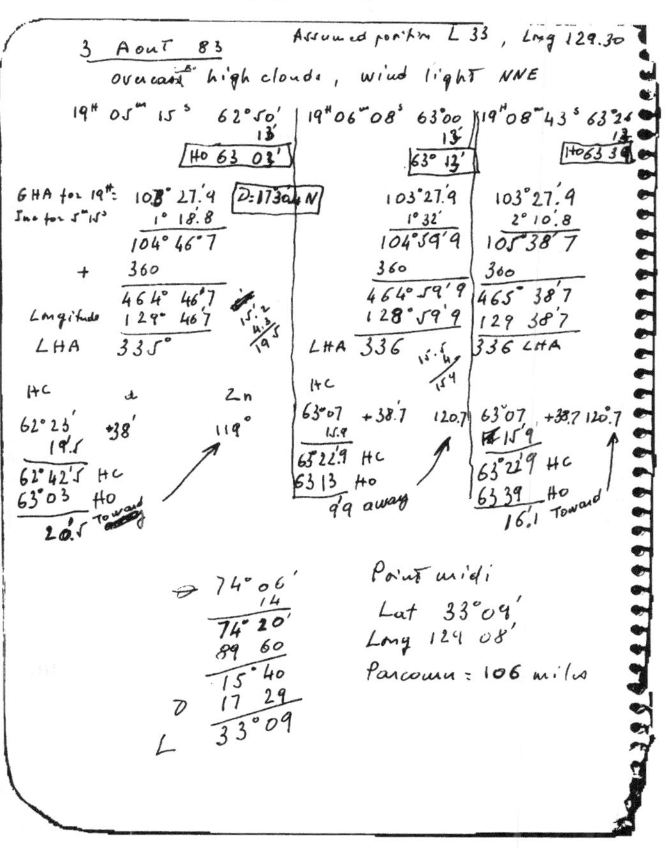

Drawing position lines (log excerpt)

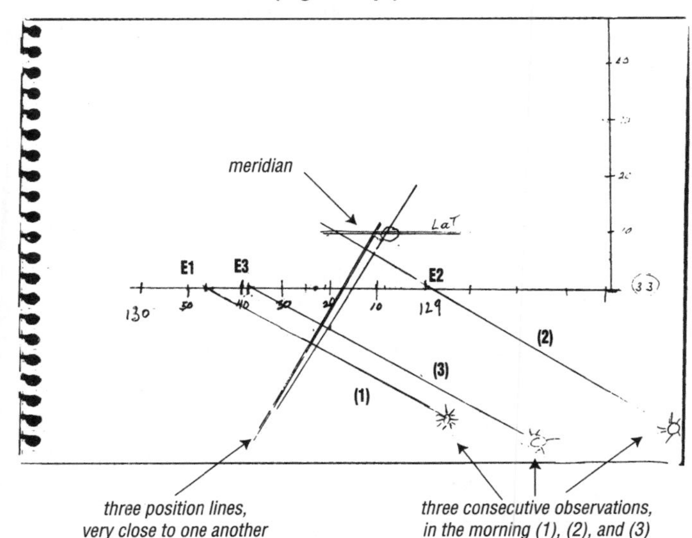

Three consecutive observations of the sun. Three different dead-reckoning positions (E1, E2, E3) to make the calculations easier. Three position lines, very close to one another, confirm the accuracy of the sights.

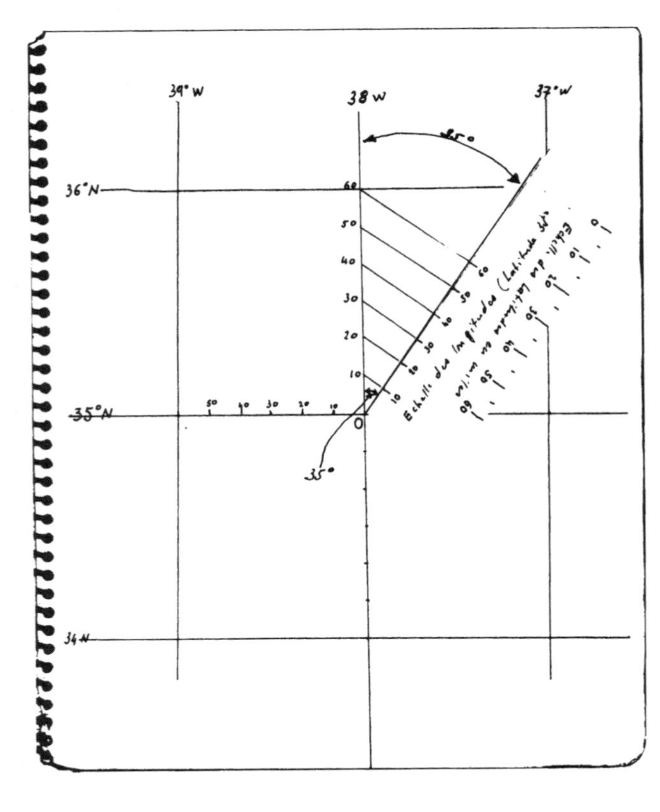

How to draw the scale of miles in function of latitude (log excerpt)

In the course of those peaceful nights, we gradually located most of the stars that are used in celestial navigation: first the easier ones, like Capella the she-goat, accompanied by her three kids; then Vega, located opposite from Capella and recognizable by the somewhat flattened four-sided figure located to its left. Naturally, we learned to recognize the splendid stars of the great lozenge in Orion: huge Sirius, almost as bright as the planet Jupiter; reddish Aldebaran; then Rigel and Betelgeuse (without forgetting the "reversed initials" rule: Rigel is blue and Betelgeuse, red.)

can be of prime importance. But for that, you need good sextant technique. On moonless nights I sometimes got very precise star fixes by keeping both eyes open and not using the sextant's telescope. This would have been impossible with the telescope.

Sighting technique

It is good if you can easily remove the sextant's telescope, so you can sight with both eyes open. For the sun, in calm seas, the accuracy is about a quarter of a mile. And in a swell, you will be sure you have brought the sun down to the horizon, and not to the top of a wave (the telescope considerably narrows the field of vision). Also, sighting is much faster with both eyes open; this is valuable in overcast weather, with the sun playing hide-and-seek among the cumulus clouds.

For star sights, there is no comparison. With the telescope, you can see the star, but the horizon is completely fuzzy; sometimes you can't even tell if you're seeing the horizon or the sky. Without the telescope

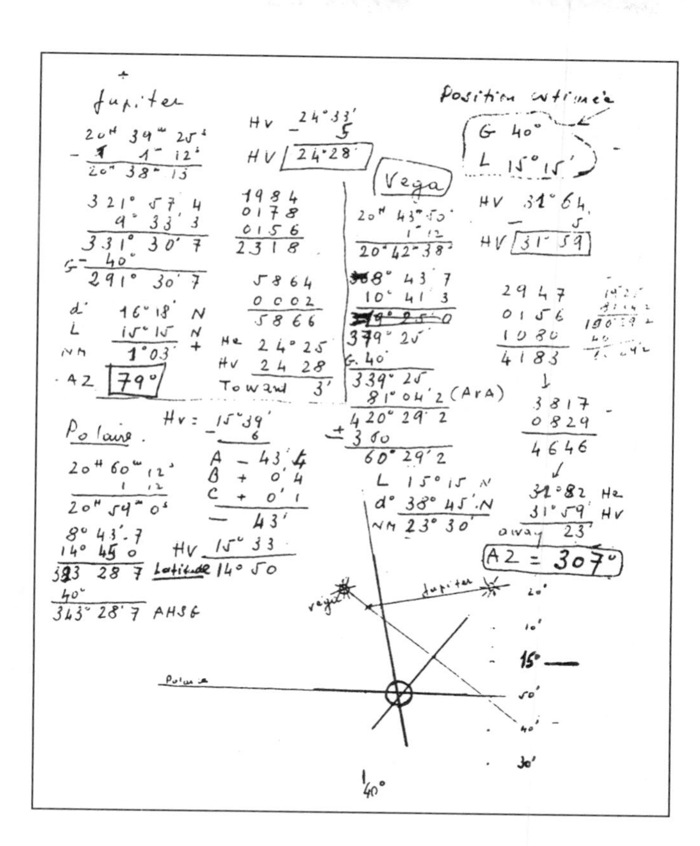

A fix using 3 star and planet lines of position (Vega, Jupiter, and Polaris). All the calculations fit on a single page of the log book.

and with both eyes open, you can not only see the star distinctly, but you also can see the horizon you are bringing it down to. On a clear night, it is possible to get an amazingly accurate fix this way. You still can even when the night isn't so clear, by more or less "dunking" the star—bringing it slightly below what you think is the horizon.

A few rules of sextant use

1) Learn to "shoot" very quickly. It's like firing a rifle; the faster you can shoot, the better your aim.

2) Always keep the sextant's mirrors and filters perfectly clean.

3) If the sky is overcast at noon, take a few altitudes just before and just afterward.

4) Take three sights at each observation, and calculate all three. You will get at least two position lines that agree.

5) Before stowing the sextant after taking a sight, wipe off the mirrors and filters, so the instrument will be ready to use next time.

6) In cold weather, bring the sextant box into the cockpit a few minutes before taking the sight, to avoid condensation on the mirrors and filters.

7) Always keep a supply of tissue paper in the sextant box, so you can wipe off the mirrors and filters in bad weather (mist and spray).

Rough times

RUNNING AGROUND

To be able to save JOSHUA in case she accidentally ran aground, her moveable ballast consisted of 50- to 70-pound lead blocks in the bottom of the hollow keel. They were held in place with removable bars, with a watertight cover bolted over everything; that way, nothing could break loose during a capsize.

SHIPWRECK

Other people's experiences with being shipwrecked suggest a few steps to take:

1) Never abandon your boat as long as you can stay aboard. A few examples: MARIE-THÉRÈSE; Anne Davison; and the Mediterranean crew that spent 13 days in an inflatable dinghy: when they abandoned ship, their boat had a 45° list, but was found in good weather three days later. There are many similar cases.

2) Don't ask for help from ships if you don't have to. Leo once asked a freighter to lift his boat onto its deck after a mistral gale; the sailboat was destroyed in the operation.

Remember what J.C. Voss said when he found himself in the water, with his boat's keel in the air: "As long as there is life, there is hope."

Surviving without water

The only way to avoid dehydration when you have absolutely nothing else is to drink the serum from fish, as Alain Bombard did. Score the flesh and squeeze the juice out; wait for rain before you eat anything; eating raw fish without extra water actually speeds dehydration.

And . . . losing your boat

Loss of MARIE-THÉRÈSE in the Chagos Archipelago (September 4, 1952)
"MARIE-THÉRÈSE was dead. The keel had vanished . . . And I wept, with my cheek against that beautiful, lifeless bow that still smelled of salt, wood oil, and adventure.
"I wept for my memories, my books, the loss of that limitless world made up of dreams and action I had so totally become a part of that I couldn't then imagine that any other could exist."

Loss of MARIE-THÉRÈSE II at Saint Vincent, in the Caribbean, (April 1958)
"True, this shipwreck was a big test, harder than the last one. But I had to take it like a man."

Loss of JOSHUA in Mexico (December 8, 1982)
"JOSHUA was a part of me, and had been for the last 21 years. I had left San Francisco for Costa Rica, where I hoped to write my next book. At anchor in Cabo San Lucas, things got nasty. There were thirty boats in the harbor. One night, a hurricane drove 26 of them onto the beach. JOSHUA's deck was swept clear, the masts downed, and the hull battered and filled with sand. A real wreck. When the sea calmed down, I slaved to get her out of there. Two guys came to help, and for a week, we struggled night and day. When the full-moon high tide came, we managed to refloat what was left of her. I didn't have a penny, and no way to fix JOSHUA up. I looked at these 20-year-old guys who were crazy about the sea, and I gave them my boat. JOSHUA had been saved, that was the main thing."

"V: Did it pain you to lose your boats?
B: Of course. When you don't have a boat, you're like a hermit crab without a shell. Life isn't very exciting. It's very painful.
V: And you felt pain?
B: Sure.
V: So what did you do to regain your peace of mind?
B: I try to build myself another boat, as quickly as possible!
V: And that has always worked?
B: It worked, at the price of many difficulties and a lot of hardship. Things gradually fall into place, but it takes work.
V: Did you ever feel that you wouldn't be able to pull it off?
B: No. You know, I try never to look too far ahead. I heave to emotionally. It's a trick I learned from reading Monfreid. When everything is going wrong, you stop thinking, you just act on instinct, you just do what has to be done every day. And little by little, things become clear.
V: And this technique has worked for you?
B: Every time."

Tahiti-Alicante, 1964

During the Tahiti-Alicante passage, we encountered a terrific, prolonged gale linked with two lows. The gale's main danger came from the secondary southeast seas raised by the first low after it had passed. The second low then kicked up extremely high westerly seas on which JOSHUA, under bare poles, tended to surf, and risked plowing into the secondary southeast swell raised by the first low. JOSHUA would have pitchpoled if we hadn't started steering so as to take each westerly sea 15° or 20° on the port quarter. That tactic had a double effect:

1) By cutting cleanly across the secondary southeast swell, which was mixed with confused, truck-sized seas coming from every direction, we were somewhat less likely to dig into one of them. If we had plowed head-on into one of those seas, JOSHUA would

Tahiti-Alicante gale

At A, JOSHUA risks pitchpoling by plowing into the secondary SE swell.
At B, JOSHUA takes the main westerly swell 15° to 20° on the port quarter. This called for steering 70 or 75 degrees, which kept her from plowing directly into the secondary SE seas. In position B, there is also less danger of surfing. The less the boat surfs, the less danger of pitchpoling.

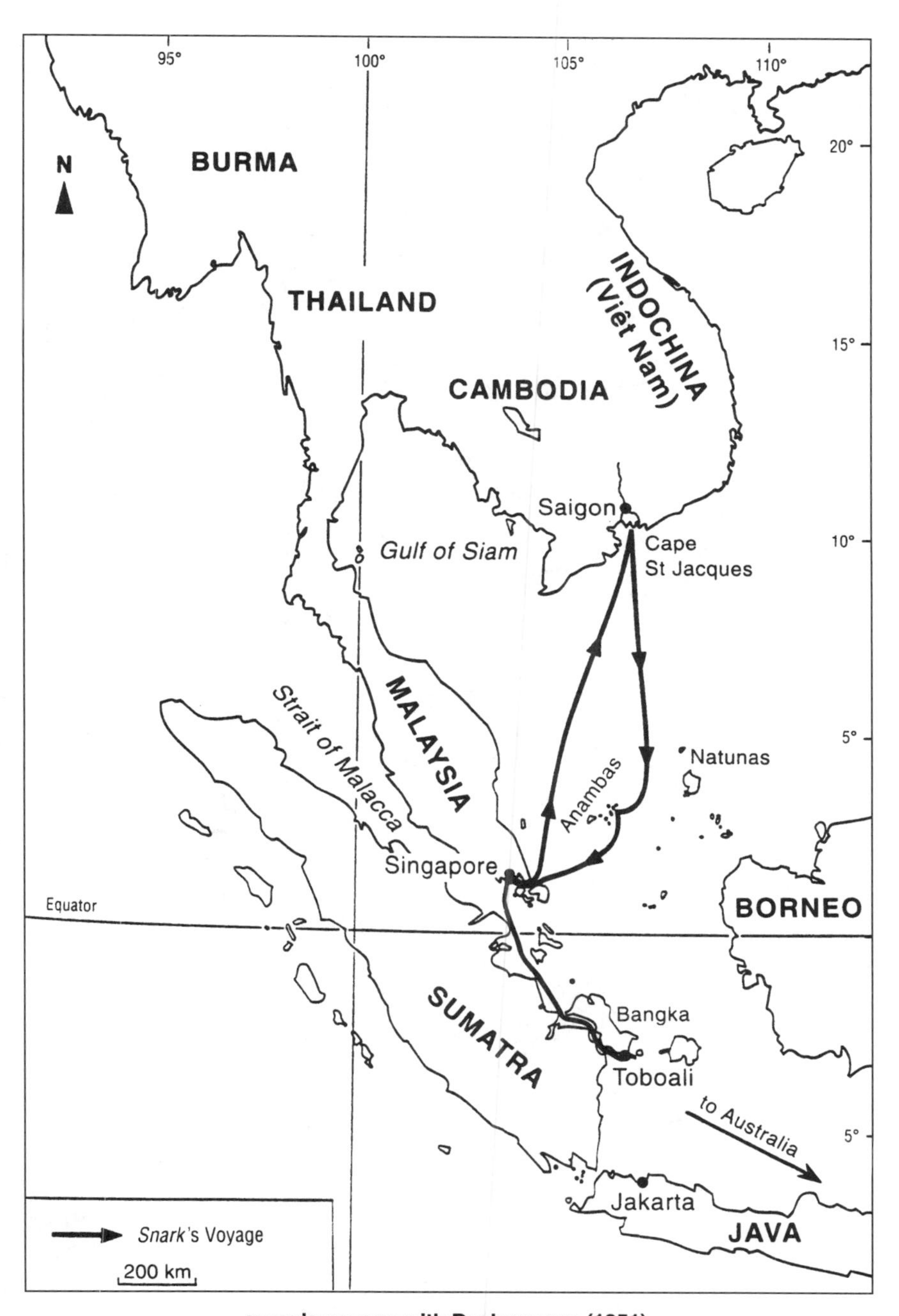

SNARK's voyage with Deshumeurs (1951)

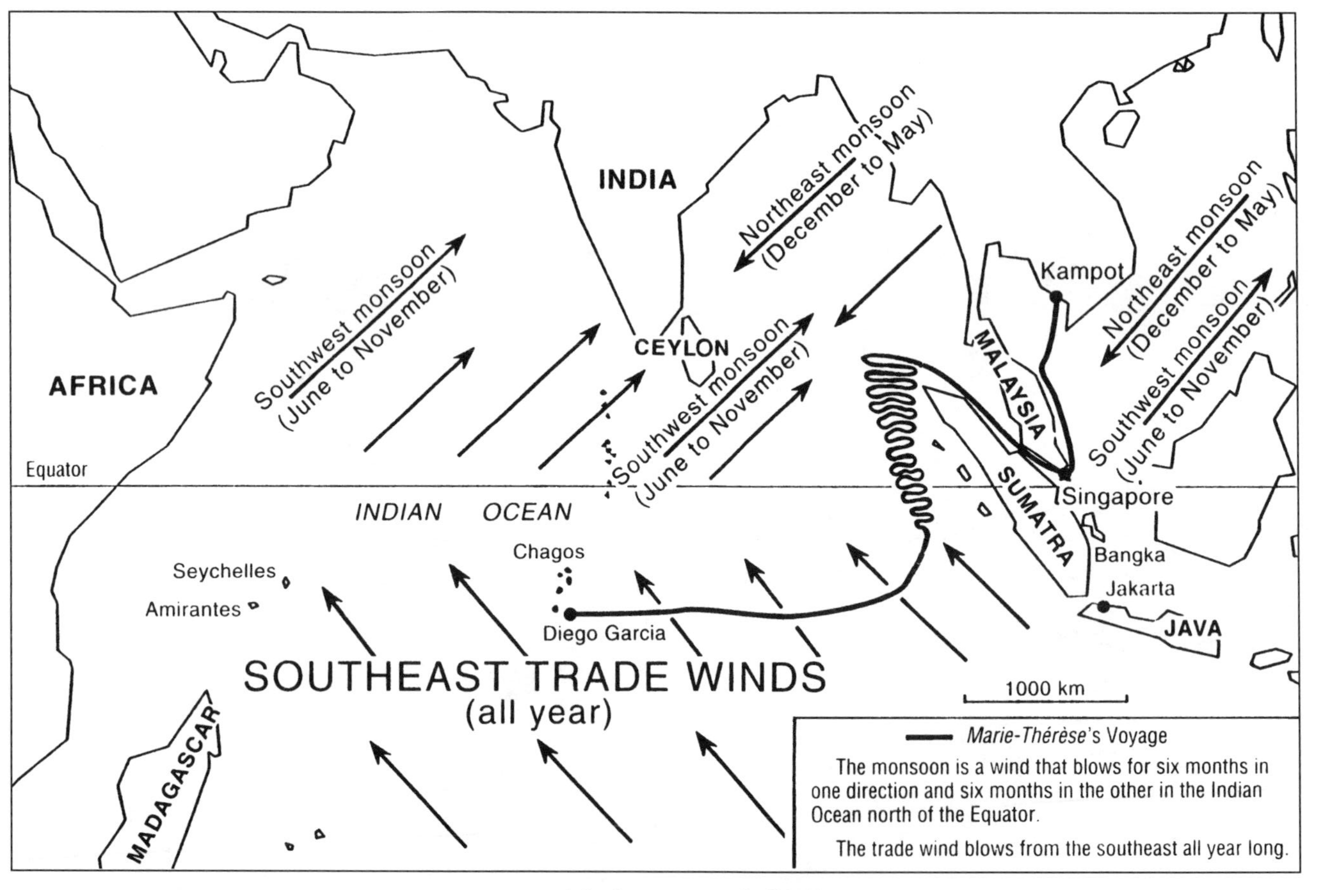

MARIE THÉRÈSE's voyage, solo (1952)

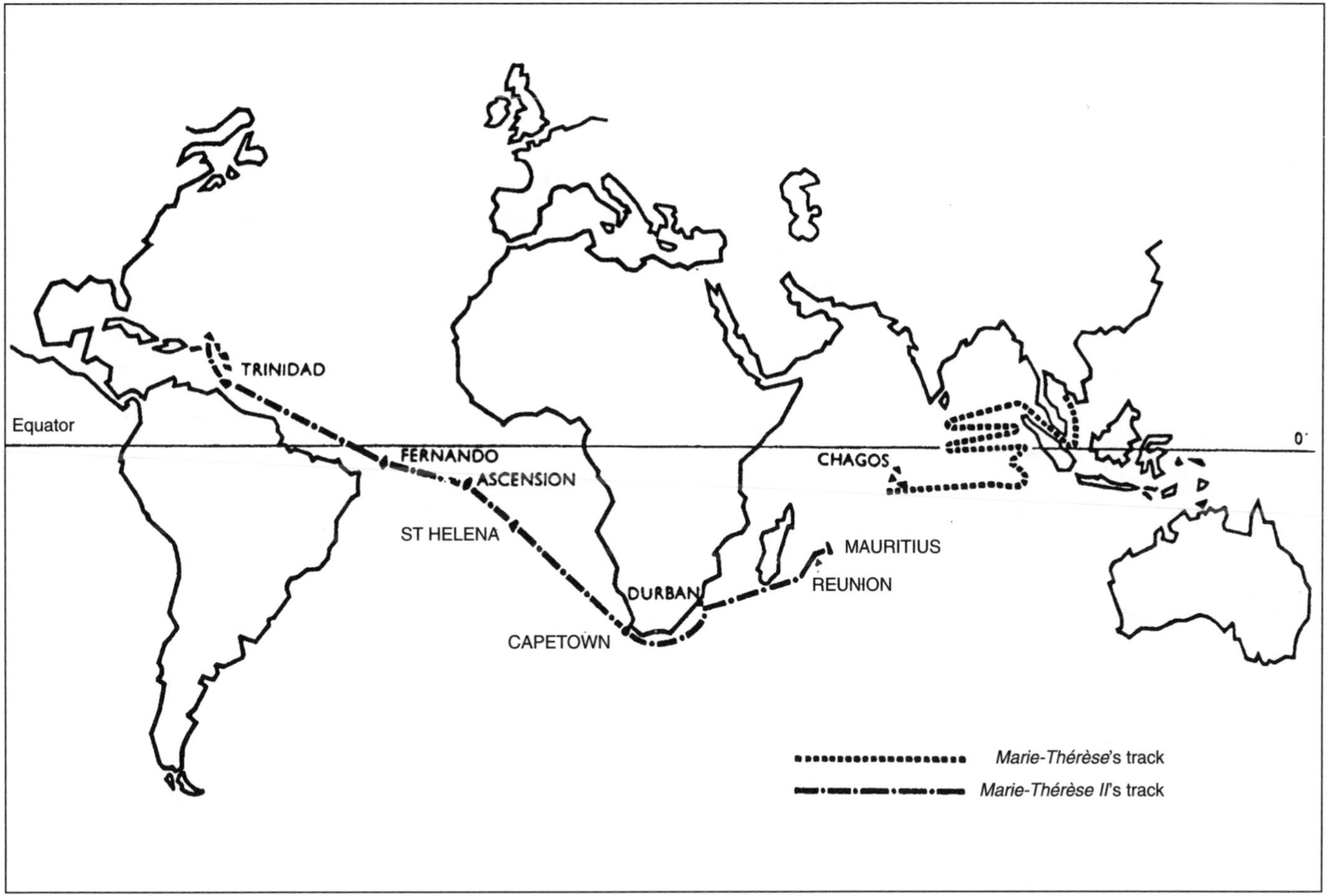

MARIE-THÉRÈSE II's voyage, solo (1955-58)

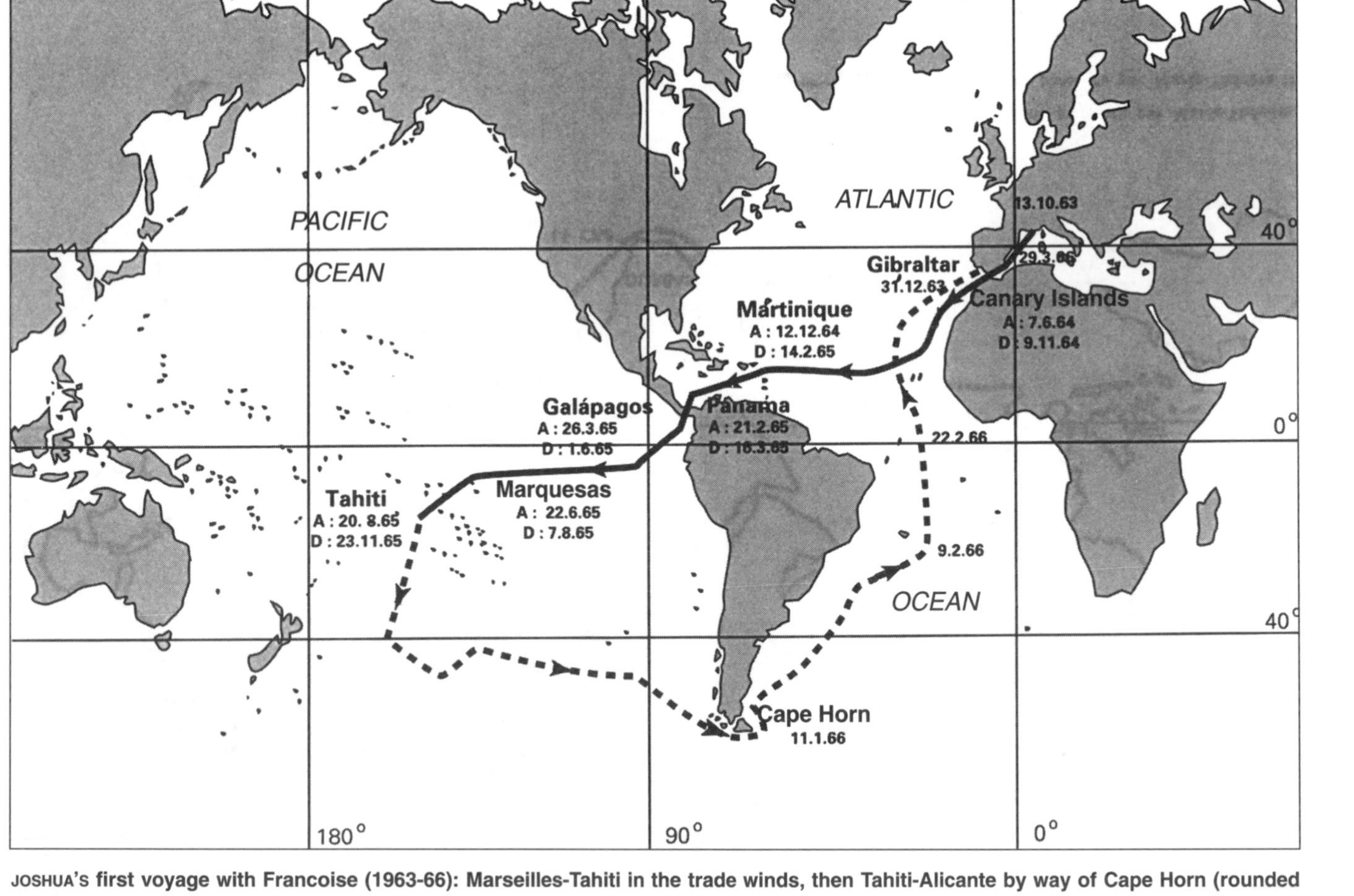

JOSHUA'S first voyage with Francoise (1963-66): Marseilles-Tahiti in the trade winds, then Tahiti-Alicante by way of Cape Horn (rounded January 11, 1966)

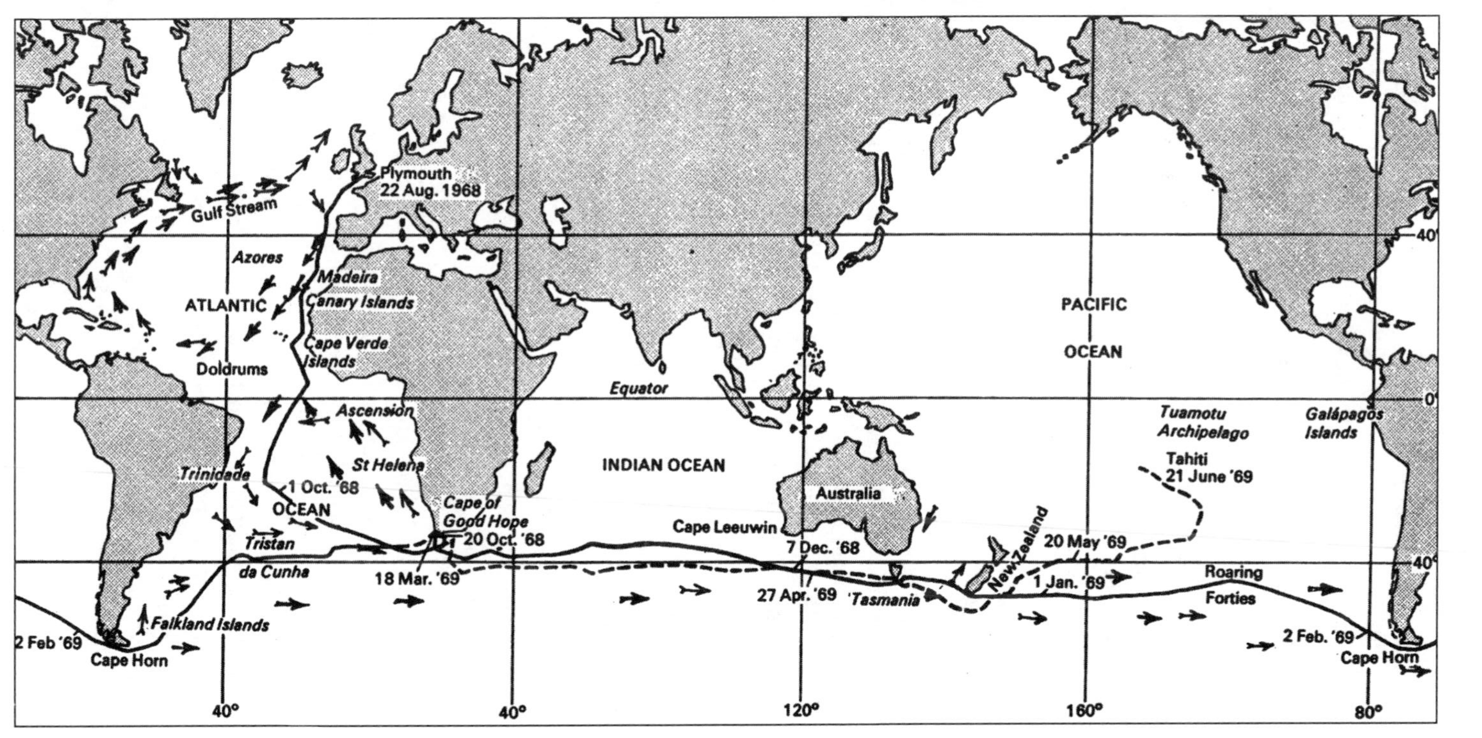

JOSHUA'S second voyage (August 22, 1968 to June 21, 1969): Plymouth-Tahiti, one and a half times around the world, solo and nonstop, called "The Long Way."

have pitchpoled—which nearly happened until we changed our steering technique.

2) Taking the main seas 15° or 20° on the port quarter caused JOSHUA to heel as she tore down the slope. The starboard side of the bow then pressed against the water somewhat like a ski or the rounded side of a spoon. This kept the bow from diving into the secondary swell.

During Tahiti-Alicante, we only had one knockdown, with the masts just below horizontal, despite conditions that were on average much worse than during The Long Way.

The Long Way
From Plymouth, August 22, 1968 to Tahiti, June 21, 1969

The Long Way totaled 37,455 miles between noon sights, in ten months. Of that, about 29,000 miles and eight consecutive months were spent in the dangerous area of southern westerlies. By contrast, JOSHUA spent only a month and a half (December 10 to January 28) in the high latitudes during Tahiti-Alicante, a fifth of The Long Way's time, with only 5,000 or 6,000 miles in dangerous waters. But whereas the sea had rumbled continuously in the high latitudes during Tahiti-Alicante, it remained relatively quiet, and even very beautiful at times, during more than a complete trip around the world: an exceptional summer, without a doubt. Only during the second passage of the Indian Ocean and the Pacific, with winter coming on, did it become constantly dangerous for nearly two months.

During The Long Way, I didn't encounter a fantastic gale like the one during Tahiti-Alicante. On the other hand, I had three knockdowns with the masts horizontal or a little below, and four more serious ones, with the masts well below the horizontal and the keel 30° and once probably 40° above the water. These last four knockdowns occurred during the second crossing of the Indian Ocean and the Pacific. The first two of this series occurred ten or twelve days apart, in the Indian Ocean, because of the boat's excessive speed for the very steep sea that was running at the time. The last two, in the Pacific, were caused by erratic breaking waves.

In all of those cases JOSHUA was under way with shortened sail, doing better than 6 knots. It is of these four knockdowns that I am going to speak now. I will call the first two the Indian Ocean knockdowns, and the second two the Pacific knockdowns. The boat always righted herself in two or three seconds, which seems normal for a boat with a weighted keel. (Though DAMIEN spent five minutes with her keel in the air after being hit by a breaking wave around the 60th parallel south.)

Indian Ocean knockdowns

The two knockdowns occurred at night, in gales from astern, as I lay in my bunk, awake. That is what usually happens when something is up: you are in your bunk, not really tense but somehow expectant. The body rests while the mind roams the deck, observing, comparing, gauging wind and sea. In the first knockdown, JOSHUA was running downwind at 6 knots under the small 75 square feet storm jib and 55 square feet staysail, with main and mizzen lowered.

The mind had shed anything that could harm it, since anything that is useless can cause harm. And animal instinct alone, which dwells deep within each of us, had come to the surface to flower, to take full possession of the "boat-man" unity, to give it the only order that made sense: hang on, whatever happened. Hold on, without trying to understand. And above all, live in the present, only the present, forgetting everything else.

When she went over, I was sure it wasn't because of a breaking sea; I would have recognized the sound and felt the dull impact. But it wasn't like that; the boat simply rolled onto her beam and lots of things went flying across the cabin. I didn't understand how it had happened. The second time, ten or twelve days later, the same thing happened again. This time, JOSHUA may have been moving a little faster, at the end of another gale, before reaching the longitude of Australia's Cape Leeuwin. Still no breaking sea. I couldn't understand it.

A few days later, I think I found the answer: I was on deck, wind force 6 to 7 full aft, speed 6.5 to 7 knots, with a winding wake due to the yawing. Suddenly JOSHUA accelerated on the advancing face of a sea and luffed, heeling quite a lot. The leeward deck dipped six or eight inches into the water, and I distinctly felt the braking effect as the heel increased. Nothing happened; the heel didn't exceed about 30 degrees and the wind vane put the boat back on course, but I felt very clearly that it wouldn't have taken much for us to get knocked down.

When seas are steep, I think it best to reduce speed considerably under self-steering, carrying just enough sail for the rudder to respond instantly. It's especially important not to start surfing down a steep sea, because if the boat luffs while yawing, and is heeling steeply as well, it can spell serious trouble for the masts.

This isn't true of ocean racing, in which hotshot crews or solo sailors tear along, riding wild tigers. Those boats are high-performance craft, relatively light, and kept on precise headings by the crew or autopilot. It's completely different for our heavier cruising boats, which have minimum crews, and are steered by self-steering gear that can let the boat yaw as much as 25 degrees to either side.

It should be noted that a boat can't start surfing down a wave unless it reaches a certain critical speed: a board floating among very large seas will stay in the same place. But if you give it a push at the right moment, it can start surfing. A cruising boat isn't designed like a surfboard; it can stay under way without starting to surf as long as it doesn't exceed a certain speed, which varies with the steepness of the waves. This threshold depends on the boat and the sea. Under 6 knots (and rather 5 than 6), JOSHUA is usually safe. A boat with a long keel is probably less inclined to luff up than one with a short keel.

But the sea will always remain the great unknown.

Adlard Coles's *Heavy Weather Sailing* is excellent, because Coles doesn't flatly affirm anything, but presents lots of facts and lets each reader weigh them in the light of his own observations. The photos of breaking waves have to be seen to be believed.

Pacific Ocean knockdowns

None of the gales during The Long Way lasted more than 36 hours. Each time, an isolated low was involved. When it had passed, another might come along, but after an interval long enough so JOSHUA wasn't affected by two lows at once, as had happened during Tahiti-Alicante.

I am going to speak of these gales in general, say what I know of them, what I see and feel, and what I usually do. First, here's a general picture of a typical gale.

1) High-latitude lows move from west to east. In the southern hemisphere the wind turns clockwise around the center. This low-pressure center generally moves eastward at 10 to 20 knots, and sometimes much faster near the Horn.

2) Most of these lows travel south of the 50th parallel. Small sailboats such as ours would normally be

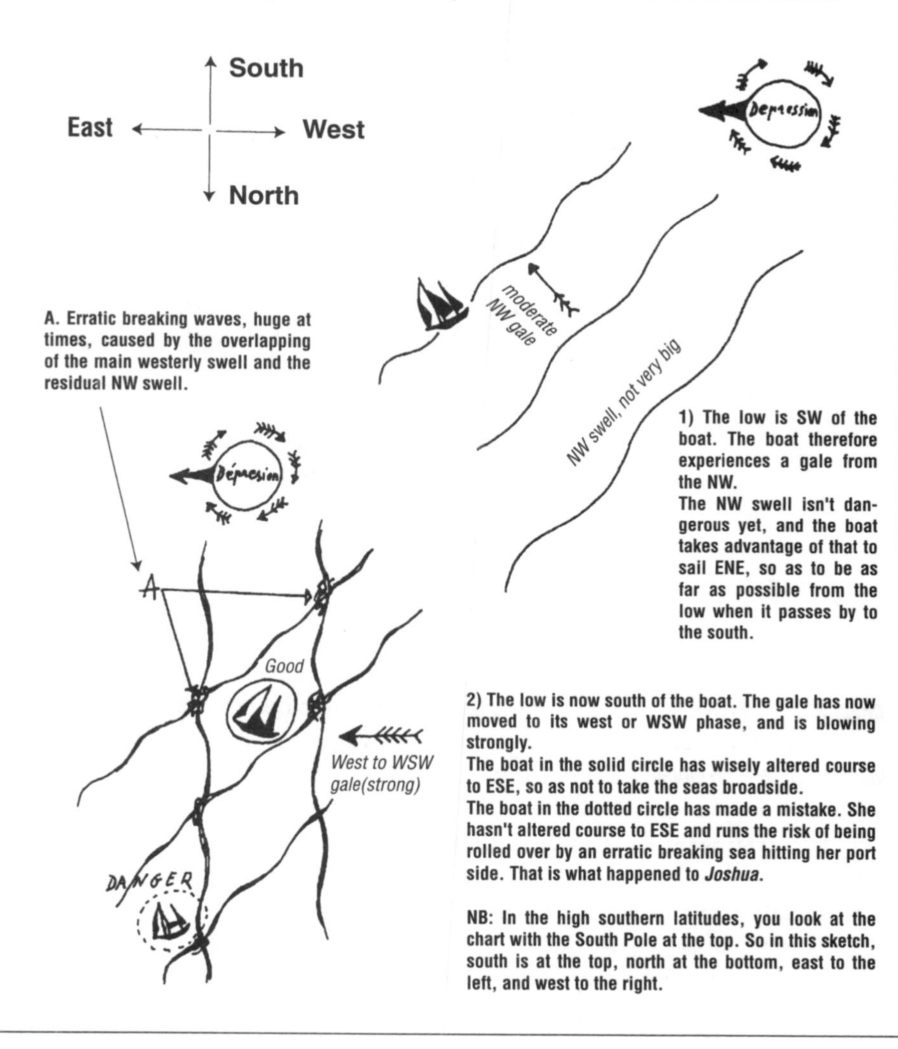

north of the low's path, since we rarely venture below the 43rd parallel, except when rounding the Horn.

3) The further you are from the center, the less violent the gale. The approach of a low is announced by a falling barometer, or by the needle's jumpiness: you can tell something is up. So I put a little bit of north in my easting (by steering 075° or 080°) to stay as far as possible from the low's center.

4) The low is approaching, and isn't far to the southwest now. The wind, which may have been variable from the north, moves to the northwest and fresh-

ens. Then, after a few hours, it starts blowing a gale. The sea builds up, but it isn't dangerous for a 40-foot boat. I keep some north in my easting, so as not to get too close to the low's path.

5) The low continues on its course eastward. Soon it is due south of the boat and closer than before, in spite of my heading, which moved me a little away from it. Still, I am a little further from the center than I would have been if I had continued due east for the preceding few days.

Now that the center is due south of the boat, the wind blows very hard from the west. The main westerly swell, which has been circling the globe since the beginning of time, builds up tremendously. In addition, the northwest swell raised by the first phase of the gale (blowing from the northwest before shifting to west) crosses the big westerly swell, at times causing enormous breaking seas.

This is where things really start to get dangerous: the main westerly swell breaks in long sections in addition to the breaking seas from the northwest. These breaking seas are often very powerful, and they frequently change direction somewhat as they break, hitting from almost north-northwest. That is why, when the gale enters its westerly phase, I prefer to alter course and steer east-southeast, so as not to risk being rolled over by one of those erratic northwest seas.

Once, when I was thirteen, Phuoc's father and I were leaving Hon Mon Tai Island to sail back to the village. It was at the end of a period of very bad weather that had kept us anchored in the lee of the island for almost a week. During the short crossing, an enormous wave nearly swamped our boat. After we had bailed for a solid hour, my teacher said: "It's right after a storm, when you think everything is fine, that you tend to let your guard down. Just then, one final, huge wave can come out of nowhere and sink your boat in a moment."

When the northwest phase of the gale has been moderate and short, these erratic breaking seas don't last long, and aren't really big. Once the wind goes to west, the boat is in no danger of getting closer to the center, since the low is moving eastward faster than the boat. So I judge it prudent to alter course to east-southeast at this time.

6) The low is still south of the boat, continuing eastward. The wind shifts to west-southwest and then generally blows hardest. The sky clears and the seas are very heavy, sometimes enormous. This lasts from a few hours to eight hours or more, depending on how fast the low is traveling, on its strength, on lots of things. It would have been wise to go on the other tack and put a fair amount of south in my east, because if the residual northwest swell is large, the erratic breaking seas coming from the port side can be very big. Obviously, these northwest seas can hit far ahead or far

astern of the boat—there's plenty of room—but they can sometimes break right on top of her. That is how the last two knockdowns in the Pacific Ocean happened, with the masts buried and the keel 30° or 40° above the horizontal.

The first Pacific knockdown wasn't my fault. I had rounded New Zealand and was heading northeast with Chatham Island some 60 miles on my right, when the gale entered its westerly phase. I couldn't alter course without running a serious risk with the reefs, because I wasn't quite sure of my position and the sea was too dangerous to go on deck with the sextant. I was on the 44th or 45th parallel, and in a hurry to reach milder latitudes, having rounded New Zealand south of the 49th parallel a few days earlier.

The last knockdown was even more severe, at only 34° South, two weeks before reaching Tahiti. And that time, it was entirely my fault. Given the very moderate latitude, I thought the gale was just for show, a sort of goodbye kiss. I was eager to catch the trade winds, so I didn't alter course when the gale went into its westerly phase. A big erratic northwest breaking wave hit, and JOSHUA, headed northeast, found herself with her keel at least 40° above the water, with lots of noise and things thrown to the cabin roof, storm jib and small staysail blown out, wind vane broken. I quickly went on deck to connect the steering wheel, and steered from inside the cabin until dawn.

Heaving to in the high southern latitudes

In the high southern latitudes, a gale from the *east* will seldom raise a truly exceptional sea, even when it blows very hard. I think it is always possible to heave to without danger of being rolled over by a large breaking sea; they remain of moderate size, and the boat (whether a 40-footer or even much smaller) can take advantage of the slick it leaves to windward. JOSHUA usually heaves to with close-reefed main sheeted flat and a small staysail aback, helm down. The slick calms the breaking waves like a layer of oil.

The picture would be very different with a gale from the *west*, blowing in the same direction as the big westerly swell that is always present in the high latitudes. Under the push of a stiff wind, this swell can very quickly become enormous, with gigantic breaking

"It is strange but true: in the high southern latitudes, where the seas can be 50 feet high and 2,000 feet long, they roll forward in endless procession, with occasionally one sea of abnormal size towering above the others, its approach visible from a considerable distance." **The Cape Horn Breed,** *by Captain W.H.S. Jones.*

seas that no slick could subdue, at least not that generated by a 40-foot boat.

In the northern hemisphere, breaking seas kicked up by a gale from the west are normally smaller, thanks to the barrier of the land masses (America and Asia), and sailboats lying hove to rarely suffer too much. But rarely doesn't mean never. In *Heavy Weather Sailing* you can see breaking waves that no yacht could ride out hove to—yet those photos were taken in the Atlantic, between 30°and 35° north latitude.

Freak waves

All sailors have occasionally noticed certain waves that are much higher than the others, even in the Mediterranean. I suppose these abnormally high seas are caused by the overlapping of several waves moving at different speeds. There is a little of everything in the

Balance sheet of ten months at sea, nonstop

"The grapefruit lasted three months, and I ate one a day or every other day during those first three months. Then I started on the lemons; they were individually wrapped in paper, and lasted nearly seven months. I used one a day squeezed in water, morning and afternoon.

"I took a single tube of vitamin C tablets during the whole trip, and a vitamin B complex tablet every day, from the third month until my arrival. I drank about half a glass of seawater per day, and put a little into my rice cooking water, to replace lost salt. I drank some twenty bottles of wine and no liquor.

"Cooking was done on a two-burner Optimus kerosene stove, without gimbals. I put a little asbestos in the cup, so the alcohol used to pre-heat it wouldn't spill when heeling; the alcohol-soaked asbestos acted as a wick. I also used a small butane stove to make tea, Ovaltine, bouillon, or coffee, and was always able to cook, even in foul weather.

"The pressure cooker saw a lot of use; it has the advantage of not spilling. I ate all I wanted and chewed well, to make the most of my food. My basic staples were white rice (I hadn't been able to find brown rice, which has more vitamins) and instant potatoes, to which I would add canned or dried vegetables (peas, green beans, carrots, sometimes asparagus). I ate quite a lot of condensed sweetened milk (a can a day, or more) and English Marvel powdered milk mixed into the dried potatoes.

"I always fixed two generous hot meals, plus a 'breakfast' of oatmeal, condensed milk, and Ovaltine two or three times a day. Two small snacks during the night. Basically, I had a little of everything, including spices (curry, chutney, *nuoc mam*, soy sauce, a few cans of smoked oysters and mussels, jars of shrimp and salmon paste, etc.).

"All in all, I ate well for the first eight months, and less well during the last two, as I had finished all the most appetizing things.

"When I left Plymouth, I weighed 139 pounds; when I returned, I weighed 143."

sea: main swells, residual swells from an old gale, and swells raised by a very distant low.

"A wave passed under TZU HANG and she slewed slightly. Beryl corrected her easily, and when she was down in the hollow she looked aft to check her alignment. Close behind, a great wall of water was towering above her, so wide that she couldn't see its flanks, so high and so steep that she knew TZU HANG could not ride over it. It didn't seem to be breaking as the other waves had broken, but water was cascading down its front, like a waterfall." (*Once is Enough*, by Miles Smeeton.)

What formed the liquid wall that plowed into TZU HANG, sweeping both masts and the doghouse away, to leave a half-swamped boat on the point of sinking, with a six-foot opening where the cabin had been? Maybe several parallel seas crossing at just the wrong time?

It should be noted that TZU HANG's accident happened in 98° west longitude and 51° 21' south latitude, just inside the extreme iceberg limit, according to the Pilot Chart for the months of December-January-February.

Daily life at sea

HEALTH AND NUTRITION

A varied diet

Before I took off on my sail around the world, Jean Rivolier—a doctor, nutritionist, and Himalayan climber—told me: "Don't worry about vitamins; just eat a varied diet."

Fresh fish

When I catch more fish than I can eat right away, I fillet them, slice the fillets in strips, and hang them to dry in the sun. You can also salt fish, or use a pressure cooker to can it.

Fruits and vegetables

It is worth drying bananas, because a stalk ripens all at once, and you don't have the time to eat all the bananas before they rot. Peel the ripe ones, slice them in thirds lengthwise, and leave them out in the sun for four to six days while protecting them from dew at

JOSHUA rushed along with the flying-fish that fell on deck during the night and got trapped under the twin staysails' poles where they are attached to the bulwark.

night. They are very nutritious, and will keep for several months.

Fresh water and collecting rain water

You can usually figure on using two and a half quarts of water per day, per person; probably a little more in the tropics.

Water usage during The Long Way

Two and a half quarts a day over ten months (303 days, to be exact) represents a consumption of 200 gallons. Since I left with 100 gallons, I therefore must have collected at least another 100 gallons of rainwater with the buckets hung under the main and mizzen booms. In fact, I collected much more, since JOSHUA arrived with her tank still half full, and I used a fair amount of fresh water to rinse clothes along the way. I could have reached Tahiti with my original 100 gallons if I had wanted to. So in those latitudes there is nothing to worry about on this score.

A tarp to collect rain water, absolutely essential in the tropics. The example shown is rigged on a ketch such as *Joshua*

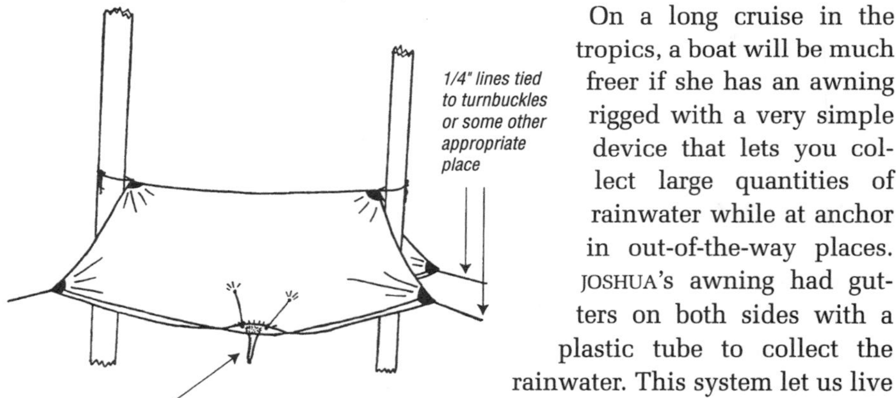

On a long cruise in the tropics, a boat will be much freer if she has an awning rigged with a very simple device that lets you collect large quantities of rainwater while at anchor in out-of-the-way places. JOSHUA's awning had gutters on both sides with a plastic tube to collect the rainwater. This system let us live for months using only rain.

WASHING

Henri and Emmanuelle used shampoo when washing with seawater; it foamed nicely and rinsed off well. So-called salt-water soaps aren't always satisfactory; they can leave white streaks on your skin.

Emmanuelle also washed her hair in seawater, using shampoo with a salt-water rinse. When her hair was dry, she gave it a good brushing to get rid of the salt.

CLOTHING

In the tropics, all you need is a hat, sunglasses, and a bathing suit or shorts. But from my Tahiti-Alicante and circumnavigation experience, I've picked up a few tricks regarding clothing that apply in the high latitudes and outside of the tropics.

God, how sweet it is to be out at sea again, with the peaceful rhythm of sails and sheets, where I can let myself live like an animal basking in the sun, filling my eyes with the thousands and thousands of miles that lay before a bow pointed toward the infinite, alone with my boat, alone with the wind and the waves, alone with the horizon and all my memories.

Boots

All-rubber boots dry quickly when they get wet; you just swab them out. But canvas- or fleece-lined boots stay damp.

Wool socks

If I put a pair of plastic bags over my socks and secure them with rubber bands, I can walk around the cabin freely when the cabin sole is damp, which is often the case when you come in after handling sail or spending time on deck. Loïck also advised me to bring a stack of newspapers along. A few sheets spread on the cabin sole soaked up the water. Very handy: you can walk on them without slipping and they last 24 hours, after which you replace them with fresh ones. Occasionally, I used the same sheets for several days before I had to change them.

Gloves and mittens

I wore leather gloves on deck, and mittens in the cabin. Even when they were soaked, my "outside" gloves kept my hands warm.

READING

There are few places and times that can be given over to really reading, to immersing yourself in a book; long passages at sea are among them.

During The Long Way, I read and reread **The Jungle Book,** *whose crystalline beauty lit up my childhood, without ever tiring of it.*

MOVIES AND PHOTOGRAPHY

For our first voyage with JOSHUA, we only had a few rolls of black-and-white film with which to record the beauty of the Galápagos, and we later greatly regretted not having color pictures. For The Long Way, I went whole hog, feeling that I absolutely had to share the experience with others. I used an underwater Nikonos, a gift from the *Sunday Times*, that worked well, produced good pictures, and saved me worrying about spray. Maurice Choquet, the head of the Beaulieu company, gave me a 16mm Beaulieu movie camera recommended by Irving Johnson, who made seven cruising-school trips around the world on his famous

During that voyage, my Beaulieu movie camera helped me see things I wouldn't have seen as clearly without it.

YANKEE. I didn't regret taking his advice. The very light camera let me take difficult shots, especially from the bowsprit and the mast. Even though I had no movie-making experience, I ruined very few shots, thanks to the Beaulieu's excellent lenses (75, 25, and 10mm) and its built-in light meter, which made choosing lens apertures easy. I also found Quéméré's book *Films et photos sur la mer* invaluable.

From the top of the mainmast, I watched my boat, her strength, her beauty, the well-set white sails in her rigging. Climbing down to get the Beaulieu was out of the question. I would lose everything, and what those dolphins were giving me was too precious; a camera lens would have spoiled it.

To replace the little nickel-cadmium battery, which must be recharged from an electrical outlet or a generator after every 15 reels of film, Choquet built me an excellent case from a waterproof flashlight that housed five ordinary batteries. Five 1.5 volt leakproof Wonder batteries lasted for ten or twelve reels shot at 24 frames per second. This gave me nearly total autonomy, since the batteries left over from the stock put aboard three years earlier still worked perfectly.

MUSIC

I take my harmonica everywhere. Music is nice to have on board, but not essential for me. It was a long time before I bought a radio with a cassette player.

SCHOOLING

Anne Falconer "boat-schooled" her two children Alexandre and Anaïs (who were 2 and 4 when the family reached Caroline Island) until the day she decided they needed the structure of more formal schooling. They then began a correspondence course from France's Centre national de l'enseignment à distance (CNED).

Despite the unpredictability of visits by passing sailboats—which brought the family mail—they followed the course on a regular schedule for nearly four years. She admits she did have a lot of trouble getting her little boy to sit still and study when he wanted to run around his atoll. After the family returned to Moorea, the children went to school and were soon at the heads of their classes!

Daniel Gazanion of KIM set out in 1987 with his wife and children on a trip that lasted six years. Arnaud and Audrey (12 and 6 when they left France) were taught according to a fairly strict schedule with CNED courses. Classes were held on board, and required discipline on everybody's part, parents and children alike. The schedule set by CNED could be modified during passages, and if the kids fell behind, they caught up during stopovers. But the family sometimes cut short its stays in out-of-the-way places like the San Blas Islands in order to reach a post office further on. Relatives and close friends back in France who knew their whereabouts handled the mail. The children's educational experience was broadened during their cruise. In addition to the CNED course, Arnaud and Audrey attended schools in the USA and Canada and easily learned English. When they got back to France, they adapted to the school system perfectly.

ROUTINE MAINTENANCE AT SEA

Always keep handy a small jar with a mixture of grease and white lead for loosening shackles, bolts, etc. It's invaluable when you have to undo a piece of hardware that hasn't been touched for years. White lead is a dangerous poison, so wash your hands and tools carefully after using it; if there are children aboard, cover the fittings with tape.

Keep an eye on wear; lubricate lines where they are exposed to chafe. Chainplate pins or shackles wear when there is play in the lee shrouds; to limit vibration, wrap a length of inner tube or shock cord around the shrouds.

Change the places where sheets and halyards bear on blocks, and splice a line as soon as it becomes necessary.

Cleaning the hull underwater: When I have to work on the bottom at sea, I usually drop the foresails and sheet the main and mizzen flat to limit rolling. I can scrub the hull in a little over half an hour.

At sea, you can't fool around too much. You must watch and see that the boat is moving well. In short, you have to be serious. You have to keep an eye out for the unexpected, cook meals, always stay in shape, be able to rest when necessary so as to be ready to stay up during bad weather. You have to keep the boat going, and do small repairs as they arise. If a sail snap comes loose, you can't wait too long before taking care of it. There may be a lot of wind later on, and then a second sail snap will fail, and then a third, and the sail will come down and rip, etc. Meditation has its limits.

SHIPBOARD DANGERS

Fires or explosions from butane or gasoline vapors

If you have a gas engine, take every possible precaution. Don't stop the motor with the ignition switch; instead, cut off the fuel supply at the tank, so as to drain the lines and carburetor. And keep the gas tank outside. Many boats have been destroyed, often with deaths and injuries, because a tank below deck exploded without warning.

Another very serious, though less obvious, danger

stems from using plastic jerrycans as spare gas containers inside the boat. A small, easily manageable fire from an overheated stove, for example, can melt such a jerrycan and turn the boat into a blazing torch. Metal jerrycans are a lot safer.

For cooking, kerosene or alcohol are much less treacherous than butane. I cook on a Primus kerosene stove that is preheated with alcohol. Using alcohol isn't dangerous if you're careful to pour it with no flame present, and seal and stow the bottle before lighting the stove.

Useful tips

When I was little, Chu helped me make my slingshots. He was the one who taught me how to cut the rubber strips across the width of the inner tube; that way, they never broke, no matter how hard you pulled.

SHOCK CORDS OR INNER-TUBE STRIPS

I always build up a little shipboard supply of rubber strips of various sizes, cut from inner tubes of different sizes (bicycle, motorcycle, car, truck). They hang near the chart table, ready for all sorts of uses: to lash the tiller, kill flies, relieve the strain on a mooring line or keep it from rubbing against the lifelines, hang a lantern in the shrouds, keep the lee shrouds taut (to avoid wear on the turnbuckle toggles), secure tools or other small items against the paneling, hold pots on the stove when attached to a length of wire, serve as antislip pads glued under the sextant case, carpet, ashtray, etc. I also stretch inner-tube strips across the chart table; that way, nautical charts and reference books stay where they belong.

VENTILATION IN BAD WEATHER

JOSHUA's air intake was a curved section of truck inner tube. When a wave washed over the deck, it flattened the inner tube, which would spring up again afterward.

LIFT PUMP

This should really be called an "Asian" pump, because I saw it everywhere in my travels there. Its genius lies in the extreme simplicity of the piston head B design. Disk B' keeps gasket B from bending downward when you pull the shaft upward on the sucking stroke. In turn, the small-diameter disk B" allows B to bend upward when you push the plunger down (the same principle as a bicycle pump).

Note that B consists of four or five rubber circles cut from an old car inner tube. The metal disks B' and B" are held in place with two clinched nails driven through the piston shaft (which can be an inch-thick tree branch).

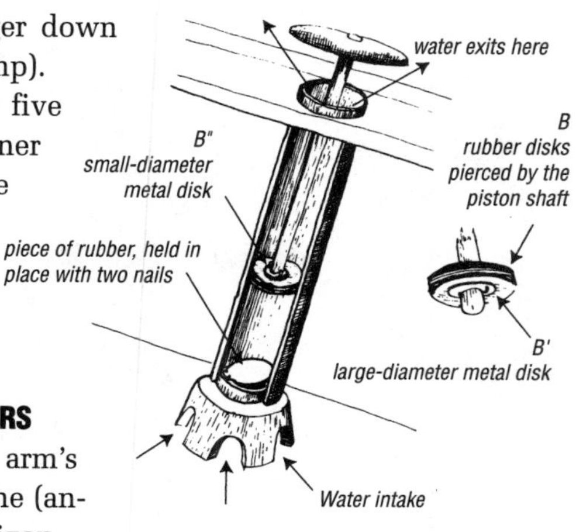

Lift pump

MEASURING ANGLES WITH YOUR FINGERS

By holding your hand out at arm's length, you can get a good idea of the (angular) height of an object on the horizon.

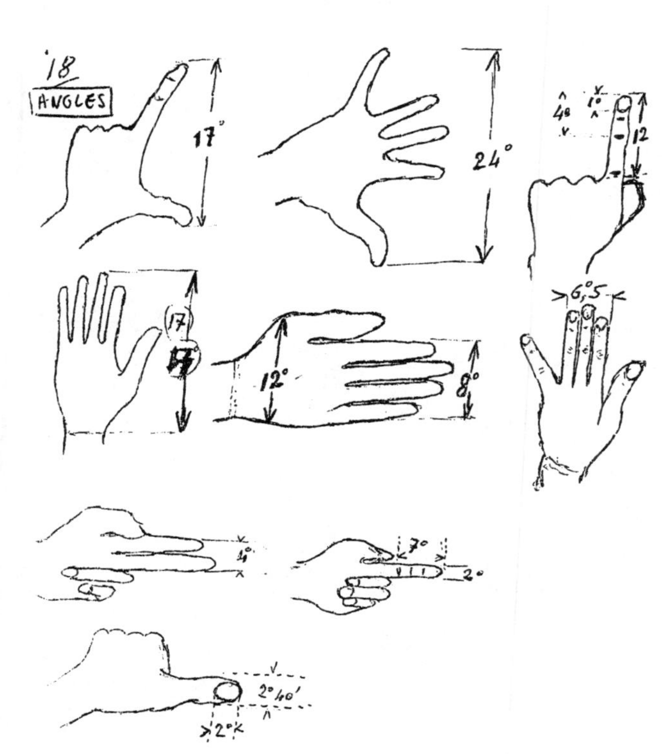

On sailing solo

Aptitude and adaptation

You don't have to be an exceptional person to sail solo, because our inborn instincts and intuition are the essence of the art of sailing.

Nor do you become a solo sailor. Unless you're born that way, you'll never be one.

John Voss and William Robinson, who were outstanding sailors, certainly didn't need anyone to help them solve their technical sailing problems. But they liked feeling the presence of a crew member nearby.

On the other hand, sailors who knew the sea far less well than Voss or Robinson when they started out have always needed to hear the singing of water on the hull, surrounded by the powerful presence of the wind and the boat, in the peace of what one thinks of as solitude. That's all solo sailing is: 5 to 10 percent of initial technical skills combined with a good dose of common sense, with, to top it off, 200 percent of the call of the open sea. Logically, this may not add up exactly right, but that's too bad; logic doesn't really have much to do with the salt-water universe.

I've always had the feeling that for me, long passages deeply cleanse me of all the grime accumulated during a stay ashore. Once the coast disappears astern, a man alone before his creator can't remain apart from the natural forces around him. His body and mind, freed from earthly bondage and attachments, can find their essence and purity in the heart of those elements in nature that the ancients made into gods. Wind, Sun, and Sea, the sailor's divine Trinity.

Problems encountered by the solo sailor

The hardest of these is just setting out. Once at sea, you have won the first round: the round against yourself, which is the most important one. Still, two challenges remain:

1) Being able to handle the boat alone, taking good and bad weather in stride. At first glance, this seems hard. But by perfecting a personal style, a solo sailor will be able to take charge even of a relatively big boat, by instinct and necessity.

"Leaving always represents the same challenge to one's self: that of daring"
Gérard Janichon

This means learning to deliver a maximum of efficient work for a minimum of time and wasted effort. That is something you learn instinctively when you have no other choice, which is exactly the solo sailor's situation.

Where maneuvering and handling sail are concerned, it is desirable to act very quickly and a little early, whenever possible. This is a skill that comes gradually. At first, you go on little outings in fair weather. Then the outings grow along with your progress in mastering the boat, in weather that goes from force 2 in the beginning to a stiff force 6 when you have a few miles under your belt.

By really stressing caution and common sense—which means sailing slowly, with an anchor ready to drop well in advance, heaving line ready, and boathook close at hand—a solo sailor will avoid collisions or botched maneuvers in a crowded anchorage. Besides, you can always drop the anchor in case of uncertainty, and return to the problem after enjoying a cigarette or a cup of coffee while you calmly decide what to do next.

Take it easy. There's no hurry.

When you're sailing alone it is certainly harder to coordinate the series of actions involved in a maneuver than when there are others aboard. On the other hand, it's harder to screw up when you're sailing solo because the powers of decision and execution are in the same hands. Commands are never misunderstood or drowned out by the wind. Man is an infinitely adaptable animal, and will almost always quickly learn what has to be done—especially once the mooring lines are cast off and one doesn't have any choice.

The days follow one another, never monotonous. Even when they seem exactly the same, they never quite are. And that's what gives life at sea its particular dimension, made up of contemplation and very small, special moments. Sea, winds, calms, sun, clouds, birds, dolphins. The peace and joy of living in harmony with the universe.

2) Being able to stay on watch 24 hours a day.

Most pleasure boaters credit solo sailors with far greater sailing skills and endurance than they actually have. It's true that watches last 24 hours a day, day after day, and sometimes week after week. But man's natural ability to adapt to the demands of his surroundings lets the solo sailor deal with two serious problems:

a) maintaining the same heading for days or weeks without exceeding the body's limits of endurance;

b) continuing to make way while remaining on the alert for several days in a row when the weather is bad or downright awful; or when sailing with a good breeze in a night full of squalls.

Thanks to self-steering, maintaining heading and speed is no longer a problem. And sleep is out of the question anyway when you're close to shore or in the shipping lanes, at least in the way we usually mean "sleep."

I believe that hearing is the sailor's most precious sense. It is so precious that while holding the wheel, my chest half-way out of the cabin so I could see through the spray, I sometimes pushed back the hood of my foul-weather gear so as not to be bothered by the false sounds of the wind whistling across the hood . . . You have to hear, above all, especially at night in total darkness, when your vision must rest, or rather, be placed on standby.

What explains the apparent endurance of the solo sailor caught between a strong need to sleep and the equally strong need to stay alert? The key lies in the way the body adapts to the long watches imposed by this kind of sailing. Of necessity, the senses become hyper-acute in monitoring the boat's safety and the sails' output. You watch while you're asleep. Or, if you prefer, you sleep while you're on watch, by taking tiny little naps, the way a dorado, a pilot fish, or that bird called a "wide-awake" does. So your body gets the rest it craves while your senses remain alert.

During this semi-sleep, a solo sailor's ear will register and give shape to any unusual sound. A tiny change of octave in the song of the water flowing along the hull may mean: be careful! While running in heavy seas, a barely audible creak in the jib-sheet block will almost always mean: watch out for a jibe!

The kinetic sense is also a precious help to the solo sailor. It will pick up an abnormal change in the boat's movements, a little roll, for example, that seems innocent but "isn't quite right."

I even think that kinetic sense can tell you when a squall is imminent. When I was starting my solo voyages, I prudently respected the wise precepts of the old-time wooden navy. At sunset, MARIE-THÉRÈSE's mainsail was always well reefed, to avoid any night-time quarrels with a force 8 wind and flying spray. But after a few weeks' sailing, I discovered that when a squall struck at night, I was always on deck long before it hit, with plenty of time to furl or drop sail. The precautions I had taken at the beginning weren't necessary (which isn't to say I was wrong to take them). After some experience, I set whatever sails were appropriate for the weather—though I usually took a couple of turns of the main's roller-furling gear before going to sleep in stormy weather.

When hearing itself is tired and is placed on standby, then your sense of touch comes into play: the feeling of the wind, spray, or rain against your cheek or neck all translate into small adjustments in your heading.

islands
and
lagoons

At the end of a passage

Work in ports of call

When you come down to it, we spend far more time in stopovers than at sea. During some of them, we putter around, fixing up the boat's interior or tackling bigger jobs, modifying her in light of our experience at sea. Or we may earn some money for the ship's kitty. These stopovers are also opportunities to meet people and share experiences. Other stops are more oriented to exploring. Instead of just repairing, restoring, or improving our floating home, we spend our days on shore, living life to the fullest in magical places, using local resources to augment the daily fare on board. And those stopovers can last a long time . . .

That little dark-blue patch, gradually rising from the horizon exactly where you expected, without daring to really believe it, and which little by little takes shape and becomes an island . . .

If you're interested in doing some serious sightseeing inland, your boat becomes a dead weight. You have to find someone to watch her or risk leaving her alone. It all depends where you are, of course. Exploring on land has never been my goal, and I feel nervous at the idea of leaving my boat without anyone to keep an eye on her. So I will just speak of islands and other places that can only be reached by sea. These are the places that, for me, justify choosing the life of a sailing vagabond.

Money

Ah, money . . . Try as we may to pick up cigarette butts and live on air, we do need some money. In any case, one thing is clear: you can go very far and lead an interesting life with very little cash to begin with, because you can always get by once you're underway—

From island to island

The Islands of the Gulf of Siam

"Great outings in the wind of the open sea, with these fishermen who were my teachers . . . Camping on desert islands with huge rays and sharks cut into strips and drying on sticks in the wind."

The Anambas Archipelago (South China Sea)

"We stayed there for nearly a week, with no desire to leave. *Snark* slept like a bird with its head under its wing, in a blue-green nest surrounded by flower-like coral reefs at the bottom of a tiny bay whose pebble beach was lined with palm trees."

Diego Garcia

"I won't speak at length about the six weeks I spent on Diego Garcia . . . Anyway, words would only be able to express very clumsily the feelings I have for those friendly people, who welcomed me to their atoll as they would a member of their own family."

Cargados Carajos

"White sand, rough coral, stunted bushes, turtles, myriads of sea-birds, and ironwood and palm trees that had survived the hurricanes. These were the surroundings in which I spent a fascinating year with my men and my boats: a dozen 20- to 30-foot sailboats and some thirty outrigger canoes."

Mauritius

"The island of friendship."

The Canaries

"Fuerteventura charmed us by the feeling of grandeur it gives off, its solitude, huge empty beaches, tall white-sand dunes, and its transparent fish-filled waters."

Saint Helena

"Greenery, scents, and colors . . . The climate here is infinitely gentle. Seen from the ocean, Saint Helena looks like a huge fortress, massive and hostile, with cliffs falling straight down to the sea."

Ascension Island

"The thing that distinguishes Ascension Island and sets it apart from most of its fellow tropical islands is the incredible dryness along its shore. The only vegetation visible is on top of Green mountain, the highest spire on the island."

Fernando Noroña

"This is a group of islands stretching about a dozen miles, topped by rocky outcroppings that aren't mountains, hills, or large rocks, but a kind of combination of all three. Some landscapes leave you dissatisfied, because they are absolutely secret. And this will remain an enigma to my senses. Not severe, or jovial: enigmatic."

Galápagos (Ecuador)

"*Joshua* was anchored a hundred yards from a big beach of very fine white sand that rings Wreck Bay. Just behind it, the village . . . consists of a dozen low houses of wood and cement with tin roofs, hammered by the sun and glare . . . Around the village was desert, a desert of lava and stone with giant cacti stuck here and there like sentinels, thin bushes, a terrifying dryness.

"At Barrington, the ballet of nature was being danced around the boat: seals, pelicans, blue-footed boobies, and fish!"

Marquesas (Polynesia)

"Entire mountains looked as if they had plunged into the sea in gigantic stone waterfalls. Here and there, ravines appeared, as if cut by some huge axe. There wasn't a sound, not a cricket chirping, not a bird singing."

Society Islands (Polynesia)

"Like conical hats pointed skyward, the Iles Sous-le-Vent, in the very heart of the Pacific, pierce the surface of the ocean, gathering the calm, green lagoon water in their wide coral edges. They form one of the archipelagos of Polynesia, where the trade wind sings."

Atolls: (Suvorov [Cook], Ahe [Tuamotu], Caroline [Kiribati])

Caroline Island:

"A minuscule atoll surrounded by immensity, a lagoon inaccessible to boats, a chain of islets, some sun-scorched, others choked by impenetrable jungles of coconut trees. There is nothing at all there, nothing to attract anyone—except a few lovers of atolls and countless sea birds."

provided you *are* underway. It's also true that there is no comparison between expenses when living ashore in town and those incurred when cruising on your boat.

ODD JOBS

In Tahiti, many of my friends did odd jobs ashore or on other boats. In general, anyone who has outfitted a boat and gone to sea has already picked up a lot of useful skills; others have already mastered some craft or other, which makes finding work even easier.

Here are a few examples taken from the 1970s as well as the 1990s.

Jory used his sewing machine to repair sails and make tarps (1970s).

Christian, who crewed on a yacht and reached Tahiti without a cent, left two years later to buy a 26-foot steel cutter in Holland. He earned the money by taking Polaroid photos of tourists as they arrived at the airport, on the waterfront, and in night clubs (circa 1970).

Jack wrote business letters in English for Tahiti's Chinese importers (circa 1970).

If you speak a foreign language very well, you can find translation work, as William Rodarmor did, who translated *The Long Way* in 1971 [and *Tamata and the Alliance* in 1995]. And I remember giving French lessons during SNARK's stopover in Singapore in 1951.

If you know electronics, you'll be able to help boat owners who have the latest gear on board—all of which breaks down sooner or later—fix or upgrade their equipment.

Dédé started a second career as a carpenter and helped build hotels and private homes in Tahiti and Moorea (1987-1992).

During their ten-year journey between France and Polynesia, Bernard and Monique used their skill at fiberglass construction in Africa, Brazil, the Caribbean, and finally Polynesia, where they set up their own business (1985-1994).

Christine got into fashion design and pareo painting in Tahiti. Beloune and Sophie became experts in painting on silk, and attracted high-class customers from among charter clients in the Iles Sous-le-Vent (1992-1994).

DELIVERIES AND CHARTER

Running charters and cruising schools have helped many sailors in the Caribbean and in Polynesia. It's a decent way to earn enough money to continue on your way, whether your boat is 45 feet long or 25. You can also hire out as a skipper to outfits that charter boats with crew; this has the advantage that you don't have to share your private home with the clients.

Klaus asked us to look after his boat for a few weeks while he delivered a rich businessman's 80-foot yacht from the Caribbean to Tahiti. That was a real coup, because this kind of delivery pays very well (1971).

Christophe provided technical support on a sailboat that accompanied a crew of Polynesian paddlers to the Cook Islands (1990). Louis did a terrific delivery with his boat to Easter Island, from Tahiti (1985).

Those are fairly unusual experiences and very well paid, but you can only land them if you are right on the spot.

WRITING A BOOK OR MAKING A MOVIE

You can also write a book.

Likewise, making a movie while sailing can be fascinating, and showing the film at stopovers is a surefire way to enrich the ship's kitty. Unfortunately, it entails a large investment and big risks, because you have to shoot in 16mm color (or video). But if you can take the chance, your cruise may turn out to be more interesting and lively, because you will notice things you might otherwise miss. If you can recoup your investment and earn your way by showing a film you love, it isn't stolen money. And if you wind up earning more than you need, you can always spend some of it doing things that don't hurt anyone—planting a tree, for example.

Daniel, Michel, Claude, and Bruno, who sailed on KIM, shot a 16mm film during their expedition (1977-1982), which took them to Antarctica. When they got back, they spent four years showing their movie on the "Connaissance du monde" circuit, which covers French-speaking countries. As a result, they were each able to build a boat and head back out to sea.

Daniel Drion, who spent ten years criss-crossing the tropics with his wife Majy and their son between 1980 and 1990, filmed their adventure in 16mm color and showed the edited film at stopovers, mainly in schools. This calls for a certain amount of planning for the editing, which is easier to do in Europe than en route. Once back home, Daniel wrote a book, *Latitudes vagabondes*. For the last two years, he has been on the "Connaissance du monde" circuit, showing his film and selling copies of the book.

MEDICAL AND PARAMEDICAL CAREERS

Christine and Michèle, who are nurses, set up a clinic in Raiatea and took turns seeing patients. This also gave them close personal contact with the local population.

TEACHING OR SUBSTITUTING

Though the popularity of the field has made it crowded, it is often still possible to practice your profession or teach in the countries where they speak your language, many of which lie along the trade-wind routes. You can also substitute for people taking scheduled leaves of absence (maternity leave, for example).

To work as a substitute, you have to inquire locally and be ready to step in as soon as a job opens up. This takes a little patience and a lot of flexibility, but these are the earmarks of a true vagabond. And the jobs can really fill the ship's cash box.

In the 1990s, Jean taught in the Marquesas for three years. Céline taught one year in the Marquesas and two on Raiatea, in the Iles Sous-le-Vent. After six years in Polynesia, they set out again with a new and bigger boat.

Maintenance and repairs

Stopovers are often the time to make small and large repairs, so where you stop may be dictated by the presence of a boatyard. A yard and a ship's chandler will have professionals who can advise you on the products best suited to your problem.

Don't hesitate to ask for advice

For serious problems, find the right person and ask for advice sincerely and without embarrassment; you'll get an answer. Don't be afraid to look ignorant. We're all ignorant, compared to those who know more than we do, and it's mainly from others that we learn.

However, it's also good to anticipate the necessity of making repairs in remote places. JOSHUA was equipped so I could handle major jobs on some lost atoll, if I had to. This made me completely independent wherever I was, perhaps needing only a friend to help me with the job. Besides the ballast and lots of other supplies, JOSHUA's hollow keel contained a few sheets of 1/16" galvanized steel and glass jars (to avoid rust) full of 7/32" rivets, along with a few dozen metal drill bits; the jars were filled with oil to keep their contents in perfect condition.

REGULAR MAINTENANCE OF A STEEL BOAT

Careening and hauling out

I regularly dive to scrub my hull, and I also haul out periodically for more serious maintenance. Whether I careen the boat or have it hoisted out depends on what is available locally.

Once the boat is out of the water, I scrub the bottom with water and put on a couple of coats of primer, if needed, followed by two coats of antifouling paint and a third coat at the waterline. It is essential to check the composition of antifouling paint (it shouldn't contain lead, copper, or copper oxide), and to be sure it adheres to the previous coat. Unfortunately, the ingredients in paints aren't always listed on the can.

Daniel, who has seen a number of steel boats come through his haul-out yard, says that the most serious mistake people made was to use incompatible copper-based antifouling paints that generate electrolysis.

Maintaining the topsides

The large, flat surfaces of JOSHUA's exterior never caused any problems. With two coats of good alkyd paint once or twice a year, I rested easy. During the three or four years after her construction, I built up layers of paint on the topsides so as to have a solid protective layer on the hull and the deck. After that, I gave her a few coats a year. Of course, fittings that are exposed to rubbing (especially sheet and halyard cleats, and mooring bitts) call for special watchfulness. Their paint should be touched up often if you want to avoid rust stains on deck—and bigger problems later on.

Waterline

This is the part of the hull that gives the most problems, but it's easy to deal with if you don't have a fit every time you see a bit of rust or a rough patch caused by electrolysis. The recipe is paint, paint, and more paint. I believe in lots of paint at the waterline, and I never hesitate to put on an extra coat or two.

Dealing with rust on the topsides

What follows is especially useful on the deck and on fittings where abrasion makes it hard to keep the paint in good shape.

1) Scrape all the rust spots.

2) Apply a phosphoric acid etching solution to destroy whatever deep rust remains after scraping. Applying the phosphoric acid is vital if you want the first coat of anti-rust primer to adhere. Rinse the surface with fresh water, and apply the primer when it is dry.

3) Put on two coats of anti-rust primer, followed by two coats of finish paint.

Maintenance summary of Tamata's topsides

– When *Tamata* was built in 1983, her topsides and deck got three coats of two-part industrial International epoxy after sandblasting, a phosphoric acid etch, and a rust-inhibitor primer.

– In 1985, two coats of two-part industrial-grade Matersol "O" epoxy on the deck, and two coats of two-part polyurethane Hempell on the hull to the waterline.

– In 1987, two coats of two-part epoxy industrial-grade Matersol "O" on the deck but nothing on the hull because the polyurethane applied two years before was still in perfect shape. (In any case, I couldn't find any more of it at the ship chandler's at Raiatea, in French Polynesia).

– In December 1989, just one coat of Matersol "O" epoxy on the deck (it was the last can available at the Raiatea store) and nothing on the hull because I couldn't find epoxy or polyurethane anywhere on the island. But the two-part Hempell polyurethane I had applied to the hull four years earlier was still like new.

– When we returned to Raiatea in February 1993, the hull and deck were in as good a shape as they had been at our previous visit, three years before. The Hempell (now seven years old) had only darkened a little, without flaking at all. The deck, in spite of some deterioration—which often happens to epoxy in sunny climates—looked freshly painted. Alas, not a drop of those miraculous two-part paints was available there. So we had to fall back on a single-component polyurethane (which is less resistant to weathering, but still much better than traditional alkyd paints).

Maintaining the interior

The interior of a boat won't give any problems, provided that a paintbrush can reach everywhere and there are no places where water can collect. If you take the precaution of giving everything seven coats of paint, you won't have to worry for years.

Though they aren't nearly as tough as epoxies or polyurethanes, alkyd paints are fine for the boat's interior.

Fresh-water tanks, if they are built directly into the hull (and are therefore not galvanized), should have an easily accessible trap door that is wide enough to make cleaning the inside easy. To protect the steel without introducing anything that might contaminate the water, I used a simple and inexpensive trick aboard TAMATA: etch the steel well, then coat it with a solution of cement dissolved in water, like whitewash.

> **Maintenance of Joshua's interior**
>
> **– *Joshua*'s interior was originally painted with two coats of a very good quality zinc chromate primer made by Galia Color (in Lyons, France), then two white finish coats, also from Galia Color.**
>
> **– After that, a couple of maintenance coats for the interior every four or five years. As on all metal boats, you have to pay extra attention to the galley, head, and the area where plexiglass is bolted to the hull around the portholes.**

Paints

Be sure the paints are compatible with each other.

Three kinds of paints, of varying quality, are available: alkyds and two-part epoxies and polyurethanes.

In general, two-part paints harden quickly and are very tough. There is no need to sand between coats. But you can't use them over a one-part paint unless you apply an isolating primer over the first coat, or sand it.

It is critical that epoxy or polyurethane paints be applied in very thin coats, as they dry in air. Three very thin coats are better than one average or heavy one. They can be applied over two-part paints.

Alkyd paints are the least tough, but they are suitable for the boat's interior. Epoxy paints are very tough, but deteriorate in sunlight.

It is worth noting that fresh-water tanks can be painted with epoxy; once completely cured, there is no

Regular maintenance and approximate schedule

STAGE	BOTTOM	HULL AND DECK	INTERIOR
Regular preventative maintenance	Scrub with water Primer: Silver Primocon (2 coats) Antifouling (without lead or copper) 2 coats (3 at the waterline) (Once a year)	Alkyd, 2-part epoxy or polyurethane (2 coats) depending on the condition of the old paint	Alkyd paint (every 6 to 10 years)
Remedial treatment in case of rust	Phosphoric-based chemical etching solution Rinse If needed, a rust-inhibitor primer (2 coats) Finish paint		

Example: TAMATA

STAGE	BOTTOM	DECK	HULL	INTERIOR
1983 built in USA	Sand-blasting 1 coat of International Inter-Zinc			Sanding International Inter-Zinc (1 c.)
	Intern. Vitaline Aluminum (2 c.) + hard antifouling (2 c.)	1 very thin protective coat (International) 3 coats of 2-part epoxy (International)		Zinc chromate (1 c.) Alkyd paint (3 c.)
1985	Antifouling (2 c.)	2-part epoxy (Matersol 0) 2 c	2-part polyurethane (Hempell) 2 c	Nothing
1987	Antifouling (2 c.)	2-part epoxy (Matersol 0) 2 c	Nothing	Nothing
1989	Antifouling (2 c.)	2-part epoxy (Matersol 0) 1 c	Nothing	Nothing
1993	Primer Antifouling (3 c.)	1-part polyurethane (2 c.)	1-part polyurethane (2 c.)	Scraping Zinc chromate (1 c.) Alkyd (2 c.)

risk of toxicity. This isn't true for all paints, so check them out.

Polyurethanes, which resist ultraviolet light well, don't deteriorate, and are therefore very suitable as a final finish coat. Note: they give off highly toxic fumes until they cure completely. I would never use them in an enclosed space, such as the cabin, even with excellent ventilation.

In general, when you aren't sure a paint is compatible with the previous coat, it's best to first put down a primer of the same brand as the paint you plan to use.

The secret to paints, as good as they may be, lies in the way you apply them. For a successful paint job, follow the manufacturer's recommended drying times (otherwise you will have to sand) and work when the humidity is very low and the temperature is right. A final word about epoxies and polyurethanes: for a given quality, whether they are labeled "industrial" or "marine" they are exactly the same . . . except for their effect on your wallet.

A trick for cleaning a painted surface

Wet the area, then spread ash on it and scrub. Ash cleans and is slightly abrasive; you'll save the expense of sandpaper.

Cold-riveting a steel hull

When you have to make repairs in some out-of-the-way place, you usually don't have the best tools or equipment. Here is a story that shows what kind of work a pair of amateurs can do, using only available materials. I was giving Henry Wakelam a hand, and the two of us riveted a dozen 1/16" metal patches over damaged sections of a 28-year-old steel boat named SHAFHAÏ. We applied sheets of newspaper smeared with red lead between the patches and the hull, then riveted the patches on. In ten days, the two of us did some 30 square feet of patching and made the boat perfectly watertight.

First we drilled 7/32" rivet holes with a hand drill, and temporarily mounted the patch with four small bolts to hold it in place. We then finished drilling the rest of the holes through the patch and the hull on 3/4" centers, and slightly reamed them out with a 3/8" bit. We removed the patch and filed off the burrs. We then laid a sheet of newspaper against the hull, swabbed it with red lead, and bolted the patch back on with the four temporary bolts. The riveting came next, with me inside the boat and Henry outside. I would push a rivet through, hold it against the hull with a hand-anvil (a large chunk of steel), and give a kick to let Henry know I was ready. He would then hit the rivet with a small hammer, mashing it into the reamed-out hole. This was cold riveting, meaning that we didn't heat the rivets first. Not a drop of water came through.

MAINTAINING A TRADITIONAL PLANKED BOAT

Watching for and preventing shipworms

Contrary to a widely held belief, shipworms aren't a major problem for a traditional planked boat. During the year I spent at Durban with MARIE-THÉRÈSE II, I worked in a shipyard that repaired and caulked wooden boats. The work fascinated me, and I observed and learned a great deal. At my other ports of call, I always visited haul-out slips, either to lend friends a hand or just because I was drawn to them, like most sailors. And I met a number of young people who were replacing planking they said had been "devoured" by shipworms. It was never necessary. I repeat: *never*. The problem wasn't shipworms, but the almost superstitious dread they inspire.

Let's look at things calmly. The planking on a 30-foot Tahiti Ketch is between 1" and 1-1/4" thick. That's much more than is needed for strength; the heavy thickness allows for a good caulk job. A few shipworm tunnels won't really threaten the hull's soundness, or even that of the plank in question—though they certainly must be dealt with.

I've often seen shipworm damage four to six inches above the waterline. It was probably due to heel during a crossing, when larvae managed to dig their way in, so there is nothing mysterious about it. When you reach port after an ocean passage, there is almost always some seaweed clinging to the topsides. It will continue to live out of water, hoping for a splash of water to give it something to eat and drink. A shipworm does the same thing: it adapts while awaiting better days. Painting antifouling to twelve inches above the waterline will avoid these kinds of surprises. It's less elegant than a pretty stripe of shiny enamel at the waterline, but much more prudent.

Treating for shipworms

And now, let's get to work. The boat is hauled out as usual. The hull, well brushed and rinsed, dries quickly. If a small damp spot appears on the hull—but outside of the caulk lines—and the damp spot is circular (an inch or so across), it's almost certainly the sign of a shipworm. Circle it with chalk. With a sharp chisel, cut horizontally across the wet spot to remove a thin sliver of wood, as if you were planing it. A tiny hole will appear; that's the opening to the tunnel. As you dig deeper with the chisel, the hole gets bigger. Stop as soon as you can poke a red-hot wire into it. To increase your chances of getting the shipworm (and any others hiding in the vicinity), heat the area as much as possible with a blowtorch. Keep at it for a while, to be on the safe side. Don't worry if the paint burns; better to scorch two or three feet of wood than to risk botching the job. (In the Gulf of Siam—and probably all over Southeast Asia—every time the junks were hauled out, their hulls were heated to the maximum with torches made of woven palm fronds.)

After the heat treatment, squirt some Xylene with a syringe into the tunnels, then paint several coats of Xylene on all the stripped wood. Plug everything with epoxy before applying the first coat of primer.

If you discover shipworms in the keel, bow, or sternpost, that's more serious, but still no cause for panic or despair. It's worth remembering that shipworms can survive out of water for a month or more in a large piece of wood. So I would leave my boat out of water for two or three months before injecting a few squirts of Xylene (or some other more effective product) from time to time, followed by the epoxy.

Caulking and waterproofing

Caulking consists of pounding cotton (or oakum) into the parts of the hull where two pieces of wood meet, notably between the planks. The cotton is driven in from the outside, of course. When the boat is put back in the water, moisture causes the joint to swell, sealing any cracks. It is important that the caulking be done evenly and tamped down well, using good, dry cotton.

A beginner may be tempted to caulk only defective areas. You should do as professionals do, and start the caulking about a foot before the leaky section, first pounding very gently, then much harder over the few inches of the leak, before gradually reducing the pressure and tapering off, a foot further on.

Leaving a wooden boat out of water for a long time isn't generally recommended, because the seams between the planks begin to spread as the wood dries out. But all will return to normal a few days after the boat is back in the water, and a long spell in dry dock provides an excellent opportunity to check the bottom caulking and to work on any suspicious areas.

On the beach, you could hear mallet blows on hulls; the junks were being caulked . . . I followed Hao's father around the beach like his shadow, hypnotized by his magician's hands as they pounded* cai tram *fiber between the planks, using wooden tools that looked like chisels. He had made them himself and soaked them in* cai dau *oil. With his machete, he would occasionally trim their edges or change their curve, depending on the shape of the cracks to be filled. As I watched him working, his eyes almost closed, I knew that the water wouldn't leak in.

A few essential points on caulking:

1) Putty, good though it may be, *only* protects the cotton. Caulking compound (even those "miracle" products that ship chandlers try to sell you) won't keep water out if the strands of oakum or cotton aren't firmly packed between the planks.

2) I've often heard it said that oakum or cotton packed very tightly between the planks can burst them, because the caulking swells under water, and that it's therefore better to caulk "light." The truth is that a "light" caulk job is much faster than a decent one in which the fiber is packed properly. People who honestly believe that "light" is better than "well-packed" may be right if the boat in question is a very old 18-foot J.I. with very thin planking, used for racing around the buoys, but certainly not for a cruising boat with normal planking.

3) Good caulking cotton produces a more watertight joint than tarred-hemp oakum. Cotton probably doesn't last as long, but it serves very well; when I have a choice, I don't hesitate to use it. There are two kinds of caulking cotton: one looks a bit like off-white string and feels fairly rough. The other is almost pure white, woolly, and very soft. Use the soft kind; you won't regret it.

The tools used are a caulking iron and a five-pound mallet. If you don't have a caulking iron, a screwdriver will do, though the job will be a little slower.

A simple technique for caulking under water

First of all, locate the leak. Then drill through the planking from the inside and push a nail through that will stick out on the other side; it will help you find the leak when you're under water.

Once in the water, test the suspicious parts of the caulk with a knife. The point will barely penetrate an area that is well-caulked, but will sink in easily when you reach the defective section. Here's another trick the Vietnamese fishermen taught me: brush your head along the bottom of the boat. When you feel your hair being sucked against the hull, you've found the leak.

You then plug the leak with dry cotton, under water. That's right! And it's very simple. To keep the caulking cotton dry, just coat it with grease. In a day or so, the water will penetrate the grease, and the cotton will get wet, swell, and seal the leak.

Preventing and treating rot

If everything on the boat is oversized, as it usually is on traditional planked vessels, a little rot in a rib, or anywhere else, isn't going to weaken the whole boat. Besides, once you start replacing ribs, there's no end to it. It means being stuck in port with a big expenditure of money and energy. It may even spell the end of a dream that at the beginning had every chance of turning into a life of long ocean passages and new friendships in different ports of call.

Here is the story of Peter, an American I met when he came through Polynesia. He had fallen in love with and bought a good used boat in the Caribbean; it was about 33 feet long, with classic planking. One day, Peter discovered a large area of rot in the inner side of the stem. Once he recovered from the shock, he started thinking. Obviously, the bow's intrinsic strength hadn't been compromised. And even if the stem were half rotten (which it wasn't, as he discovered by carefully sounding the entire bow after his disturbing discovery), the piece was so thick, that it wouldn't be a problem. The trick was to stop the rot and keep it from spreading. His reasoning was sound, and so was what he did next.

Peter hauled out in Panama and spent two months there.

1) To let the humidity out, he started by drilling tiny holes—the width of a large syringe needle—in the affected area.

2) He then heated the area with a blowtorch a few times a day for about or a month while continuing to air out the boat.

3) For several days running, he injected acetone into the holes he had drilled. Acetone is extremely volatile; as it evaporates, it draws out the last traces of humidity.

4) Finally, he gave the stem massive injections of

Everdur, totally impregnating the entire rotten area, which was now perfectly dry. *Everdur* is a very fluid two-part epoxy that acts as a fungicide as it vitrifies the rotten area. If you soaked a dry sponge with *Everdur*, it would become as hard as a brick.

The hauled-out junks had been waiting for months, shaded from the sun by a thin layer of palm fronds spread on their decks. That way, air could circulate between the leaves, letting the boats slowly dry out without any play developing between the planks. Each week during the rainy season the hulls had been sprinkled with seawater, so the salt—the basic protection against rot here—would protect their pitch-scented wood.

A few tricks

Plugging small leaks

On an old wooden boat, a bag of sawdust can be valuable in plugging small leaks. Here is what you do: fill a bucket with sawdust, dive about six feet beneath the keel while holding the bucket upside down so the sawdust doesn't get wet, then turn it over, open side up. A cloud of sawdust will float up (you can shake the bucket to spread it around). Once it reaches the hull, the sawdust will be sucked into the cracks and stick there. It will swell in a few minutes, and plug the leaks. I used this Asian trick from time to time on MARIE-THÉRÈSE's hull during her Indian Ocean crossing. It worked for between several hours and several days; a matter of luck. When you're at anchor, and the boat's hull isn't working, it can remain watertight for months.

Making a temporary repair under water

You can repair a large hole in a wood, fiberglass, or metal hull under water using an Asian method that involves a compound made of two parts ordinary cement mixed with one part of clay. It hardens underwater in about twelve hours. In the Indian Ocean, I plugged serious leaks in MARIE-THÉRÈSE's hull this way.

Later, Henry Wakelam greatly improved the method. Here is the result of our experiments. Mix equal parts dry plaster and cement. In another container, mix water and clay (not kaolin) until you get a very liquid mud. Pour this into the plaster and cement and stir until you get a putty with the consistency of modeling clay. You now have to work very quickly, because the putty will remain soft for only a couple of minutes. You apply the plaster-cement-clay putty under water; it hardens

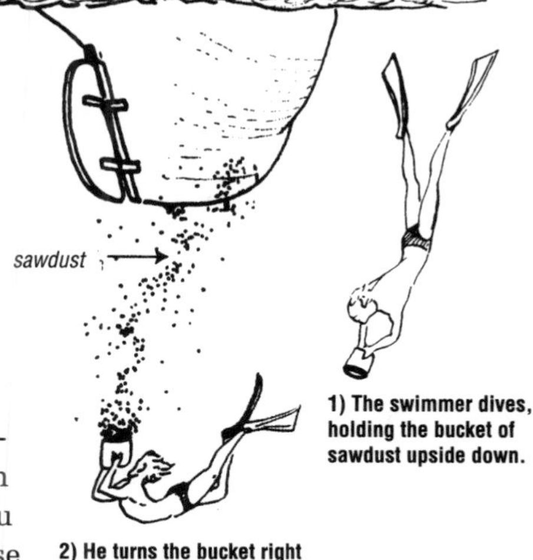

Plugging small leaks temporarily

in under a quarter of an hour. Be sure to first drive a few nails into the damaged part of a wooden hull as an armature, to help the putty adhere in case the surface is too smooth.

There are now two-part products on the market that will even stick to wet wood, and which can be rubbed onto the damaged part of the hull, under water. I know of a boat where a section of the hull two hand's breadths across had been scraped bare on a coral head and needed to be protected against shipworms. The boat was about to leave on a long charter trip to the Tuamotus and the skipper couldn't wait for a haul-out slot to become available. The skipper used a two-part American product called Underwater Patching (from Pettit Paints in San Leandro, California). He returned to haul out seven or eight months later, and found that the underwater repair had held amazingly well. When the plastic patch was torn off, the bare wood showed no sign of shipworms.

<u>Checking a water tank's joints</u>

Spread soapy water over the seams, and ask some passer-by to blow into the filler hole. Soap bubbles will appear at the cracks in the welds (there are always a few).

<u>Working underneath a motor, or in other places where you can't see</u>

Use a mirror and a flashlight.

REPAIRING SAILS

When sewing Dacron, I use #16 sail needles (the smallest I know of) or even ordinary round needles, so as not to damage the fibers. To repair sections with several thicknesses of cloth (head, tack, or clew), I use the stronger #14 or #15 needles; otherwise, they wouldn't penetrate. A sailmaker's palm is invaluable, as is a supply of strong Dacron thread and sewing wax. Don't pull directly on the thread with the needle; you'll break its eye; pull the thread by hand. For heavy thicknesses, a good pair of pliers is very useful.

When using a sewing machine, here is how to tell if the needle is the right size: thread it, and stretch the thread vertically. If the needle slides down on its own, the eye is large enough; if it sticks, it's too small, and will put tension on the thread between the needle and the spool.

REFILLING A BUTANE TANK

Henri Cordovero on CHALLENGE figured out a way to refill a small butane tank from a larger drum. What's in the drum is a liquid, so it can flow from one tank to another. But you have to vent the small tank from time to time, otherwise the pressure build-up will keep the liquid from flowing. It's a good idea to hang the full drum in sunshine and to cool the tank to be filled, for example by covering it with palm fronds or ice.

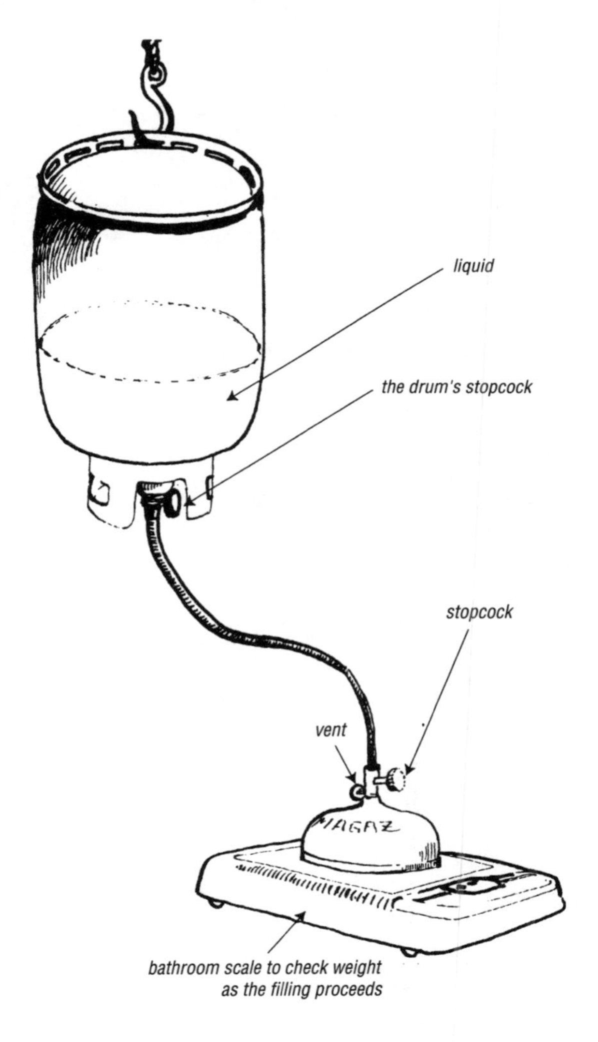

Refilling a small butane tank from a large drum (proceed with caution, and always out of doors)

The atoll

Living the beachcomber life

"You either love an atoll from deep in your guts, or you don't love it at all. If you just love it a little, the feeling soon changes to not at all. There are mosquitos, gnats, flies drawn by the smell of fish, rats that scavenge everywhere, dangerous sharks that cruise the tide flats in a foot of water, terrible stonefish disguised as chunks of coral among all the rest of the coral, animals that sting and animals that bite. Coconuts fall without warning, seemingly aimed at your head. The sun blazes straight down, then is reflected back up in flames from the calm water to hit you again from below. So it's understandable that some people might not love atolls . . . But when you look more closely, you notice the colors of the lagoon, the shining pass, the living coral, the atoll's breathing. And you see further, you begin to learn—and the rest comes very quickly . . ."

Like an inner sea, protected by the barrier reef that breaks the thrust of the great ocean swells into millions of pearls, the lagoon is connected to the open sea by passes.

The coral reef islands or islets that surround an atoll's lagoon are called *motu*. They are the only strips of land above water, and are usually covered with coconut trees. Some *motu* can be five miles long, others are tiny. Between the *motu*, the coral shallows are cut here and there by passes, which link the ocean and the lagoon, and by *hoa*, shallow channels in the outer coral flats that don't reach the lagoon. Some atolls have no pass at all, others may have several.

Sailing to an atoll

THE GOOD SEASON

Beware of the hurricane season. Remember, hurricanes occur above 10° latitude north and south, during the rainy season.

Here is my experience of the Pacific atolls I've had the occasion to visit, especially during recent years:

At 10° south latitude in the Pacific, Caroline Island is at the extreme limit for hurricanes and their effects. But it can be hit by tropical storms, as my friends Ron and Anne Falconer, who lived on Caroline from 1987 to 1991, can attest. In February 1990, Anne wrote: "We just came through a storm that turned into a hurricane southwest of us . . . We got 19 inches of rain in five days . . . Our cistern overflowed for the first time."

Suvorov atoll, at 13° south, was hit by a strong hurricane during Tom Neale's time there. The good season for Suvorov would be from May to November, and the hurricane season from January to March.

French Polynesia extends over a very wide area. The Marquesas stretch from 8° to about 10° south and normally don't get hurricanes. The Tuamotus, which stretch between 14° to 20° south, and the Society Islands (which include Tahiti), between 16° to 20° south latitude, are in hurricane latitudes (they had five cyclones in 1983). The risky period is from December to March-April.

Outside of the rainy season, the dominant winds are the trades, and especially the *mara'amu*, a south-southeasterly trade wind that can blow hard during the Polynesian winter (July to September).

This morning, the Fairy Tern came out to say hello, flying around JOSHUA's masts to tell me I was within twenty miles of the atoll. I already knew that; the stars and my sextant had told me before dawn. But to make her feel appreciated, I pretended to be a bit lost and thanked her for her welcome, which she had carried so far on her light wings.

MAKING A LANDFALL ON AN ATOLL

It's important to keep an eye out when nearing an atoll, because you won't see it until you're almost there; only its coconut trees stand out. All your senses must be on alert, as you listen and watch for signs: the thunder of the barrier reef or perhaps a greenish reflection on the bottoms of clouds. You will first see the tufts of coconut trees, then waves on the barrier reef, and then the pass.

Sea birds

The fairy tern (*Gygis alba rothschildi*) is the only sea bird that never flies further than 15 or 20 miles from the coast or its island. It can warn us that we are getting close to land.

At night, beware of unexpected currents

The first time I encountered the Tuamotus in 1964, I distrusted them: an archipelago of low, dangerous atolls, they were scattered like a mine field between the Marquesas and Tahiti.

"Everything is shipshape on board; nothing is keeping us. The moon will be full in a few days; we will wait for it to cross the Tuamotus. The currents there are treacherous, powerful at times, and can move a boat in unexpected directions. Considering how unhealthy the area is, it's best to hold as many trump cards as possible and take advantage of the full moon, which is essential to get reliable star sights when you need them."

What happened to Patrick years later confirmed the need for extreme vigilance. He was sailing from Tahiti to the Tuamotus one night and had reached the vicinity of the atolls. He was tired, and decided to go below for a nap. He checked his position, which put him several dozen miles downwind of the nearest atoll. In other words, no reason for concern. He reduced speed, estimated his drift, and went to sleep. Against all logic, Patrick wound up on the reef. An unexpected current toward the land had caused him to drift much faster than expected, and not in the anticipated direction.

At night or in bad weather, be especially careful. Stay awake and heave to occasionally, to listen.

Listening

The only way to have the slightest chance of hearing the sea breaking on a reef is to heave to, and of course to remain alert. Here's a perfect illustration. One beautiful full-moon night, I was sailing along Bora Bora's barrier reef, about a half mile off. I was in the lee of the island, on a broad reach. The wind was light, force 2 at the most; the boat was making about 3 knots. The sea was absolutely calm with a long southwesterly swell which I could distinctly see pounding on the reef in huge breakers. And yet, try as I might, the only thing I could hear was the rustle of water at the bow. So I closed to within a quarter-mile and continued to sail along the reef, struck by the beauty of those terrific breakers illuminated by the full moon. And I still couldn't hear anything! I wanted to make sure, once and for all, so I hove to. And then I heard real rolling thunder! I could even hear it in the cabin when I went below to light the stove for a cup of coffee. From that experience, I can say at least one thing with certainty: even if your boat is barely moving, you won't be warned by the sound of even a very large swell breaking on a reef, much less a gentle one.

Don't blindly rely on your instruments

In 1993, Antoine was sailing not far from the Bora Bora reef at dawn, reassured by the presence of a GPS and a radar set on board. And wham! He suddenly had the fright of his life: the boat was caught in a wave about to break on the reef. Instinctively, Antoine slammed the tiller over and saved his boat—at the cost of some gut-twisting terror. If he hadn't been alert and ready to take action . . . His radar hadn't picked up the breaking waves, and his GPS didn't sound the alarm as he neared the barrier reef.

On a radar screen, you can see land well inside the barrier reef without getting any echo of the reef, even though it's closer. As for the GPS, I wouldn't trust it, since the atolls aren't yet perfectly charted. Putting too much faith in instruments alone can lead to catastrophe if you cut things close. When you're near an atoll, having electronic aids aboard is no reason not to look and listen.

PICKING THE RIGHT MOMENT TO TAKE A PASS

So the atoll is finally in sight, and the crew is feeling relieved. Great! The boat is tearing along. I'm so happy to arrive after a week at sea, I'm hypnotized . . . Careful now . . . It might be a good idea to make sure the outgoing current isn't too strong before taking the pass, and to coil my halyards a bit better so as not to risk a last-minute tangle. I heave to, which gives me all the time I need to straighten everything on deck and to calmly choose the best way to take the pass.

Tides in the Tuamotus

Against all logic, the tide in the Tuamotus is high when the moon rises and sets, and low when the moon passes the meridian (upper and lower). I've often confirmed this phenomenon from late-19th century *Sailing Directions*, whose information is laid out much more clearly than in our modern volumes.

Thanks to Kipling's stories, I know how Pau Amna the giant crab invented the tides in the Time of the Very Beginnings, and why all crabs today have pincers (it's because of the little girl's golden scissors).

It's best to enter with minimal current running through the pass. Currents near an atoll are complicated and can be very powerful in certain narrow passes. Some passes, in fact, are hard to take without a motor.

When the tide is rising, the flow is into the pass. But if the swell is large, it can submerge the coral shelf, filling the lagoon. In that case the overflow runs out through the pass in the form of an outgoing current.

Given this complexity—which varies with the atoll's layout—my principle is to take a pass with minimal outgoing current around low tide, in other words when the moon is passing the upper or lower meridian.

The 1894 *Sailing Directions* give the following advice for landing in the Tuamotus:

"Where the pass meets the sea, with an outgoing current, and where the pass meets the lagoon, with an incoming current, an eddy line (*opape*) forms, which, in the first case, looks convex to an observer coming in from the sea, and concave in the second case. By climbing into the rigging, one can determine with certainty, before taking the pass, whether the current is flowing in or out, or whether there is no current. This eddy line raises a chop, very stiff at times, in the middle of the pass. One must therefore, especially with a small boat, stay close to the side, as by sailing in the middle one would be exposed to having the deck swept by seas, and even being turned sideways, no longer able to steer."

PASSES AND ENTRANCES

Passes are more or less navigable, depending on the shape of the atoll. Suvorov's deep emerald-green pass is wide and clear, and can be taken under sail alone whatever the state of the trade wind. The Ahe pass, on the other hand, would have given me serious problems without the help of a motor. It is relatively narrow and parallel to the direction of the trades, so you have to tack through it. Tacking under sail alone would be unthinkable for a heavy, long-keel boat that isn't very maneuverable in tight quarters. It's best to check ahead of time, observe carefully, and use your motor. One of the toughest and most spectacular passes I know is Blind Passage, Caroline Island's windward pass; it's a dead end, since it doesn't actually go through to the main lagoon.

I remember Ron explaining to me in 1987 how to take it:

"It doesn't look like much on the chart, but when you see it from outside, directly upwind of the atoll, it

The sun was already high and sparkled on the crests of the waves, which turned into millions of fine pearls as they crashed on Suvorov's barrier reef.

To the right and left, coral just below the surface raced by, sparkling with greens, browns, purples, reds, blacks, with everything mixed with the small surface wavelets of a very slight favorable current. This jewel of light was like a setting for the pass, a long streak of light green paved with splashes of color, with large brown pools when the coral rose to create eddies we rushed through. The tide was slack . . . JOSHUA was tearing along . . . I had never been so much at one with my boat . . . And suddenly there we were in the blue of the lagoon, almost speechless . . . And I began perhaps to better understand Gerbault, who spoke of taking passes under sail alone . . . with that light around the boat . . .

really looks nasty: unbelievably narrow, with breakers on either side. But if you sail by it along the reef a few times and look carefully, you can see that it can be done in fair weather. And once you're inside, it's heaven!"

Véronique Lerebours and I went there, and this is how I described our arrival in an article for *Neptune* magazine:

"TAMATA skirted the reef, jibed, went over onto the other tack, jibed again. Véronique had the tiller and I was in the spreaders, absorbing Blind Passage's essence. It was both impressive and terrific; just a dark-blue line through the breakers leading to the coral shelf far in the distance . . . I climbed down from my perch. Véronique dropped the staysail to clear the foredeck. We came in with the wind full aft under jib and mainsail, the sun high but still behind us, so we wouldn't be blinded by reflections. The anchors were at the ready, the mooring lines faked out, halyards neatly coiled and ready to loose, Zodiac ready on the cabin roof, diving mask under the bench with our reef sandals . . . The breakers drew nearer, rumbling on the coral that defended the pass like huge, drooling fangs . . . And all at once, it was over, the rumbling was lost in our wake and TAMATA was running on flat water. Véronique uncleated the jib halyard and held it taut with both hands, ready to drop the sail. We had nearly reached the dead end and I quickly slowed us down by sheeting the main flat, then cut our speed further with big sweeps of the tiller. 'Jib!' . . . the jib dropped like a stone. 'Anchor!' . . . the anchor splashed and Véronique jammed the chain, because the bottom wasn't far down."

The lagoon welcomed us into its open arms and dressed up for the occasion, with luminous colors and silvery pearls thrown up by the bow. We were charging along on a broad reach under a cloudless southeast trade-wind sky. The dangerous coral heads stood out against the surrounding blue and could be spotted well in advance. My belly was filled with terrific joy.

THE LAGOON

It is easy to sail in a lagoon, provided you take a few basic precautions: the sun should be high and somewhat behind you. Colors show how deep the water is. Dark blue: very deep, no problems. Turquoise: watch out, the bottom is shallow, but it's sand, and not too nasty. Brown spots: beware, that's coral, and you want to get clear of it quickly. One person should always be up the mast or at the bow, pointing out which way to go.

WATCH THE ANCHORAGE

In the atolls, you usually anchor in the lee of a *motu*, which is fine so long as the wind doesn't shift.

But when the lagoon is wide and the wind begins to change direction, the boat can be in real danger. The wind blows toward shore and a chop can come up quickly; the bigger the lagoon, the bigger the chop, of course. In the Tuamotus, the least sign of bad weather usually sounds the alarm for the crew, which has to be ready to cross the lagoon and find another more or less questionable anchorage while waiting for good weather to return. And you can get in serious trouble if you're slow to make up your mind.

Some atolls have safe anchorages, protected on more than one side. Ahe has an anchorage of the kind you only dream of, protected by a horseshoe-shaped coral outcropping that is awash at low tide. At Caroline, Blind Passage is a narrow slit with a slight bend, just 40 feet wide and about 200 yards long, that cuts through the reef and ends at the coral flats. TAMATA was in safety at the bottom of this pass, lying to four anchors, surrounded by coral that was level with the water.

I wanted to play with the wind and the coral, skim past the great scattered polyp-covered shelves, their carpets of sea urchins close enough to touch, the bottom dropping from zero to a hundred feet and more. Here, sailing took on a whole new meaning. After the ocean swell, it was wonderful to crisscross this beautiful calm, blue water in every direction, to make love to this lagoon which had seduced me from the very first moment, to breathe in the scent of the nearby islets that protected us from the great waves beyond.

Local resources

When visiting atolls, it's best not to count on finding much by way of local supplies. In soil richness, atolls and coral islands are like deserts! And for the ones with villages, as in the Tuamotus, contact with the outside is often limited to visits by local trading schooners, which carry passengers, food, and materials. Their trips are neither frequent nor regular. At Ahe, for example, the schooner came about once a month.

WATER

You can always find fresh water on an atoll; just dig a well. That's a discovery I made one day on Suvorov, when I started digging in the sand. You would think that there can't be water on an atoll, whose altitude is practically sea level. The sand doesn't filter out the salt, so common sense would say that sweating to dig a well would yield only seawater. But a small miracle softly said "no" to big old common sense. During the rainy season, water from the sky penetrates the sand to gently overlay that from the sea. Fresh water is lighter than salt water, so it floats on top, and the underground stillness keeps the two from mixing.

Deshumeurs had his second great flash in the water, when he went skindiving. We had a speargun and a mask. He dove first, and stuck his head out ten seconds later, saying, "It's beautiful! It's so beautiful!" The undersea world, which he had never seen before, was an incredible revelation for him.

You can therefore find fresh water on all the world's coral islands, provided they have a rainy season. The supply will dwindle after a prolonged drought, but you can almost always find some water in the middle of the island.

We had that experience on the Poro Poro *motu* at Ahe, which was about an acre in area. After spending ten hours breaking through a concrete-hard layer of coral with a crowbar, we hit the water pocket—and found it as pure as on Suvorov!

It is also wise to collect rainwater, and even wiser, if you plan a long stay, to build a cistern. Tom Neale had one on Suvorov, Ron Falconer built one on Caroline, and I had mine on Ahe.

Peter told me of an easy way to build a cistern: just dig a cylindrical hole in the ground and line it with a very strong plastic bag. The bag should be slightly wider than the hole, so it doesn't get stretched. Close the top of the bag, leaving only a hole for the rain gutter or filler hose.

But having water isn't enough, you have to use it carefully. Before drinking our water, we ran it through a porous clay filter. And we didn't waste a drop. We showered over a large wash basin, and used the water on our garden; we recycled our dishwater the same way.

FISH

I get fish in a couple of different ways: by spearfishing in the pass and outer reef; throwing the *patia* (Polynesian spear) in the shallows; and by using a fish pen, which is the least tiring.

In the passes

The pass, with its jacks, groupers, and parrotfish, remains the best source of fish. You slip into the water and choose your dinner with a *pupui* (Tahitian speargun).

You have to be careful, though; the trigger on a Tahitian speargun is dangerous, because the gun can go off if you bump it against a piece of coral. So we designed a safety catch: a small wooden chock wedged between the handle and the trigger. You put the chock in when loading the gun, remove it while hunting, then replace it before climbing out onto the reef.

When fish are plentiful in the pass, watch out for sharks. A grey shark can grow to six feet, and become aggressive if you spear a fish under its nose. To each his own, it seems to say, and you don't have to speak shark to get the message.

The Suvorov and Ahe passes deserve a special mention written in big red letters: even small sharks can be dangerous there. You have to stay on your guard. If possible, hunt with someone else and stick together. One person keeps an eye out while the other hunts; the lookout warns of danger by slapping the water as hard as possible. And when you spear a fish, try to hit its lateral line so it dies instantly, without flapping.

Since I started spearfishing in tropical waters, I have come to a few conclusions about the behavior of sharks and skindivers:

1) Sharks are timid, and, except perhaps for some rare species, won't attack during daylight. They are usually afraid of people and hard to approach.

2) The most timid of sharks can become enraged if there is blood in the water, and speared fish nearly al-

Spearfishing with Polynesians is a real treat. They become gods underwater, masters at holding their breath and stalking, and unbelievably good shots. I am a good swimmer, with plenty of wind, and I was the best carbine shot on the* GAZELLE*. But mastering the* pupui *isn't only a matter of swimming, wind, and aim. To even begin to approach the skill level of a Polynesian, you have to be on totally intimate terms with the fish and the water, to* become *them.

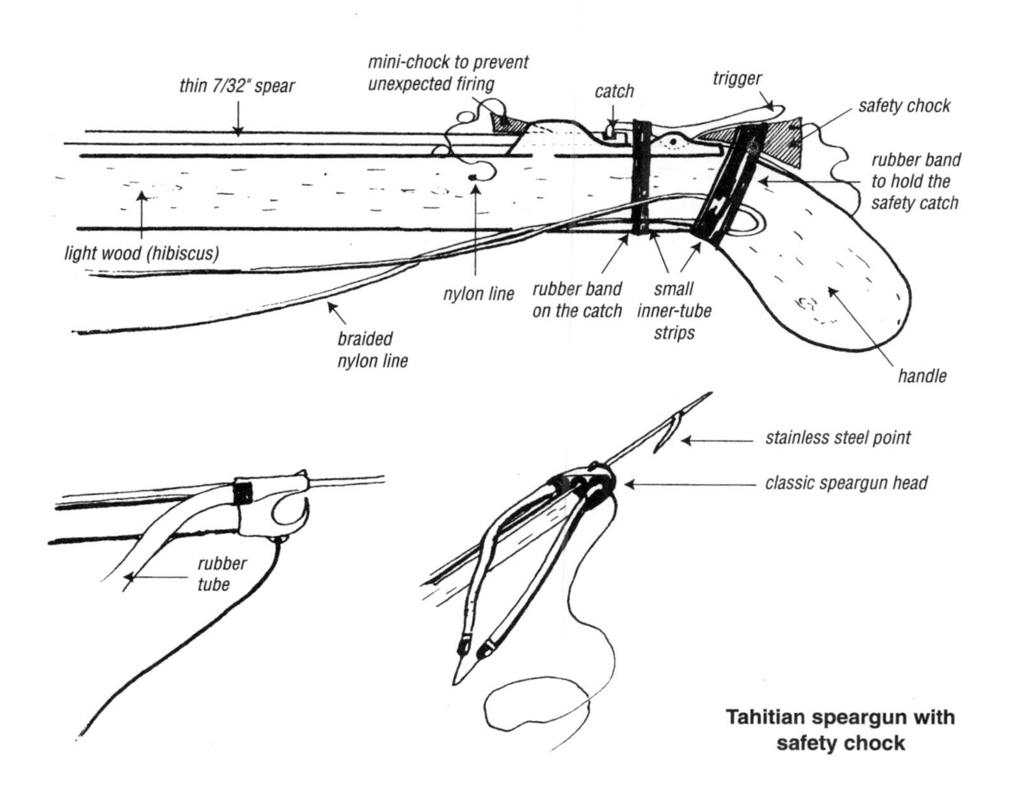

Tahitian speargun with safety chock

ways bleed. Moreover, the vibrations from a fish struggling at the end of a spear will almost always attract sharks. Caution may dictate that you hunt elsewhere.

3) A shark about to charge will start to quiver in a particular but immediately understandable way. You should immediately wave your gun aggressively, even if it doesn't have a spear.

4) A shark can be bluffed by an aggressive attitude, but you have to be able to see it first, so beware of murky water. Personally, I won't swim in the tropics unless the water is clear.

5) Sharks feed mainly at night, so skip those midnight dips in waters where sharks are found. You won't see them, and—to make things worse—it's their dinner time.

6) Sharks prefer to attack light-colored, slender parts of the body: arms, legs, hands, feet. (I was once bitten on the foot by a shark in the Indian Ocean in 1953.)

7) Even if you are bitten, all isn't lost: keep on bluffing. There's nothing else you can do, in any case.

Hunting sharks

Sharks have no vertical vision, and therefore can't tell what is happening above them. You can therefore get within point-blank range if you dive directly down on one. Dick wore a weighted belt that allowed him to sink when he stopped swimming; he was motionless and sank in total silence, so the shark wasn't alerted.

Spearing a shark isn't easy. All of the vital organs, located in the upper forward part of a shark's body near the head, are protected by the thickest layer of skin. Its belly, which a spear can penetrate easily, contains no vital organ. The heart, which is located behind the anterior lateral fin, is protected by very strong cartilage. Finally, a shark speared through the side might attack the diver.

Assuming you are above the shark, the best place to aim is the top of the head between the eyes and the gills. Hitting the shark there will snap its spinal cord and virtually paralyze it (See position 1 in the sketch). Note that this calls for a powerful speargun. It takes a Tahitian speargun with two pairs of rubber tubes to penetrate the very tough skin over that part of a shark's body. And if the shark is over six feet long, don't bother trying; the spear won't go in.

If you can't shoot for the head, aim for the gills. Whenever I have hit a shark in the gills, it has corkscrewed around and tried to bite the spear, but without being able to swim. These were sharks under five feet long. I once shot at a shark a little longer than five feet long and missed my target, hitting it well behind the gills. The shark struggled furiously, swimming in a circle at the end of the cord—while I mentally made out my will.

Where on a small shark do you aim?

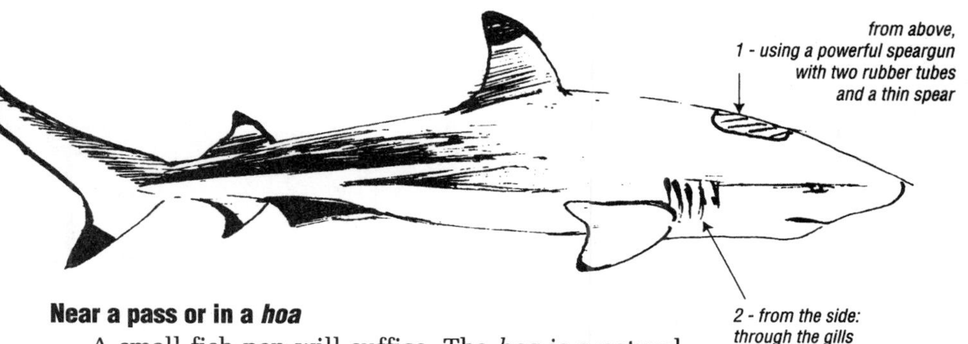

Near a pass or in a *hoa*

A small fish pen will suffice. The *hoa* is a natural, not very deep (3 to 6 feet) trench that goes from the sea to the lagoon.

In *Tamata and the Alliance*, I describe planning to build our fish pen on Ahe: "Using the crowbar to dig with, we would set eight posts in the coral at the *hoa*'s mouth in a circle a dozen feet across. We would connect the posts with poles nailed to their tops and tack chicken wire around the circle, to a depth of six feet. We would then snip an opening a foot across, and stick a short cylinder of chicken wire through it, close to the water's surface and open to the current, with its end curving downward into the pen. That was how the fish would get in. Once inside, they would swim in circles in the trap, never thinking of leaving through the hole above them. Then we would build two low walls with chunks of coral collected on the tide flats. To work properly, the walls had to extend about a hundred feet on either side of the pen entrance at a ninety-degree angle, like a pair of arms, so the fish would be herded toward the trap."

Inside the lagoon

There are often fewer fish in the lagoon than in the passes, but if you look carefully around the coral

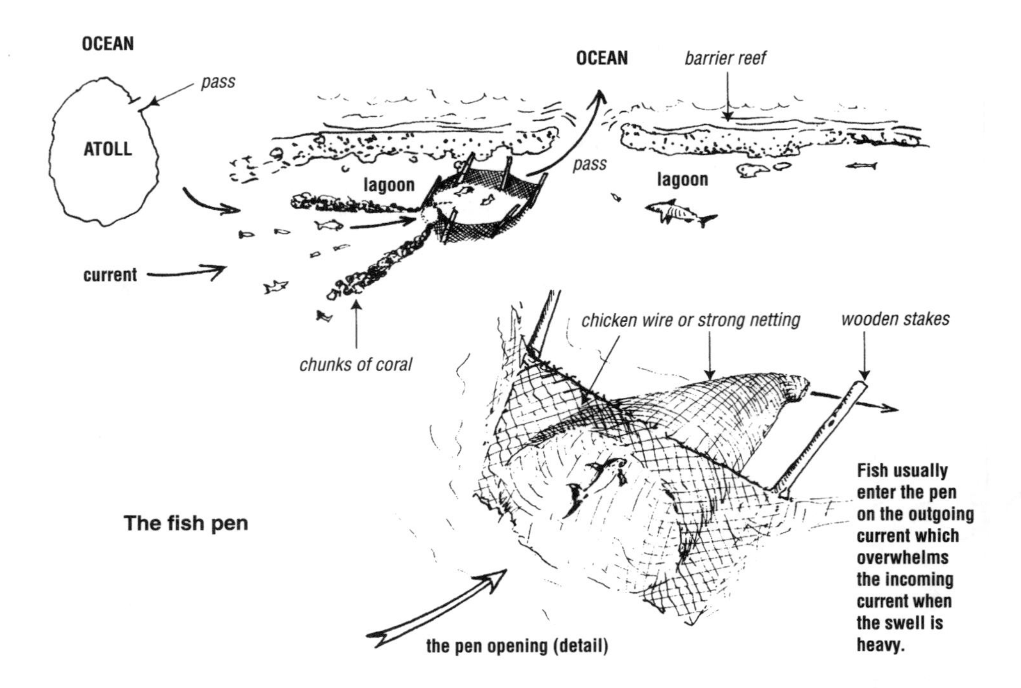

The fish pen

heads, you can find groupers, parrotfish, soldierfish (*ihi*), and surgeonfish. But watch out for black-tip lagoon sharks. They normally never attack unless there is blood in the water or a fish struggling at the end of a spear. But I have become a lot more alert since almost being attacked by a four-foot black-tip shark at Ahe.

On the coral flats

In the coral flats on the outer reef, the *patia* (Polynesian spear) is king. A good *patia* should be as long as its owner is tall, then half again as long; this usually means about nine feet, including the points. These can be picked up in local hardware stores, where you can also get spare rubber tubes for your *pupui*.

Mastering the *patia* is extremely difficult and requires serious training, patience, and determination. At first, I practiced by aiming at a sheet of paper on a sandy bottom (so as not to dull the points), or at sea cucumbers. In fact, sea cucumbers are a perfect target to help you learn to account for refraction, which varies according to the angle of your shot and the depth of the fish you are aiming for.

In the shallows, you can use the *patia* to spear parrotfish, small groupers, and surgeonfish.

Also in the shallow, you can pick up pencil sea

urchins, lobsters, octopi, and clams of every color—turquoise, electric blue, and violet. Tahitians smash urchins open on the coral, wash them off in the tide pools, and eat them on the spot.

Small sharks can be extremely dangerous in the shallows when you are walking in water up to your calves: they see only a small proportion of your body, and can attack "by mistake." You can lie down to give them a better idea of your size, threaten them with a *patia* or stick, or slap the water with the flat of your hand to chase them away.

I strongly recommend wearing plastic sandals when you walk on a reef, because coral is sharp, and wounds get infected easily in the tropics; protect yourself with a hat (of *niau*), sunglasses, and T-shirt, because the sun can be scorching on the shallows. (The rest of the time, we go barefoot in a bathing suit or a *pareo*.) In any case, it pays to keep your eyes open when you're walking on an atoll—or in a boat, for that matter!

Other dangers on the shallows: moray eels, but especially stonefish (*nohu*).

The stonefish is a real menace. Chameleon-like, it changes color to blend with its environment; you can hardly see one, even on a sandy bottom. Its lateral fins are soft as silk and completely harmless. But on its back are three dagger-like spines that can

Raumati was the* patia. *The undisputed champion of Ahe, he used his* patia *the way Paganini used a violin bow. Seeing him from afar on the edge of the reef where the waves broke, he looked like a ballet dancer, in total symbiosis with the coral. Raumati had insisted on making me my* patia *himself. It was almost identical to his, eight feet long and straight, but a little lighter, to suit my slighter build.

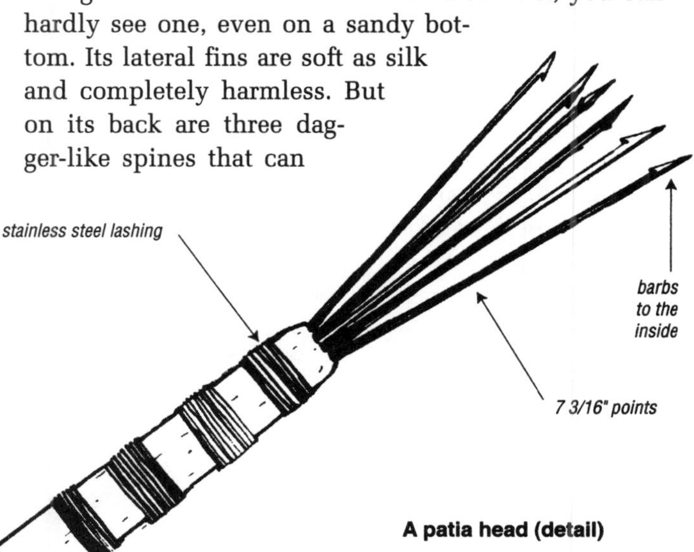

A patia head (detail)

Stephan caught on fast, with his whole body, and his feet had eyes that could see thorns and sharp coral.

cause an incredibly stabbing pain. It feels like being bitten by a cobra, which has a similar venom. Those deadly spines can pierce a plastic sandal. To avoid them, Polynesians walk slowly across sandy bottoms, shuffling their feet. The *nohu* lies motionless; if you brush against one, it will move elsewhere without complaint. You have to be especially cautious when the sun is in your eyes.

A sturdy woman friend once stepped on one of these filthy beasts in aptly named Opu Nohu Bay, on Moorea. A year later, she was still walking with a cane and the deeply ulcerated sole of her foot was painful to look at. More recently, my friend Bernard Champon got stung by a small *nohu* in a foot and a half of water (in spite of his plastic sandals); he spent several days in bed before being able to walk, and painfully, at that. He suffered from the wound for several months. Treatment consisted in taking antibiotics for one month, and wrapping the wound in alcohol-soaked bandages for two and a half.

A "sucking" syringe exists that can limit the damage if used as soon as you are stung. An injectable serum also exists, but it is unfortunately fragile: it must be kept refrigerated and has a limited shelf life. The poison is said to be volatile; immediately exposing the wound to as much heat as possible is probably a good idea.

Danger: ciguatera poisoning!

Captain Cook's log mentions several islands with fish that were violently poisonous because of ciguatera. Things haven't changed much since then. Whether a fish is edible depends on where it was caught. A parrotfish taken off one point will always be safe to eat; an identical parrotfish taken off some other point can leave you paralyzed for a month.

Toxic algae on dead coral produces the ciguatera poison. Herbivorous fish feed on the coral, and are eaten in turn by carnivorous ones. So both lagoon and ocean fish contain the poison, and humans can get it from either. Atolls that haven't been "developed" and are rarely hit by hurricanes seem the least at risk for ciguatera, because of the link between the poison and the destruction of coral reefs. Suvorov, Caroline, and Ahe have been spared this curse, whereas in the Gambier Islands, the only fish you can safely eat is the bait goatfish (*vété*). They are from 6 to 10 inches long and have barbels that they use to rake the bottom. They swim in compact schools in sandy shallows, and aren't too hard to spear with a *patia*; if you miss one, you'll probably hit the one next to it.

Ocean and lagoon triggerfish (*motuoiri* in Tahitian) are extremely poisonous the world over, and pufferfish are deadly everywhere. On the other hand, soldierfish (*ihi*), which are small red fish with large eyes that live in caves and grottoes, are considered always safe to eat, except perhaps in the Gambier Islands.

The first signs of ciguatera poisoning are headache, pain behind the eyes, pains in the joints, diarrhea, and sometimes vomiting. This is followed by occasionally intense itching, and sometimes nervous disorders; the sense of touch can be affected, including the ability to feel sensations of heat or cold.

Ciguatera can really knock you out. I have friends who couldn't eat the smallest piece of fish a year after getting ciguatera poisoning without experiencing a return of the original symptoms.

On all atolls, in all parts of the world, caution suggests initially eating only small fish, which are less likely to carry ciguatera than large ones. And of course, ask people in the know. Domestic animals such as cats and dogs are apparently more susceptible to ciguatera. Some people use them as guinea pigs to test fish toxicity, when they don't have any other way.

In case of ciguatera poisoning, it's important to get to a clinic or hospital.

As a point of interest only, here is a treatment prescribed by the late Tahitian healer Tiuraï: 1 tablespoon vinegar, 1 tablespoon brown sugar, 1 green (unripe) *nono* fruit (*Morinda cyclifolia*). This fruit grows on a shrub, and has pineapple-like nodules; its size varies from that of an egg to a tennis ball. It is found on many islands of the Pacific, and on the atolls. The recipe is as follows: crush the entire *nono* fruit (skin, seeds, and all), extract the juice (by squeezing it through a cloth, for example), mix it with the vinegar, pour it into a glass of water, add the sugar, and drink. Repeat next day; no more.

This, of course doesn't take the place of a good ship's pharmacy.

Here are some more recent thoughts from Doctor Paul Zumbiehl, who lived for a long time in Polynesia, including a year on Ahunui atoll (where he went through three hurricanes in a row in 1983): "Since we don't yet have an antidote [to ciguatera], drugs are used to treat the symptoms, and vary according to the clinical situation: atropine, vitamin B, antihistamines, heart stimulants, and, of course, resuscitation."

Food and cooking habits

When Tuamotu islanders eat fish, they don't eat only the best parts, as Westerners often do. Except for the gills, intestines, and the biggest bones, they eat the whole fish—including the fins, skin, eyes, brains, and small bones. When I learned this during my stay on Ahe, it reminded me of what Professor Jean Rivolier once told me when I asked his dietary advice while preparing for The Long Way. Rivolier said that an entire Swedish polar expedition had once died of malnutrition because they used only the "best" parts of the seals they killed. A group of Eskimos got through the same winter without any trouble because they ate every part of the seal, including the fat and organs. It's worth knowing that meat contains six or seven different proteins; if one is missing from your diet for too long, you can be in trouble.

One easy way to cook fish is to place it on the fire, protected by a layer of young palm fronds (wide ones, with a single stalk), then cover it with another frond to create an oven. You can also cook fish on hot stones, but this takes a long time, and the coral tends to crumble.

Another method, which takes even longer, is to use a Tahitian oven, or *himaa*, as follows: Dig a hole about five feet across and two feet deep, and light a fire in it. Place stones on the coals, and let them get red hot. Cover the stones with a layer of banana leaves, and place the food to be cooked on it. Cover the food with more leaves, then with dirt or sand, and leave it to slowly cook.

Eaten with rice (which you can cook in a tin can with a home-made wire handle) and washed down with coconut milk, food baked in a *himaa* is absolutely delicious. For a salad, you can cut out the heart of a young coconut tree (taking care to select one from among several that are crowded too close together).

You can also eat marinated raw fish, Polynesian style. Cut a fillet in slices as thick as your thumb. Put them in a bowl with minced onion, sprinkle with salt and lemon juice (five to six lemons per pound of fish), and allow to marinate for an hour or two, to taste. With rice and coconut milk, it's delicious.

OTHER ISLAND RESOURCES

Coconut crabs

Ashore, you can find coconut crabs (*kaveu*, or *Birgus latro*), which abound on out-of-the-way atolls. A *kaveu* looks like a giant hermit crab, but without a shell. It can grow to eight or nine pounds and has huge claws that can crush your wrist. The biggest ones I've seen were almost a foot and a half long. You can sometimes spot them in daylight, but they usually spend the hot hours in underground holes. By day, you may be able to attract them by burning a couple of split dry coconuts. You can also dig into their burrows with a strong stick, if they aren't too deep, or smoke them out with burning palm fronds. *Kaveu* come out at night, and it's easiest to hunt for them using a flashlight or a pressure lantern (or with a torch of woven fronds, which is simpler).

Their gigantic claws aren't dangerous if you use this simple technique. When a *kaveu* sees you, it sometimes stops dead for a second; from behind, quickly flatten it to the ground with your foot or the palm of your hand.

To tie up a *kaveu* (to carry it, for example), make a cord from the tough stem of a palm frond, which you tie with a series of half-hitches. You can kill a *kaveu* quickly and painlessly by snapping its head backward, but you have to yank hard.

According to Tom Neale, *kaveu* are best roasted over a fire. They cook in just a few minutes (three to five for a large crab), and should be eaten very hot, especially the fatty ventral pouch.

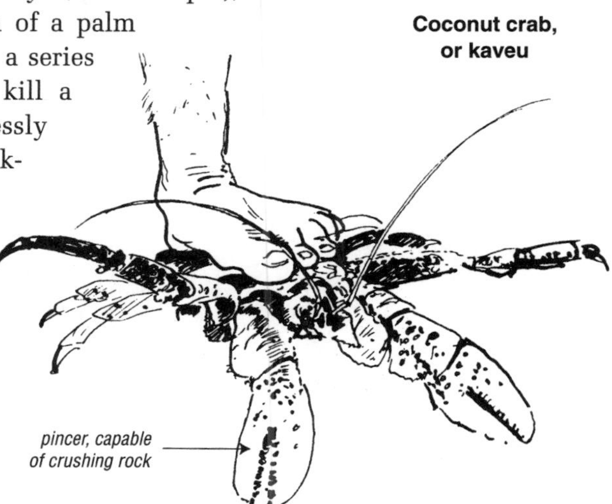

Coconut crab, or kaveu

Seabird eggs

On Suvorov, several thousand seabirds, mainly terns, lay their eggs on several of the atoll islands, starting in October. They wheel above the island in a terrifying racket, and lay their eggs on patches of open ground, and sometimes on bare rock. When we took an egg, they would lay another, but we didn't take too many and tried to leave them alone as much as possible. We also saw noddies, frigatebirds, red- and blue-footed boobies, and masked boobies. The fairy tern, with its long black beak and eyes like black marbles, lays a single egg, perfectly balanced on a branch; it's a miracle that it stays there.

To test an egg for freshness, Neale used to drop it into a bowl of water. If it was fresh, it sank and lay on the bottom. If the embryo had started to develop, the egg would pivot, with one end up. And if it was old, it would float to the surface.

The coconut tree and its many uses

A green coconut provides a delicious drink, but you have to climb the tree to get it. And climbing a coconut tree requires strong muscles combined with careful technique. I can't share the magic formula in an explanation or sketch, since it's a combination of poetry and physics. But I can try to explain the basics of my own technique, which I learned in Asia.

Two main rules:

1) Tie a loop around your ankles. This can be a knotted towel or pareo, or a loop of hibiscus bark.

2) Always set the sole of your foot flat against the tree.

Each person will choose a method suited to his physical shape. In my case, my toes always point upward. For Ugo Conti,

Climbing a coconut tree

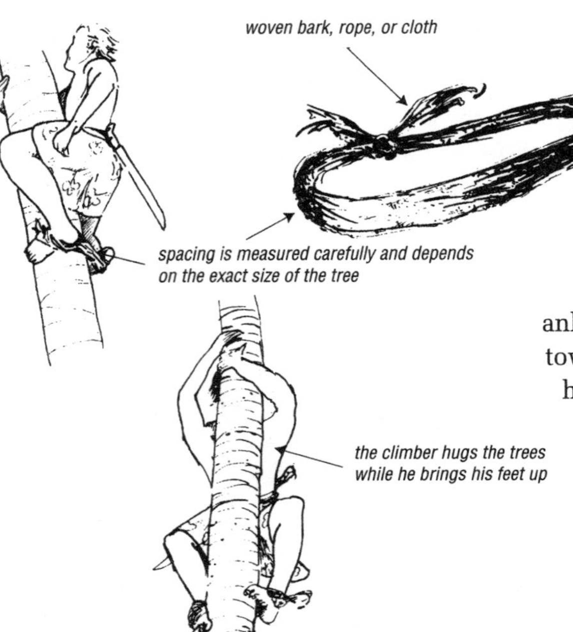

to whom I taught this method, his toes had to point downward.

Then climb slowly.

There is one rule you should really take to heart, if you don't want to end your days in a wheelchair: never—and I mean never—hang from the lowest palm frond. It can break loose without warning, and you could fall.

To drop a young coconut without breaking it, spin it like a top so it lands point first.

On the coral flats, you often find long bamboo poles with metal hooks that Korean fishermen use. They are very handy to hook a coconut without having to climb the tree. But watch the falling nut out of the corner of your eye: a second one may be coming down just as fast.

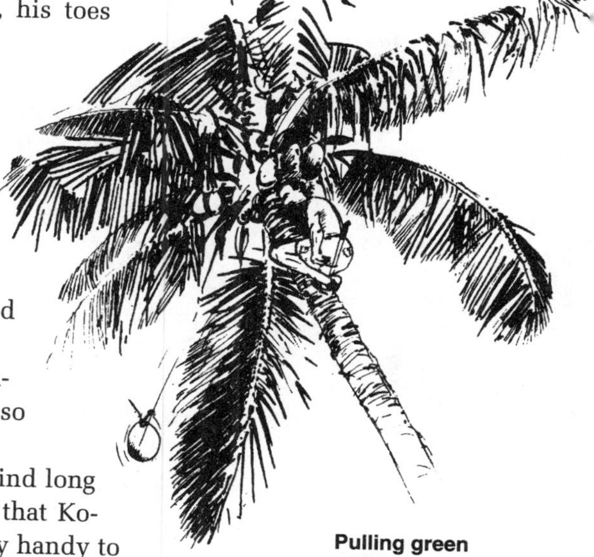

Pulling green coconuts from the tree

To open a green coconut:

— if you don't have a machete: bang the weaker (stem) end against a tree trunk;

— with a knife: cut into the stem end, if the coconut is young enough;

— with a machete: cut slices from the non-stem end (the way you sharpen a pencil) to reach the kernel. Then cut across the kernel, and make a hole in with the point of the machete.

A long coconut hook (from Korean fishermen)

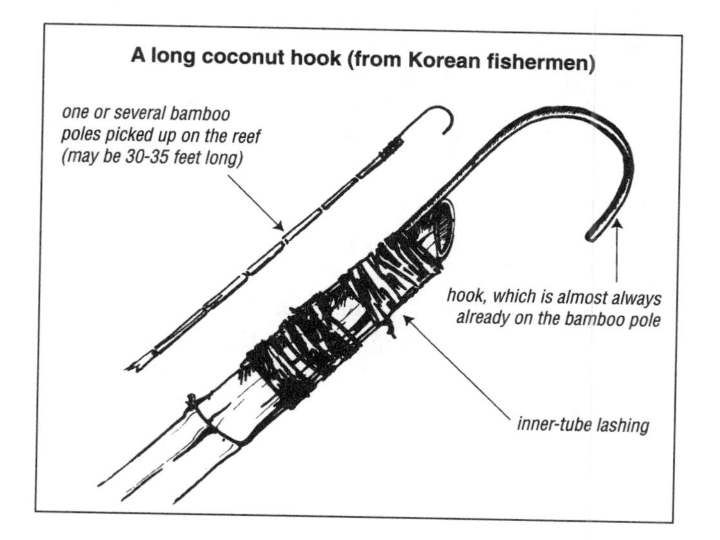

Opening green coconuts to drink them

Here is a trick for carrying several coconuts. Starting with the coconut's stem end, pry up one end of a strip of bark (without cutting it completely off). Tie the coconuts together in pairs with the strips of bark, then drape them across the spine of a stripped palm frond.

A sprouted coconut (*uto*), writes Tom Neale in *An Island to Myself*, "forms when a coconut falls from the tree and remains on the ground until it starts to germinate. At that point nature creates a fascinating metamorphosis. Miniature fronds begin to emerge, while inside, the water and meat gradually change into a spongy substance. This is *uto*. You can eat it raw or cooked, though too much *uto* can cause indigestion."

To cut a coconut, aim for its midline and give it a good chop. I admired Anne Falconer's skill at this. She never missed; one chop, and it was on to the next nut. After two years on the atoll, she had found her style and sharpened her gestures.

slice through the fleshy end

A mature, brown-husked coconut that falls from the tree, but hasn't spouted yet, is a dry coconut, and the meat inside is firm. You can eat it as is, or make coconut milk. To do this, you first have to husk the nut, ridding it of its protective covering. Slam the nut onto a sharpened stake or a pointed piece of coral, and twist. A strip of husk will come loose. Tear it off, and repeat the operation all around the nut: slam, twist, loosen, tear. Once the nut is husked, hold it in your left hand and hit it with the back of the machete all around its circumference until it breaks in two. You can then scrape out the meat with a coconut scraper. To make coconut milk, squeeze the scraped coconut in a cloth, or in hibiscus bark, or the kind of fibrous tissue you find at the base of coconut trees (it looks like sacking). Serve the milk at meals with fish and vegetables.

Tying coconuts in pairs with their own bark

1 - cut here with the machete point

2 - rip the strip of bark loose

In his 1960 dissertation, Dr. Paul-Henri Pétard writes:

"On some of the waterless Paumotu [Tuamotu] islands, the inhabitants drink co-

Carrying coconuts

conut water when the rainwater cisterns dry up. This massive daily intake causes no problems . . .

"Coconut water is generally sterile. It can be injected without ill effect subcutaneously, intramuscularly, or intravenously. It advantageously replaces glucose or artificial saline solutions, helping to flush out the kidneys . . .

"Coconut meat—fresh albumin—can be eaten at any stage of the nut's growth. The soft meat of *nia* coconuts (mature but not dry, and therefore picked from the tree) is given to babies and to weaned piglets."

Coconut scraper

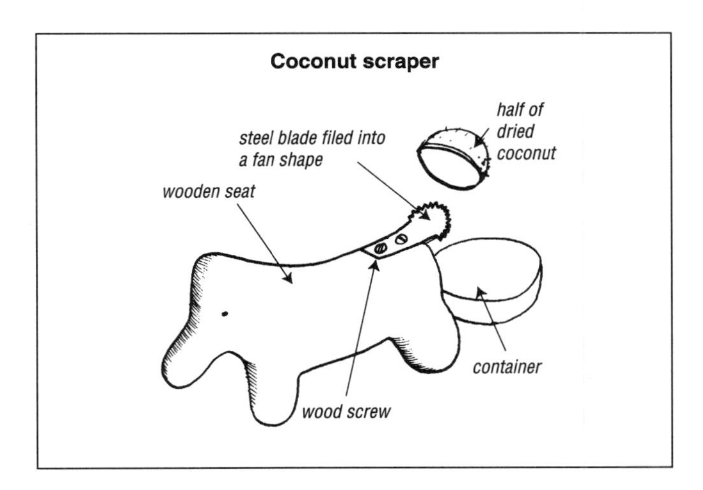

Purslane (pulli pes)

The purslane is a creeping plant whose small, thick leaves are rich in vitamin C and trace elements; like the coconut, it's a good source of fats and carbohydrates. Its flavor is refreshing, but a bit bland.

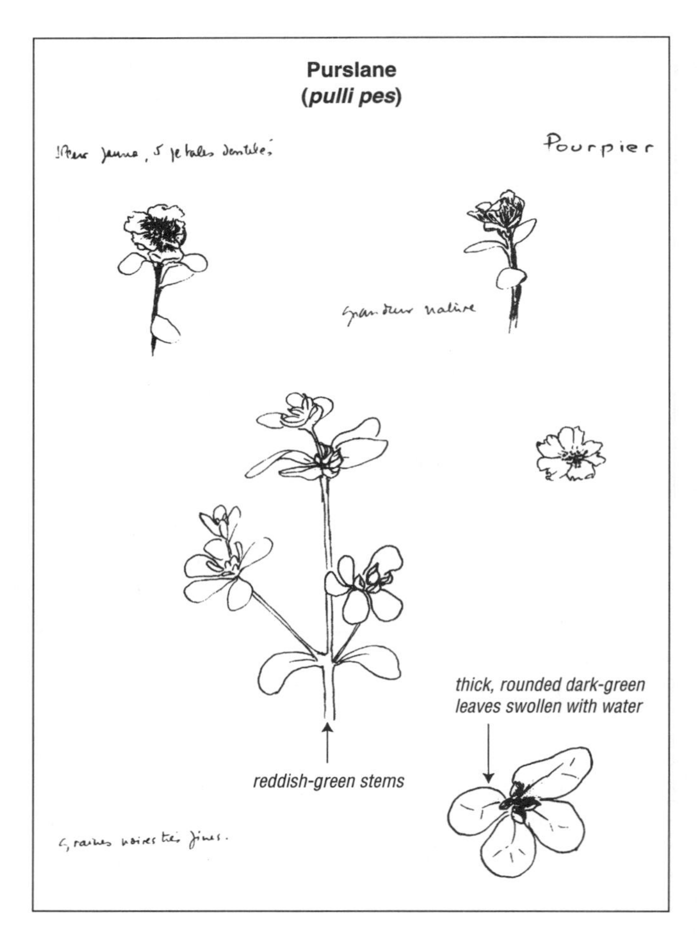

Purslane
(*pulli pes*)

Tubers

Arrowroot is a small plant with leaves shaped like spearheads. Grate the starchy roots onto a cloth laid across a bowl, run water over the mixture, and stir it; a white liquid will flow out. Finish by squeezing the cloth. Wait two hours while the flour sinks to the bottom, then pour off the water and dry the flour in the sun. Anne tried making it a couple of times, but gave up: it was too much work for a couple of pounds of flour. Be careful: arrowroot tubers can be dangerous to eat if they aren't washed properly, as they contain a poison.

Papaya

You can make excellent salads of grated green papaya. To make a grater, us a triangular file to cut teeth in the edge of a large spoon; the teeth must be larger than those of a coconut grater, which are too fine.

ADVICE FOR A LONG STAY ASHORE

If you plan a long stay in the atolls, it's smart to ship a good supply of lemons and grapefruit. We put ours aboard quickly and a bit carelessly in Tahiti, and some of them spoiled; the rest lasted for three months. Bring along plenty of onions and garlic, and beans and seeds for sprouts (lentil, soy, alfalfa, and watercress), which are rich in vitamin C. Don't forget rice and flour, and bring a speargun with spare rubber tubes.

Here is a tip about garlic: crush the clove with the flat of a knife before mincing it; this gets rid of an acid that upsets some people's stomachs, if they eat a lot of garlic. Also remove the clove's inner stem. Remember to chew garlic well; the extra saliva makes it easier to digest.

To sprout lentils, soak them for a few hours, drain, and put them in a glass jar sealed with a piece of muslin held with a rubber band. Lay the jar down and roll it to spread the lentils around, then put it in a dark cabinet. The sprouts will give you fresh greens every day, ashore and at sea.

Iléana bought fresh butter on our trips to Tahiti. To extend its life, she filled jars with one third salted water and then packed the butter very tightly in order to avoid air bubbles that would make it rancid. Water covered the whole thing.

Settling on an atoll

ESSENTIAL TOOLS

A machete and a crowbar are the two essential tools for living on an atoll. A small hatchet is also often useful to have.

You rarely see a Marquesan without his machete. It's like a short sword with a sharp blade, carried in a hand-sewn leather sheath. A second small sheath, sewn onto the bigger one, holds a whetstone. You can do anything with a machete: clear a path through the forest, sharpen stakes when build-

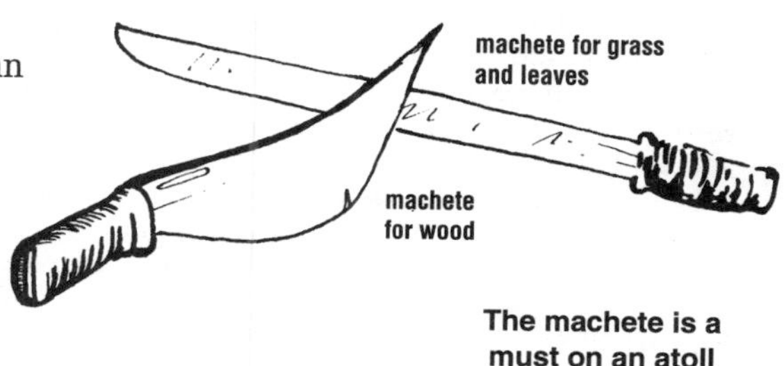

The machete is a must on an atoll

I visited Tom for four months over three visits to Suvorov . . . The fourth time, he was no longer there . . . But when I returned a fifth time, I saw that Suvorov had become a magic atoll. With only his hands, his faith, and his courage, with his magic shovel and machete, and with his sweat and his love, a man had shared in the creation of the world.

ing a house, peel hibiscus to make cord, open coconuts . . .

The crowbar is useful for breaking through coral.

THE FARÉ

It's best to build a *faré* on stilts. This adds a kind of basement for storage and keeps the interior free of sand, and much cleaner. On Ahe, the posts and beams of our *faré* were *kaaia* wood; the bark came off easily, in sheets, when pounded with a mallet. We charred the ends of the posts to prevent rot, a trick known to farmers the world over. We dug the post holes with a crowbar, and in three days the posts were up.

The pressing problem of a roof was solved with *nono*—wood rafters and fronds woven Polynesian-style. *Niau*, or woven palm fronds, is the main component of a Polynesian roof. Green fronds last about two years, dry ones at least three, but they require some preparation. On Ahe, Iléana spread them out near the tide flats with the leaves facing up, and soaked them with seawater three times a day. The salt treatment kept our roofs in good shape for four years instead of three . . .

But words are pale things to describe Ahe. You have to live an atoll, not just with your head, but with your whole being.

On Caroline, Anne soaked fronds overnight in the lagoon (weighted down with a stone, so they didn't float away). That both cured them and made them

Settling on Ahe (Tuamotus, 1975)

JOSHUA's cargo when we sailed from Tahiti to Ahe to settle on the atoll:
"A ton of topsoil in hundred-pound sacks, plus four bags of chicken manure to get our garden plants off to the best possible start; three rolls of wire fencing to keep the village chickens from wrecking our tomatoes and pumpkins; five lemon trees in pots; four 5' x 3' sheets of glass I could use to make a still to condense seawater into fresh . . . ten bags of cement for a cistern; four sheets of aluminum, two glass panes, and styrofoam, which I was thinking of using to build a solar oven for cooking . . . three mattresses . . . ten five-gallon drums of kerosene . . . seventy pounds of nails to build the main faré and Iléana's studio; four gallons of Xylene; three lengths of wide-diameter plastic piping for gutters to collect rainwater from the roofs; a large clay filter which could produce five or six quarts of drinking water a day . . . four bundles of empty sacks . . . a year's worth of food, not to mention essential tools and gadgets . . .
All the floor boards for our future faré, which would be built on stilts, all the beams for the floor joists, and sheets and sheets of old plywood that was still useable . . . and four empty fifty-five-gallon drums were lashed to the railing, which would hold our precious water supply while the cistern was being built."

more flexible and easier to weave. She then split their stems lengthwise with a machete; this produced two symmetrical half-fronds, which were then woven together. Weaving *niau* take a lot of practice, and it helps if you're a Tuamotu graduate.

Once the fronds were on the roof, we built a gutter on top of them to collect rainwater. It led directly to our tanks, which we covered with cloth to filter the water.

One month to the day after anchoring off Poro Poro, we moved into our *faré*.

I now know that it's possible to build a traditional* faré *on a deserted atoll, using only a machete and a sharpening stone. Instead of nails, you would use coconut-fiber lashings, as was done all across the Pacific before the great European voyages of discovery.

FRUIT TREES AND GARDEN

When we settled on Ahe, our little one-acre *motu* was a desert. But I wanted to plant a garden, so as to have green vegetables and fresh fruit. "You're wasting your time," the best gardener in the village told me. "Nothing will ever grow on Poro Poro; it's all sand and there's too much wind. You can build your house there, but don't bother trying to grow anything." But I had been in Israel, where I saw forests growing in what had once been desert. So I tried to transform this coral desert. It's hard to imagine the work involved; it was like gardening on the sun, in an absolute wasteland. We protected our little garden from the wind with a row of *aito* trees, a fast-growing pine that makes a good windbreak. Around the *faré*, and well behind it, we covered the sand with dry coconut fronds gathered on a neighboring *motu*, a job that took us nearly a month.

Gradually, the garden turned green. We managed to grow bok choy, watermelons, cucumbers, pumpkins, and tomatoes. Each time we left Ahe for a few months, we first planted some seeds of avocado, mango, and lemon trees. When we came back a few months later, we had small saplings to plant in our garden and in the village.

Very few pests attacked the vegetables, except for

Gutters and drums for collecting rainwater

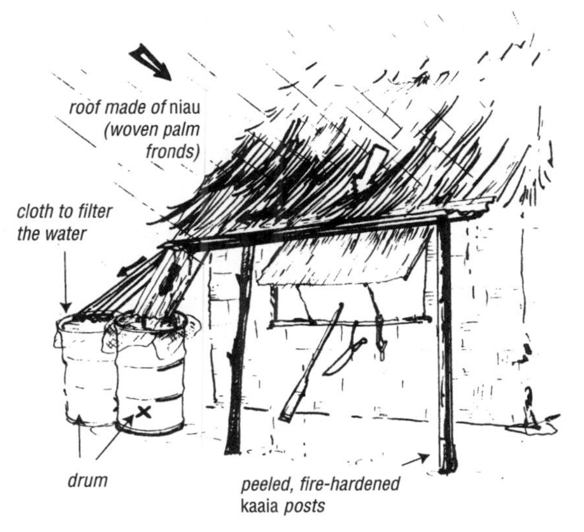

Without a stick of furniture, we lived the way you do in Asia, on mats and cushions, with mattresses on the floor. You have lots of room in a small space, coolness, with a roof of woven coconut fronds, extremely low walls so you can see out while sitting down, very large windows all around the* faré *so you can open everything up and have the impression of being inside and outside at the same time: inside to be in the cool shade, outside for the view and contact with your surroundings and the lagoon.

snails and the *tupa* sand crabs, which we hunted at night with a lantern. For lack of pollinating insects, we had to pollinate the watermelon flowers ourselves, by hand.

Tom Neale also had a garden on Suvorov, but it was just big enough for him. He grew tomatoes, peas, a few papayas, some banana trees that yielded poorly, and some breadfruit in season.

COMPOST

Trying to grow anything in an atoll without compost would be pointless. The fleshy leaves and stems of the *tahinu* plant make excellent compost, as do banana tree trunks, if you chop them up with a machete.

Make a chicken-wire cylinder, stand it on end, and fill it with minced leaves and stems and lots of chopped sea cucumbers, fish guts, kitchen scraps, and other organic matter. Sea cucumbers abound on the sandy shallows, and they are rich in nitrogen and trace elements. Urine and excrement complete the mixture. I figured that on Poro Poro my family—two adults and one child—produced 50 to 80 gallons of human fertilizer a year.

It's a good idea to add good humus to the compost. It can be found under *miki miki* thickets, but in a layer so thin you have to scrape it up with a spoon. You can find much more humus in the groves of pandanus (*Pisonia grandis*), which are huge trees that grow on Ahe and Caroline, and probably on most atolls. Seabirds nest in the trees, and the ground beneath them consists of a rich mixture of humus and phosphoric acid from the birds' droppings.

Once the compost heap is complete, let it sit for a week before mixing it again, adding more sea cucumbers, human waste, urine, and kitchen scraps. A good compost heap takes a solid week of work by two people to get started and a lot of sweat to feed and stir at regular intervals. but the results are better than you could ever hope for. A thermometer stuck into the heap would burst at 130 degrees; I've even used this amazing heat to brew myself a cup of instant coffee.

Turn the compost heap over at least once a month, so the heat doesn't only stay in the center. It's a good idea to have two compost heaps going at the same time.

LIGHTING

To improvise light for night fishing or hunting:

1) Make a torch by weaving three coconut fronds together. It burns for about ten minutes, long enough for a walk around the atoll to gather lobsters on a rising tide or to hunt fish with a machete in the coral flats' *hoa*.

2) I have often used a trick devised by the Deroys, a family of scientists living in the Galápagos. A quick blaze of light from a cigarette lighter lets your eye "photograph" the details of the ground along a forest trail for a short distance (two to ten yards). You walk in the darkness between flashes. Screen the lighter with your left hand so you aren't blinded by the glare. You can do the same thing with a flashlight, by switching it on and off every few seconds, which saves on batteries. But using a lighter is much better than a flashlight, as it gives a very bright light.

On Ahe, we lit the *faré* with kerosene lamps. I found that the 200-candlepower pressure lantern burned the most fuel. Next came a kerosene lamp with a circular wick and shade; it gave good light once it was properly trimmed, but had to be protected from drafts. Last in line were lanterns and candles. (Today of course, you could use solar panels, which are very efficient in the tropics.)

But we lived according to the rhythm of the sun. We got up early, at 6 a.m. (Stephan went to school at 7), and went to bed at nightfall, which comes quickly in the tropics; by 8 p.m., we were all asleep.

MEALS

Our meals on Ahe were very simple. The menu consisted of fish twice a day, grilled or baked, with rice and vegetables from the garden: cucumbers, radishes, tomatoes, or bok choy.

We made soups with the radish greens. We picked lettuce and bok choy leaves as they appeared; the plants were always sown very close together.

The rest, such as fruits and eggs, depended on the schedule of the schooner, which usually called once a month. The village supplied us with *uru* (breadfruit) and fresh lemons.

Iléana baked bread a couple of times a week on a

camp oven set on the Primus stove, but it was often easier to make crepes or porridge at breakfast. We roasted green coffee from the Marquesas in a heavy aluminum pot.

TIPS AND SHORTCUTS

Making ropes

Take a coconut frond and strip off a length of the tough fiber from the upper part of the stem with a machete. The only knot you can tie with it is a series of half hitches; square knots don't work.

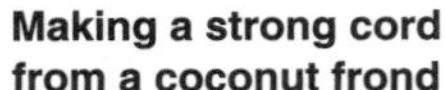

Making a strong cord from a coconut frond

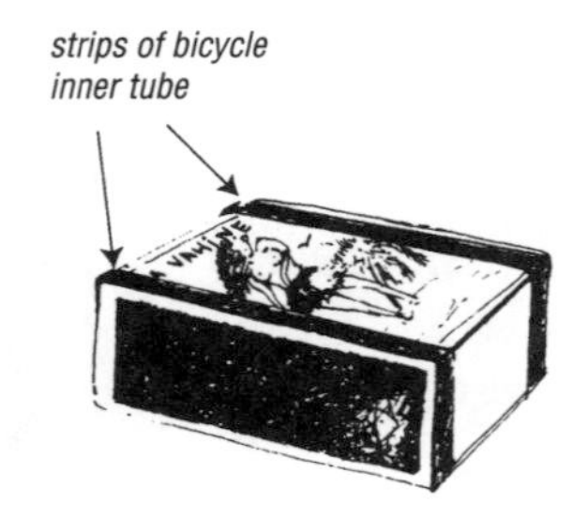

The hibiscus (*purau*) is one of the most common seashore trees in the tropics. You can recognize it by its yellow flowers, which bloom, turn red, and die in a day, falling on the ground or in the lagoon. Strips of *purau* bark make strong cords that can be used to lash building timbers, or to loop around your ankles when climbing coconut trees. The tree also yields good wood: it is straight, light, and easy to work; Polynesians use it for canoe outriggers.

Banana leaves

When you hold a banana leaf over a flame, its edges curl, its color deepens, and the leaf becomes so soft you can use it to wrap cakes, meat, etc. for a Tahitian oven, for example, without its splitting.

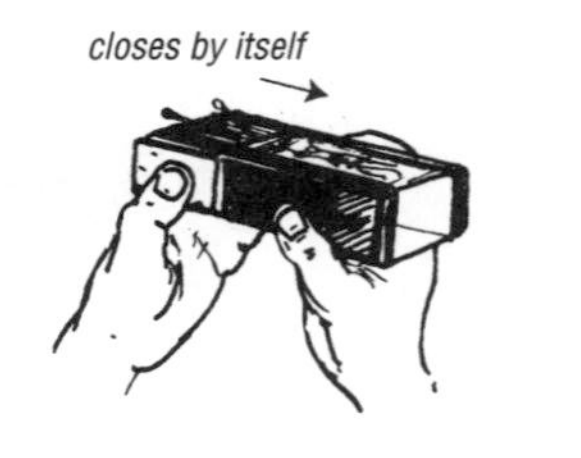

Self-closing matchbox

Self-closing matchbox

Use two strips of bicycle inner tube (see sketch).

GETTING RID OF PESTS

Eliminating mosquitos

1) Prevent standing water: turn coconut shells over, cover reservoirs, and don't leave open containers out in the rain.

2) Pour kerosene into any holes. Mosquitos lay their eggs in fresh water, and the pupae hatch into adults in ten to twelve days. The larvae need to rise to the surface to breathe, which a thin film of oil can prevent. In Indochina, we used to fight malaria and dengue fever, which are mosquito-borne, by putting a few spoonfuls of kerosene in our cisterns. On Ahe, we poured a little kerosene mixed with a jug of water into the sand crab (*tupa*) holes, using a plastic hose so the mixture reached the underground water layer without soaking into the sand.

This is what made digging the Panama Canal possible when the project reached the swamps and malaria broke out among the workers: somebody had the idea of pouring drums of kerosene into the water.

To get rid of any remaining mosquitos, burn coconut debris.

The acrid, delicious smell from the coconut debris we burned to drive the mosquitos away stung my eyes, while it carried me back to the time of my vacations in Indochina with the fishermen of the Gulf of Siam, when I would sleep on the beach in a sack of reeds.

Ants

You can avoid ants by wrapping the base of the *faré* posts with a rag soaked in diesel fuel, motor oil, or kerosene.

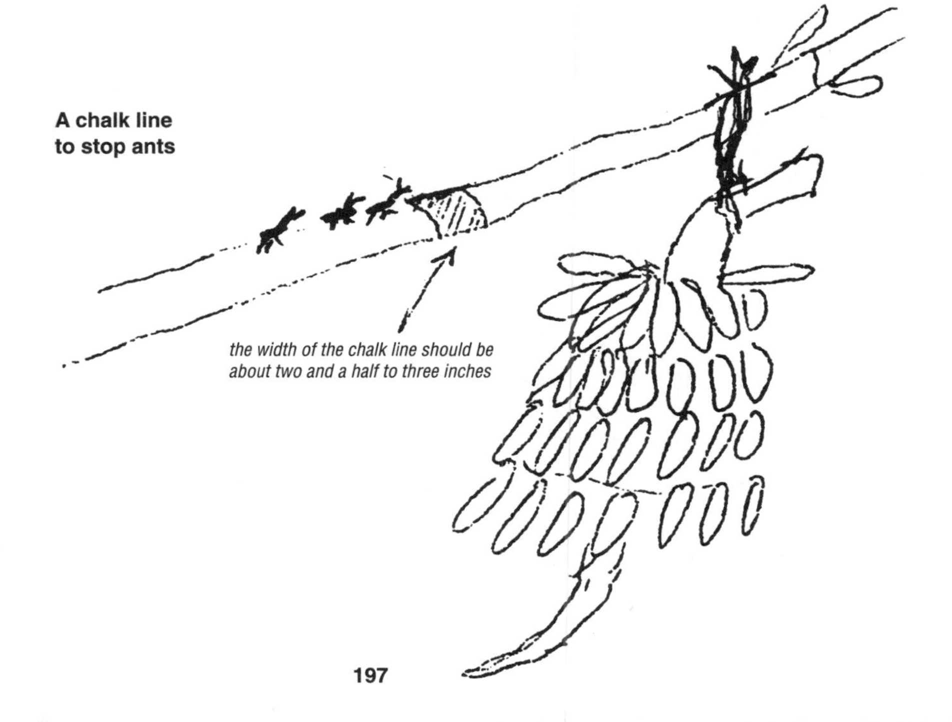

To keep fish, meat, or other food safe from ants, hang it from a kerosene-soaked string. If the string is thick enough, this will last several days.

Another trick: draw a heavy line of chalk around the legs of the food storage bin. For it to last several days, make the line very wide (two or three inches).

Sand flies (*nono*)

Nono, also called biting midges (*yeng-yeng* in the Caribbean) are very small gnat-like flies whose bite can itch terribly. They are abundant on beaches, and bite at nightfall. There isn't much you can do about it. You can drive them away by burning coconut debris, and avoid getting bitten by covering exposed skin with a mixture of citronella and suntan oil; they don't like the smell of citronella, and the oil makes the skin slippery.

A Robinson Crusoe family

Ron and Anne Falconer lived for seven months on Suvorov (800 miles west of Tahiti) after Tom Neale's death. They moved into his *faré*, cared for his chickens, dug and fertilized his garden with compost, and thinned the young sprouts in the coconut groves to keep the atoll from getting overgrown. They worked hard to make the miracle last, and preserved Suvorov's magic with fresh sweat. Seven months later, the Cook Islands government evicted them as trespassers.

With Suvorov still in their hearts, they left for Ahe, in the Tuamotus. They built a *faré*, were welcomed by the villagers, and spent twenty months there. But Ron wanted someplace new and empty. He dreamed of a deserted atoll where he and his family could live the life of freedom that Neale had known during his nearly twenty years on Suvorov, alone with his magic shovel and machete, far from everything and everybody, visited only by a few friendly sailboats. An atoll that would become magic in turn, like Suvorov. They found Caroline Island (400 miles north of Tahiti) and spent three and a half years there with their two children.

So they have a lot of experience in surviving on an atoll.

We witnessed how they settled on Caroline.

From Ahe, they shipped 12-foot floorboards for a *faré* in the cabin of their small 28-foot sailboat, while towing an 11-foot aluminum dinghy crammed with a pile of lighter material, carefully covered with a tarp.

They built the main *faré* in a month, a separate kitchen dominated by an oven raised on coral blocks, and an "open" faré where they ate their meals. These were soon followed by a cistern made of cement reinforced with chicken wire, a compost heap powered with chunks of shark and sea cucumber, a chicken coop, and a garden.

Ron took care of the odd repair job, cooked, baked, ground wheat flour, and tended two beehives he set up near the cistern. The hives produced twenty pounds of honey the first year, and thirty pounds thereafter.

Anne fished, wove palm fronds, fed the ducks and chickens *uto* (the meat of sprouted coconuts), and taught the children. Alexandre wasn't easy to keep still; Anaïs studied well.

And we could see how happy they were to have fully lived out their dream.

Conclusion

So here we are at last. Driven by our instincts, we decided to leave; maybe even chose to just drop everything and go. We have smelled the air of the open sea, felt the intoxication of those first passages, racked our brains over the many problems we faced along the way, and sweated over ways to solve them—and found our island in the tropical sun. Together, we walked around the magical lagoon, the shallows where the powerful swell from the horizon rumbles, the atoll with its green palm trees stirred by the eternal gods of the trade wind. It is time to spend a few minutes in the hammock in the shade of the *tahinu* bushes, to rest up after this all-important overview.

Before closing though, let me pass on a tip I think is priceless: it's worth making friends with the gods. They enjoy it, and occasionally lead us into the fourth dimension, where things become clear and the obvious effective. I know what I'm talking about, and I've often enjoyed the gods' company—both here and beyond.

Finally, let's go to the heart of the matter, the center of the center, to what justifies the birth of this book:

> Dear Pat,
>
> You came upon me carving some kind of little figure out of wood and you said, "Why don't you make something for me?"
>
> I asked you what you wanted, and you said, "A box."
>
> "What for?"
>
> "To put things in."
>
> "What things?"
>
> "Whatever you have," you said.
>
> Well, here's your box. Nearly everything I have is in it . . . [especially] the indescribable joy of creation . . . And still the box is not full.
>
> *John Steinbeck,* East of Eden

Replace "Pat" with "reader," "carving" with "raising sail," "box" with "book," etc. In other words, read between the lines and you will understand why I can now leave in peace.

And may the gods be with you in your search for that enchanted island . . .

Glossary

Aback. A sail is said to be aback when the wind strikes it on its back side and its sheet has been left on the windward side of the boat. Often used when heaving to.

Ahe. An atoll in the Tuamotu Archipelago (French Polynesia) located at 146° 20' W and 14° 25' S.

Aito (Tahitian). The ironwood tree; also called filao.

Altitude. The angular distance of a heavenly body above the horizon.

Antifouling paint. A toxic paint designed to prevent seaweed or barnacles from growing on a boat's bottom.

Atoll. A low coral island, four to six feet above sea level, shaped roughly like a donut and surrounding a lagoon.

Azimuth. The bearing of a heavenly body, measured from north or south in degrees.

Ballast. Heavy material placed in a boat's bilge or keel to stabilize her.

Batten. A small strip of wood or plastic slipped into a pocket sewn at the luff of a sail to stiffen it.

Bare poles. Running under bares poles is a heavy-weather tactic in which no sails are set.

Bearing. The direction of an object from the observer, measured in degrees.

Beaufort Scale. A numerical system for representing wind strength. It originally went from force 0 (dead calm) to force 12 (hurricane). The modern version goes up to force 17.

Becket. A metal loop or eye on a block, to which a line can be attached.

Bitt. A strong vertical fitting on deck to which mooring lines or the anchor cable are secured.

Block and tackle. A set of pulleys and a line, used to multiply the force pulling on a line.

Boathook. A strong pole, several yards long, with a rounded hook at the end. It is used to retrieve a mooring line attached to a buoy, fend off from a dock while maneuvering in port, etc.

Bobstay. A steel cable or chain connecting the end of the bowsprit to the bow at the waterline.

Bolt rope. Rope sewn into one or more edges of a sail to reinforce it or to allow the sail to be fed into a grooved spar.

Bonnet. Strip of canvas laced to the foot of a sail (e.g., staysail) to increase its area when the wind is light.

Boom. A horizontal wood or aluminum spar to which the foot (bottom edge) of a sail is attached.

Bottom. The submerged part of a boat's hull from the keel to the waterline. This is in contrast to the topsides, the part of the hull from the waterline to the gunwales.

Bowsprit. A wood or steel spar extending forward from the bow.

Broach. A boat broaches when she slews around and luffs up uncontrollably, heeling dangerously as she does so.

Broad reach. Point of sail in which the wind strikes the boat's aft quarter.

CQR. The brand name of a plow anchor with very good holding strength.

Cable clamp. A U-shaped fitting used to secure the standing end of a shroud after it goes around the thimble.

Careen. To beach a vessel and haul her over onto one side so the other side can be cleaned, repaired, and painted.

Caroline Island. An atoll 400 miles north of Tahiti.

Caulk. To seal the joints between the planking of a wooden boat.

Centerboard. A keel that can be drawn up into the hull, as opposed to a fixed keel.

Chafe. Damage or wear resulting from friction.

Chainplate. Metal plate bolted or welded to the boat's sides to anchor a shroud.

Chine. The intersection at an angle of the bottom and sides of a flat- or V-bottomed boat.

Ciguatera. A serious food poisoning caused by eating certain coral-reef or ocean fish.

Cirrocumulus. High white clouds: dappled, rippled, or mackerel sky.

Cirrostratus. High clouds shaped like wispy cloth. They often produce a halo around the sun or moon.

Cleat. A wood or metal fitting around which a line is cleated (wrapped) to secure it.

Clew. The lower aft corner of a sail.

Close-hauled. A point of sail in which the boat sails into the wind at an angle of about 45 degrees. As the angle increases, she is successively on a reach (60 degrees), a beam reach (wind at 90 degrees to the boat's axis), a broad reach, and a run (wind directly astern).

Cockpit. A protective open compartment on deck behind the cabin. You normally steer from the cockpit.

Cold-molding. A boat construction technique in which several thin layers of wood veneer are glued together with epoxy.

Colin. French brand of pivoting-fluke anchor, e.g. Colin Tripgrip.

Cumulus. A fluffy, fair-weather cloud.

Cutter. A sailboat with one mast, two forestays, and two headsails (jib and staysail).

Danforth. Brand of pivoting-fluke anchor.

Declination. 1. Of the sun: the latitude directly above which the sun passes at noon. 2. Magnetic: The difference between magnetic north (shown by the compass) and true north (the direction of the meridians).

Draft. The vertical distance between the waterline and the lowest point on the keel.

Ephemeris. A nautical almanac, published annually, that gives the positions of heavenly bodies hourly or daily throughout the year; used in celestial navigation.

Equation of time. The difference between mean solar time and apparent solar time, i.e. the difference between time related to the visible true sun and time related to the imaginary mean sun on which mean time (as in GMT) is based.

Fairlead. An open metal fitting on the bulwark through which the anchor line runs.

Fall off. To steer the boat away from the eye of the wind; the opposite of luffing up.

Faré (Tahitian). House.

Fiferail. Strong horizontal rail fitted to the mast to which running rigging is belayed (secured).

Fitting. General term applied to gear that is not part of a boat's structure, but is attached to hull, deck, rigging, etc., such as cleats, fairleads, etc.

Flogging. Violent flapping of a sail.

Fluke. The part of an anchor that digs into the bottom.

Foot. The lower edge of a sail, between the tack and the clew.

Foredeck. The part of a deck between the forward mast and the bow.

Forestay. A steel cable usually running from the bow to two-thirds of the way up the mainmast. It steadies the mast and lets you set a staysail between the jib and the mainmast. (See also headstay.)

Freeboard. The height, measured at the boat's center, between the upper part of the deck and the surface of the water.

Furl. To tie a sail down along its boom, after it has been lowered. Headsails, which don't have booms, are bundled and tied with short lines.

Gaff rig. A fore-and-aft rig with a trapezoidal sail, the head (upper edge) of which is attached to a gaff while the foot is extended by a boom.

Gale. 1. Generic term for a violent wind. 2. Wind strength corresponding to force 8 on the Beaufort Scale (34-40 knots).

Garboard. The plank immediately above the keel.

Gasket. A short line used to furl a sail.

Genoa. A large jib set when the wind isn't too strong.

Global Positioning System (GPS). Satellite-based system for finding one's position.

Greenwich Mean Time (GMT). The mean time at Greenwich, England; the Universal Time reference.

Ground tackle. The anchors, cables, and other gear required when anchoring.

Gunwale. The board or railing running along the top edge of the hull (usually where it meets the deck).

Halyard. A line or steel cable that runs through a pulley (called a block) at the top of the mast and is used to hoist a sail.

Head. The upper edge of a sail.

Heading. The direction of the boat's axis relative to magnetic north, as measured by a compass.

Headsail. Any sail set forward of the mast (or of the foremast if there is more than one mast), such as the jib or staysail.

Headstay. A cable that runs from the bow or the end of the bowsprit to the top of the mainmast. It helps to steady the mast and is the attachment for the luff of the jib, storm jib, or genoa.

Heave to. A heavy-weather maneuver in which the sails are sheeted flat or aback, the tiller put down to leeward, and the boat allowed to slowly drift.

Heel. The sideways inclination of a boat caused by wind pressure on the sails.

High latitudes. In general, those latitudes below 40° S, with powerful westerly winds.

Hoa (Tahitian). Shallow channel in a reef's coral shelf.

Hull. The portion of a boat between the keel and the gunwales.

Ihi (Tahitian). Soldierfish (*Myripristis murdjan*).

Intercept. The difference between the true zenith distance and the calculated zenith distance of a heavenly body, measured in nautical miles from the assumed or dead reckoning position along the line of bearing of the body's geographical position (azimuth).

Jib. A triangular sail at the front of the boat.

Jibe. To bring the sails (deliberately or by accident) from one side of the boat to the other, with the wind blowing from astern.

Keel. A boat's main longitudinal member, to which the stem and sternpost are attached.

Ketch. Two-masted boat whose smaller, after mizzenmast is forward of the rudder post.

Knot. Unit of speed when sailing. One knot equals one nautical mile per hour.

Landfall. Land first sighted after a long sea voyage: may also be a lighthouse or an island.

Latitude. The angular distance between the equator and the observer's position; the meridian arc between that position and the equator.

Leech. The aftermost or trailing edge of a sail.

Leeway. The sideways drift of a boat caused by the wind.

Limber holes. Notches or holes cut in ribs or floors to allow bilge water to flow freely.

Line of position. A line drawn on the chart by the navigator perpendicular to the azimuth of the sun or some other heavenly body. The boat should be at some point on the line.

Longitude. The angle between the observer's meridian and the Greenwich meridian.

Luff. 1. To bring the boat's heading closer to the eye of the wind; the opposite of falling off. 2. The forward edge of a sail.

Mainsail. Triangular sail attached to the mast.

Mast step. The support for the bottom of the mast.

Mara'amu (Tahitian). South-southeasterly trade wind that can reach 40 mph and blow for days.

Meridian passage. The upper meridian passage occurs when a heavenly body is on the observer's meridian, i.e. it is due north or south of the observer; the body is then at its maximum altitude and the local hour angle is 0°.

Miki miki (Tahitian). Small gnarled seaside shrub or tree (*Pemphis*).

Mizzen. 1) The rear mast on a two-masted boat. 2) The sail attached to that mast.

Mooring line. A line used to tie the boat to a dock, buoy, or another boat.

Motu (Tahitian). An island formed on top of the reef and built of reef debris torn off by cyclones. Plants take hold as soon as the sediments reach above the tide level.

Nautical mile. Unit of length equal to 6,076 feet or 1852 meters.

Niau (Tahitian). Woven palm fronds, used for roofs, etc.

Nohu (Tahitian). Stonefish (*Synanceja verrucosa*).

Nono (Tahitian). A small gnat-like fly, whose bite can cause intense itching; also called Biting Midge.

Oakum. Tarred fibers pounded between the seams when caulking a traditional wooden planked boat.

Pass. A natural channel connecting a lagoon and the ocean.

Patia (Tahitian). Polynesian spear.

Pintle. A rudder fitting with a long pin, which fits into a socket (gudgeon) to form a hinge about which the rudder pivots.

Pitch. The motion of a boat in a seaway or when close-hauled, as she seesaws up and down about her horizontal athwartships axis.

Pitchpole. To capsize forward, stern over bow.

Port. The left side of a boat when facing forward.

Pulpit. A steel frame which encircles the forestay.

Pupui. Tahitian speargun.

Purau (Tahitian). The hibiscus, a common tropical seaside tree recognizable by its yellow flowers, which drop off at day's end.

Reef. 1. To make a sail's area smaller by lowering the sail part way, and tying the lower part in a bundle (usually on the boom). 2. Coral or rocks close to the water's surface.

Reef band. A horizontal row of holes in the sails, reinforced by eyelets or grommets, through which reef points are threaded.

Reef points. Small lines used to tie down the bundled sail when it is reefed.

Rig. The arrangement of mast(s) and sails on a sailboat: sloop, ketch, cutter, etc.

Rigging. All the ropes, lines, wire, and gear used to support the masts and to control the spars and sails. Standing rigging: the shrouds and stays that support the mast. Running rigging: the halyards, sheets, etc. that control the booms and sails.

Rode. The cable attached to the anchor, whether line, chain, or wire rope.

Rolling hitch. A knot used to attach a smaller line to a larger one or to a chain, when the direction of pull is along the line.

Rudder trunk. Watertight casing that houses the rudder post when the rudder is hung beneath the hull.

Running. Point of sail with the wind dead astern.

Sail slide. A small metal or plastic slide sewn to the luff of the mainsail, which slides along a sail track on the mast or boom.

Sail snap (hank, snap shackle). A fitting made of steel, bronze, etc. that holds the luff of a headsail to a stay. Once a jib is attached by its snaps, it is said to be snapped or hanked on.

Sail track. A slot or groove running the length of the mast into which the sail slides fit, securing the luff of the mainsail.

Scope. The ratio of the amount of anchor cable veered to the depth of the water in which the boat is floating.

Sextant. Precision navigational instrument used to measure the angular distance of a heavenly body above the horizon.

Shackle. A U-shaped metal fitting with a pin or a bolt across the open end, used to connect stays, anchor chains, etc.

Sheet. A line used to orient the sails relative to the wind, and attached to the clew (lower aft corner) of a headsail or to the boom of a mainsail. Each sail has a sheet, which you sheet in (or harden) or ease to adjust the sail.

Shipworm. A destructive wood-boring marine mollusc (*Teredo navalis*).

Shiver. The light flapping of a sail that isn't properly set.

Shroud. A steel cable used to steady the mast from side to side, anchored to a chainplate on the hull.

Slick. The area of calm water to windward of a boat driven broadside downwind, as when hove to.

Sloop. Single-masted boat with a jib and mainsail.

Spar. Any long piece of wood used in a boat's rigging, such as a mast, boom, or bowsprit.

Spreaders. Pairs of short horizontal spars, usually two-thirds of the way up a mast, which maintain the shrouds' angle and tension on the mast.

Spring stay. Cable connecting a boat's two mastheads.

Starboard. The right side of a boat when looking forward.

Stay. A steel cable used to steady the mast from front to back. The headstay goes to the masthead; the forestay usually goes to the level of the first spreaders.

Staysail. A headsail carried between the mainsail and the jib. The staysail's tack is usually aft of the bow.

Stem. The forward member that is attached to the keel and forms the bow.

Sternpost. The member running vertically from the keel, from which the rudder is usually hung.

Storm jib. A very small, strong jib used in heavy weather.

Surf. Of a boat, to sail very fast down the face of a wave, with danger of broaching.

Suvorov. Isolated atoll in the Cook Islands (New Zealand), 800 miles west of Tahiti.

Tack. 1) A boat is said to be sailing on a port tack when the wind is coming from the port side, and on a starboard tack when it comes from starboard. 2) The corner of the mainsail where the boom meets the mast; the corner of the jib where the headstay meets the deck. 3) To come about, to change from one tack to another with the bow passing through the eye of the wind.

Tahinu (Tahitian). Small tree (*Messerschmidtia argentea*), ten to thirty feet tall.

Thimble. An eye or ring made of stainless or galvanized steel, brass, etc. with a concave groove on the outside in which the rope or wire rope lies.

Tiller. A wooden or metal bar attached to the rudder which allows you to steer from the cockpit.

Topping lift. A line used to hold up the end of the boom when the mainsail (or mizzen) is not set.

Topsides. The part of the hull between the waterline and the gunwales.

Trade winds. The steady, dominant easterly winds in the tropics. They blow from the northeast in the northern hemisphere, from southeast in the southern hemisphere.

Transom. The flat structure extending across the stern of a hull.

Triggerfish. Omnivorous fish with a strong dorsal spine, powerful teeth, and prominent eyes, found near coral heads or in the open ocean; can cause ciguatera poisoning.

Trim tab. An auxiliary rudder attached to the main rudder, and part of a self-steering system.

Tupa (Tahitian). Sand crab.

Turnbuckle. A threaded metal link used to tighten a shroud.

Uru (Tahitian). Breadfruit (*Artocarpus communis*).

Uto (Tahitian). The meat of a germinated coconut.

Vété (Tahitian). Bait goatfish (*Mulloidichthys samoensis*).

Warp. 1) The lengthwise direction of thread in cloth, perpendicular to the weft. 2) A heavy line used for mooring. 3) To move a boat by hauling or winching a warp.

Waterline. The line where a boat's bottom and topsides meet.

Whisker stay. A stay that steadies the bowsprit horizontally. (See also bobstay).

Winch. A small revolving drum with a crank handle used to tighten lines (sheets, halyards, etc.).

Windage. All those parts of a boat that contribute to total air drag increase windage, including the rigging, mast, and cabin.

Windlass. A kind of capstan used to pull up the anchor chain. It typically has two drums, one for line (gypsy) and one for chain (wildcat).

Wind vane. The aerial (as opposed to underwater) part of a self-steering rig.

Yaw. The boat swings first to one side and then to the other side of her course when she yaws.

Chronology

Dates in Bernard Moitessier's life

April 10, 1925. Moitessier is born in Hanoi, North Vietnam. His family settles in Saigon a few months later.

1947. Coastal shipping aboard a junk in the Gulf of Siam.

1951. Departure aboard SNARK with Pierre Deshumeurs. They sail from Cap Saint-Jacques, Vietnam, to Singapore by way of the Anambas islands, then to Toboali, Indonesia, en route to Australia. They are forced to return to Saigon six months later.

1952. Solo departure from Kampot, Cambodia aboard MARIE-THÉRÈSE. He sails across the Gulf of Siam to Singapore, then into the Indian Ocean. Shipwrecked in the Chagos Bank. A Royal Navy ship takes him to Mauritius, where he works at various jobs until 1955. MARIE-THÉRÈSE II is built in nine months, and he sails from Mauritius to South Africa (Durban and Capetown). He sets out in the Atlantic, sailing alongside Henry Wakelam on WANDA: Saint Helena, Ascension island, Fernando, the Caribbean.

1958. Shipwreck in the Caribbean.

1960. He writes *Sailing to the Reefs* in France.

1961. Construction of JOSHUA, followed by two seasons of cruising school in the Mediterranean.

1963-1966. Long cruise (with wife Françoise) to French Polynesia by way of the Caribbean, Panama, and the Galápagos, with return via Cape Horn.

1966. He writes *Cape Horn: The Logical Route.*

1968-1969. Solo nonstop race one and a half times around the world from Plymouth, England to Tahiti by way of the three capes: Good Hope (twice), Leeuwin (twice), and Cape Horn.

1969-1971. He writes *The Long Way.*

1975-1978. He settles on Ahe, an atoll in the Tuamotus, with Iléana and their son Stephan. Regular visits to Tom Neale on Suvorov, an atoll in the Cook islands.

December 8, 1982. JOSHUA is wrecked at Cabo San Lucas, Mexico.

1983. Construction of TAMATA and departure for Hawaii, then to Tahiti via Suvorov.

1985-1993. Writing in Paris, with trips on TAMATA to the atolls (Suvorov, Caroline) with Véronique.

1993. *Tamata and the Alliance* is finished in July, at Raiatea, French Polynesia.

June 16, 1994. Moitessier dies near Paris.

Bibliography

	The Glénans manual of sailing (David & Charles, 1992)
ANTOINE	*Mettre les voiles* (Arthaud, 1993)
BARRAULT, Jean-Michel	*Navigation de plaisance* (Flammarion, 1971)
COLES, Adlard	*Heavy weather sailing* (Adlard Coles, 1996)
DRION, Daniel	*Latitude vagabondes, dix années à la voile autour du monde* (Editions Sillage, 1992)
JANICHON, Gérard	*Damien* (AEJ, 1994)
KIPLING, Rudyard	*The jungle book* (Wm. Morrow, 1996)
	Just so stories (Wm. Morrow, 1995)
MOITESSIER, Bernard	*Sailing to the reefs*
	Cape Horn, the logical route (Grafton, 1987)
	The long way (Sheridan House, 1995)
	Tamata and the alliance (Sheridan House, 1995)
NEALE, Tom	*An island to oneself: the story of six years on a desert island* (Wm. Collins, 1966)
OLIVEAU, Maurice	*La navigation astronomique àla portée de tous* (Pen Duick, 1981)
PARDEY, Larry & Lin	*The self-sufficient sailor* (W.W. Norton)
PÉTARD, Paul-Henri	Thèse de doctorat sur les plantes et la médication traditionelle en Polynésie (Faculté de médecine de Marseille, 1960)
QUÉMÉRÉ, Erwan	*Cinémas et photos sur la mer* (Editions Blandel-la-Rougerie, 1965)
SIZAIRE, Pierre	*Le guide des étoiles (Delachaux et Niestlé*, 1989)
SMEETON, Miles	*Once is enough* (Grafton, 1991)
STERN-VEYRIN, Olivier	*Solitaire ou pas* (Arthaud, 1987)
	Navigation en haute mer (Arthaud, 1985)
VAN DE WIELE, Annie	*Pénélope était du voyage* (Flammarion, 1954)
WATTS, Alan	*Instant weather forecasting* (Sheridan House, 1996)
ZUMBIEHL, Paul	*Un atoll et un rêve, une île, un homme, une femme* (Albin Michel, 1985)

ARTICLES

Revue *Bateaux* série "Vagabondages marins" no. 34, 35, 37, 39, 41, 42, 44, 46, 48, 50, 58, 60, 62, 64, 70, 72, 75, 77, 79, 84, 86, 105, 114, 118.
Revue *Neptune Yachting*, no. 46, "Le paradis selon Moitessier".

index

y

PHOTO CREDITS

Erwin Christian: page 168
Bernard Moitessier: pages 38, 70, 74, 144
William Rodarmor: pages vi, 6

ARTWORK CREDITS

Bernard Moitessier provided all the artwork, except for the following:
Iléana Draghici: page 190
Goudis: pages 19, 20, 21, 22, 23, 24, 26, 53, 56, 57 (top), 58, 59, 65 (bottom), 66, 87, 90, 91, 109, 113, 121, 143 (top), 165, 167, 177, 179, 180, 181, 185, 186, 187, 188, 189, 191, 193, 196.
Jeremiah B. Lighter: pages 11, 69, 149

Also published by Sheridan House

Tamata and the Alliance
by Bernard Moitessier
Translated by William Rodarmor

"The picaresque life of a seagoing vagabond, a fascinating tale told with remarkable insouciance by the wanderer himself....Risk-taker, romantic, holistic environmental philosopher (his "alliance" with nature), biodynamic horticulturalist, husband and father and national hero, and a fine writer to boot—a character who brought brio and dash to all he undertook." *Kirkus Reviews*

"To 20th-century ocean sailors, Bernard Moitessier was what Kit Carson had been to the 19th-century Western pioneers; yet so far as I know Carson wrote no books, and Moitessier wrote beautifully." **Tristan Jones** in *Encounters of a Wayward Sailor*

"Bernard Moitessier was one of the great free spirits of sailing, a man who preached and practiced a simpler way of life free of the complications of civilization. His book is a delight, but be warned—you may find normal life difficult to follow after you have read it." **Robin Knox-Johnston**, author of *A World of My Own* and *Sea, Ice and Rock*

"When the call to lone adventuring sounds clear, a Bernard Moitessier appears. Nothing stops him. He sweeps toward his fate, carrying our hearts with him. This call illuminates Bernard's last book. It is a final testament, the tale of a free soul adrift in a crippled world, looking for harbors, finding few, a mystical Pied Piper whose home became the sea." **Hal Holbrook**, actor, sailor and author of *Mark Twain Tonight*